About the authors

D0222834

Roger Burbach is director of the Center for the Study of the Americas and a visiting scholar at the University of California, Berkeley. He has written extensively on Latin America and US foreign policy for over four decades. His first book, *Agribusiness in the Americas* (1980), co-authored with Patricia Flynn, is regarded as a classic in the research of transnational agribusiness corporations and their exploitative role in Latin America. His most notable book is *Fire in the Americas* (1987), co-authored with Orlando Núñez, which is an informal manifesto of the Nicaraguan revolution during the 1980s. With the collapse of twentieth-century socialism in the Soviet Union and eastern Europe he began to study the emergent system of globalization and to write about the new Latin American social movements and the renewed quest for socialism in the twenty-first century.

Michael Fox is a former editor of *NACLA Report on the Americas*. He has worked for many years as a freelance journalist, radio reporter, and documentary film-maker covering Latin America. He is the co-author of *Venezuela Speaks!: Voices from the Grassroots* (2010) and the co-director of the documentary films *Beyond Elections: Redefining Democracy in the Americas* and *Crossing the American Crises: From Collapse to Action*, both available through PM Press. He is on the board of Venezuelanalysis.com and his articles have been published in *The Nation*, *Yes Magazine*, *Earth Island Journal*, and more. His work can be found at blendingthelines.org.

Federico Fuentes edits *Bolivia Rising*, is on the board of Venezuelanalysis.com, and is a regular contributor to the Australian-based newspaper *Green Left Weekly*, serving as part of its Caracas bureau from 2007 to 2010. During his time in Caracas he was based at the Fundación Centro Internacional Miranda as a resident researcher investigating twenty-first-century political instruments and popular participation in public management. He has co-authored three books with Marta Harnecker on the new left in Bolivia, Ecuador, and Paraguay. His articles have been published with *ZNet*, *Counterpunch*, *MRZine*, Venezuelanalysis.com, *Aporrea, Rebelión, America XXI, Comuna*, and other publications and websites in both Spanish and English.

Contents

Illustrations | viii Acknowledgments | ix
Abbreviations | xii Map | xiv

Introduction: turbulent transitions and the specter of
socialism 1

1 Globalization, neoliberalism, and the rise of the social
movements 12

2 The pink tide and the challenge to US hegemony. 26

3 Between neo-extractivism and twenty-first-century socialism . . 38

4 Venezuela's twenty-first-century socialism. 48

5 Bolivia's communitarian socialism 78

6 Ecuador's *buen vivir* socialism (by Marc Becker) 98

7 Brazil: between challenging hegemony and embracing it . . . 114

8 Cuba: 'updating' twentieth-century socialism?. 142

Conclusion: socialism and the long Latin American spring . . 153

Appendix: nationwide elections in Venezuela, Bolivia and
Ecuador 159

Notes | 161 Bibliography | 183
Index | 201

Illustrations

1 Argentine *piqueteros* demonstrate in Buenos Aires during the 2001–2 financial crisis to protest neoliberal state policies and forced evictions of worker-led factory takeovers, and show solidarity with the worker occupation of the Zanon ceramic factory in southern Argentina 12

2 The presidents of Saint Vincent and the Granadines, Bolivia, Cuba, and Venezuela embrace during a 2009 ALBA summit in Cumaná, Venezuela, where the organization ratified a new regional currency, known as the sucre. 26

3 Bolivia begins testing to exploit the world's largest reserve of lithium on the Uyuni salt flats in November 2009 38

4 Hundreds of thousands of supporters of Venezuelan president Hugo Chávez flood Bolívar avenue in Caracas for a campaign rally in support of Chávez's 2006 re-election 48

5 Thousands of Bolivian *campesinos* and indigenous farmers raise their hands during a people's assembly in La Paz, Bolivia, in 2005, in support of making a recently passed hydrocarbons law even tougher on multinational companies 78

6 An indigenous Ecuadoran blows a conch shell at the opening march for the June 2010 Meeting of Original Peoples and Nations of Abya Yala in Quito, Ecuador 98

7 Brazilian president Luiz Inácio Lula da Silva and presidential candidate Dilma Rousseff attend a campaign rally in São Bernardo do Campo, São Paulo, on the eve of the first round of the 2010 presidential elections 114

8 Santiago de Cuba, 2010 142

9 Seven hundred women from Vía Campesina and Brazil's Landless Workers' Movement march against a 44,000-acre eucalyptus plantation in Rio Grande do Sul, Brazil, in early 2009 152

'*Latin America's Turbulent Transitions* makes sense of Latin America's leftward turn, both in terms of its origins and what this turn means for some of the main countries involved. As such, it is an essential resource for the general reader and for students of the region. The case study of Venezuela is especially useful in helping us understand Hugo Chavez's historic legacy and the advent of twenty-first-century socialism.

Gregory Wilpert, author of Changing Venezuela by Taking Power

'Anyone seeking to understand the complexities and tensions of the struggles to turn the radical social transformations in contemporary capitalist Latin America into a sustained socialist project needs to encounter this book's rare combination of open-hearted commitment and hard-headed analysis.'

Steve Ludlam, University of Sheffield

'A profoundly important book. Latin America is the last place in the world where a broad enlightened left not only survives but thrives, setting an idealistic agenda of solidarity, equality, and freedom – though often times rhetoric doesn't match reality. Deploying a rigorous comparative framework, *Latin America's Turbulent Transitions* takes an unflinching look at socialism in the region, both as it is and as it could be.'

Greg Grandin, New York University, author of Fordlandia: The Rise and Fall of Henry Ford's Forgotten Jungle City

More praise for *Latin America's Turbulent Transitions*

'Burbach, Fox, and Fuentes have written a thoughtful account of the radical projects that have arisen in Latin America in the wake of the collapse of the "old" socialism and the simultaneous weakening of US hegemony in the region.'

Fred Rosen, editor of NACLA Report on the Americas

'This is a vital guide for anyone seeking to understand where the left is headed in Latin America, as well as the vexing political and social challenges confronted by charismatic leaders and progressive forces on the ground.'

Nikolas Kozloff, author of Revolution! South America and the Rise of the New Left

'In a continent of ferment and change like Latin America, where we often live through tumultuous moments, a serious, documented, and critical book like *Latin America's Turbulent Transitions* is a valuable contribution to deepening our discussions and orienting us in the construction of a new world. Burbach, Fox, and Fuentes' vast and comprehensive chapters tackle many of the current themes and conflicts and serve as small compasses to help us understand where we are and suggest possible paths forward.'

Raul Zibechi, Uruguayan journalist, author of Dispersing Powers: Social Movements as Anti-State Forces

'Little by little, inch by inch, the thick, dark velvet curtain thrown over daily events in Latin America by uninterested editors and nervous journalists in the Western media is being tugged back. Roger Burbach, Michael Fox, and Federico Fuentes have produced a sparklingly up-to-date account of the "pink tide" of new thinking for the general reader. The lives and politics of the present-day political giants of the Western Hemisphere – Chávez, Lula, Correa, Raúl Castro, and many more – are set out with admirable clarity by three authors who know what they are talking about. No student of the New World should be without it.'

Hugh O'Shaughnessy, author of Priest of Paraguay

Latin America's turbulent transitions

the future of twenty-first-century socialism

ROGER BURBACH, MICHAEL FOX, AND
FEDERICO FUENTES

Fernwood Publishing
HALIFAX | WINNIPEG

Zed Books
LONDON | NEW YORK

Latin America's turbulent transitions: the future of twenty-first-century socialism was first published in 2013.

Published in Canada by Fernwood Publishing, 32 Oceanvista Lane, Black Point, Nova Scotia, BOJ 1BO and 748 Broadway Avenue, Winnipeg, Manitoba, R3G 0X3

www.fernwoodpublishing.ca

Published in the rest of the world by Zed Books Ltd, 7 Cynthia Street, London N1 9JF, UK and Room 400, 175 Fifth Avenue, New York, NY 10010, USA

www.zedbooks.co.uk

Copyright © Roger Burbach, Michael Fox, and Federico Fuentes 2013

The rights of Roger Burbach, Michael Fox, and Federico Fuentes to be identified as the authors of this work have been asserted by them in accordance with the Copyright, Designs and Patents Act, 1988.

Fernwood Publishing Company Limited gratefully acknowledges the financial support of the Government of Canada through the Canada Book Fund and the Canada Council for the Arts, the Nova Scotia Department of Communities, Culture and Heritage, the Manitoba Department of Culture, Heritage and Tourism under the Manitoba Book Publishers Marketing Assistance Program and the Province of Manitoba, through the Book Publishing Tax Credit, for our publishing program.

FSC
www.fsc.org
MIX
Paper from
responsible sources
FSC® C013604

Set in OurType Arnhem and Monotype Futura by Ewan Smith, London
Index: ed.emery@thefreeuniversity.net
Cover design: www.alice-marwick.co.uk
Printed and bound by CPI Group (UK) Ltd, Croydon, CRO 4YY

Distributed in the USA exclusively by Palgrave Macmillan, a division of St Martin's Press, LLC, 175 Fifth Avenue, New York, NY 10010, USA

All rights reserved. No part of this publication may be reproduced, stored in a retrieval system or transmitted in any form or by any means, electronic, mechanical, photocopying or otherwise, without the prior permission of Zed Books Ltd.

A catalogue record for this book is available from the British Library
Library of Congress Cataloging in Publication Data available

Library and Archives Canada Cataloguing in Publication
Burbach, Roger
    Latin America's turbulant transitions : the future of twenty-first century socialism / Roger Burbach, Michael Fox and Federico Fuentes.
Includes bibliographical references.
ISBN 978-1-55266-560-2
    1. Socialism--Latin America--History--21st century. 2. Latin America--Politics and government--21st century. I. Fox, Michael, 1977- II. Fuentes, Federico III. Title.
HX110.5.A6B87 2013   320.53'1098   C2012-907759-3

ISBN 978 1 84813 568 0 hb (Zed Books)
ISBN 978 1 84813 567 3 pb (Zed Books)
ISBN 978 1 55266 560 2 pb (Fernwood Publishing)

Library
University of Texas
at San Antonio

Acknowledgments

This book is comprised of chapters that were initially drafted by one of the co-authors and then enriched by collective discussion. It is a multi-continental effort, receiving support and assistance from the Americas, Europe, and Australia. It is telling that in this globalized world, a book on Latin America must tap into a myriad of sources around the planet.

The two most important contributors to the book were Marc Becker and Greg Wilpert. Marc wrote the chapter on Ecuador. Greg was critical in drafting the first three chapters with Roger, and had to withdraw from the project because of other commitments. Without his early work, this book may never have become a reality.

The three co-authors have many people to thank. I, Roger, received support from my comrades at the Center for the Study of the Americas, namely Miguel Altieri, Cecile Earle, Patricia Flynn, and Peter Rosset. Early ideas about, and concepts of, the social movements came out of the course on social movements that I taught with Maria Elena Martinez at the University of California at Berkeley. Adam Sgrenci, our reader for the course, is a long-time collaborator who served as a sounding board for my thoughts on the new left in Latin America. Laura Enriquez was very helpful in taking me on as a visiting scholar in the sociology department of the university, giving me access to the library and its research facilities. David Parkhurst, as well as being a good friend, kept me electronically and digitally connected with the world during the writing of this book.

On the east coast, Fred Rosen, Bob Armstrong, and Karen Judd were very helpful on my trips back there to work on the book. Tim Draimin of Toronto, Canada, also helped me in my travels. I was deeply dismayed and saddened by the death of Hank Frundt, a dear friend and brother for almost four decades. He counseled me on personal matters, and advised and assisted me on every book I have written, including this one.

I am also indebted to medical doctors Michiyo Kawachi

and Jeffery Wolf for keeping me alive during the writing of this manuscript. In February 2004 I was diagnosed with multiple myeloma and told I had three to five years to live. Eight and a half years later I am in remission after undergoing a stem cell transplant. I owe my survival to their willingness to work with me in devising and researching new medical approaches at moments when it looked like the end was near.

Glenn and Marilyn Borchardt are lifelong friends who assisted me through thick and thin in this project. My sisters Ann and Miriam Burbach also provided moral support. Tanya Kerssen commented on an early draft. Eric Leenson, Monica Marini, Jesse Clarke, and Margot Pepper are personal as well as creative *compañeros*, who stimulated my spirits over the course of this project. My son Matthew batted around some of the ideas in this book. He and my daughter Allie provided unswerving love, support, and loyalty, enabling me to carry on.

I, Michael, am, above all, grateful to my loving wife and partner, Sílvia Leindecker, for her patience, advice, and support during the drafting of the book. Our precious little girl, Rosa, was born in the final rounds of editing the manuscript, and she has been an extra inspiration to me. This book would have been impossible without the insights of countless individuals. Of particular importance were Igor Fuser, the ABC Metalworkers' Union, Bernardo Cotrim, Jefferson Pinheiro and Coletivo Catarse, Erick da Silva, Ubiratan de Souza, Raul Pont, CIDADE, the editors of *Brasil de Fato*, Daniel S. Pereira and many other members of Brazil's Landless Workers' Movement, Pablo Morales, Paulo Kliass, and the authors of the March/April 2011 Brazil issue of *NACLA Report on the Americas*.

Thank you to Ben Dangl for taking a look at a late draft. Many thanks also to the friends and family that supported us throughout the process. Deserving special recognition are Sam Dodge; JoJo Farrell; Chris Michael; Kate Fox, Maryann and Michael C. Fox; Gabriela, Joshua, and Marcel Kirst; as well as Paula, Stephane, Tiago, and Bela Leindecker Gutfreund.

As always, it is impossible to thank by name all those who have helped in the writing of this book, but I, Federico, would like to note the important encouragement and assistance received from comrades in Australia, especially the various editors on *Green Left Weekly*, who over the years have been a constant sounding board for ideas; in Canada, particularly John

Riddell and Richard Fidler for their ever insightful views; and in Venezuela, above all, Marta Harnecker and Michael Lebowitz, whom I had the great pleasure of both working with and learning from.

My contribution to this book would not have been possible without the constant support and back-up from my family, in particular my mother and father, Cecilia and Adrian Fuentes. My partner, Kiraz Janicke, who had to put up with me during this writing period, was an essential factor in keeping me on track and helping me to see this project to the end.

We are grateful to our editors at Zed Books, including Ken Barlow, Kika Sroka-Miller, and many others, for their patience and insight, which helped focus the project and guide it in new exciting directions. Many thanks also to the photographers – Tim Russo, Noah Friedman-Rudovsky, Sílvia Leindecker, Marc Becker, Lewis Watts, and Jefferson Pinheiro – for their excellent images.

Above all, thanks must go to the amazing people whom we have met and learned from during our time in Latin America. Their lives and struggles are a constant source of inspiration to us, as they are for millions around the world. They provide living proof that a better world is possible.

Abbreviations

ALBA   Bolivarian Alliance of the Peoples of Our Americas.
            Previously known as the Bolivarian Alternative for the
            Peoples of Our Americas and the Bolivarian Alternative for
            the Americas. Also referred to as ALBA-TCP or Bolivarian
            Alliance of the Peoples of Our Americas – Peoples' Trade
            Agreement.

BANCOSUR   Bank of the South

BRIC   Brazil, Russia, India, China

CADAFE   Venezuelan state electricity company

CAN   Community of Andean Nations

CELAC   Community of Latin American and Caribbean States

COB   Bolivian Workers Central

CONAIE   Confederation of Indigenous Nationalities of Ecuador

CTV   Confederation of Venezuelan Workers

EZLN   Zapatista National Liberation Army

FARC   Revolutionary Armed Forces of Colombia

FTAA   Free Trade Area of the Americas

GDP   gross domestic product

IMF   International Monetary Fund

IPSP   Political Instrument for the Sovereignty of the People
            (Bolivia)

MAS   Movement Toward Socialism, also known as the MAS-IPSP
            or Movement Toward Socialism – Political Instrument for
            the Sovereignty of the People (Bolivia)

MERCOSUR   Common Market of the South

MST   Movement of Landless Rural Workers (Brazil)

MVR   Movement for a Fifth Republic (Venezuela)

NAFTA   North American Free Trade Agreement

NED   National Endowment for Democracy (United States)

OAS   Organization of American States

OPEC   Organization of the Petroleum Exporting Countries

PB   participatory budgeting

PDVSA   Petroleum of Venezuela SA

PPT   Homeland For All (Venezuela)

PSOL   Socialism and Freedom Party (Brazil)

PSUV	United Socialist Party of Venezuela
PT	Workers' Party (Brazil)
SADC	South American Defense Council
SAPs	structural adjustment programs
sucre	Unitary System for Regional Compensation
TCP	Peoples' Trade Agreements
TIPNIS	Isiboro-Secure National Park and Indigenous Territory (Bolivia)
UN	United Nations
UNASUR	Union of South American Nations
UNETE	National Union of Workers (Venezuela)
USAID	United States Agency for International Development
WSF	World Social Forum

Introduction: turbulent transitions and the specter of socialism

Latin America today is largely relegated to the back burner of global affairs. The conflicts in the Gulf and the Middle East, the economic crisis gripping Europe, China's march onto the world scene, and the political dysfunctionality of the United States are the broad trends that shape our headlines. When Latin America does break into the news it is usually over the drug wars or immigration issues. It goes virtually unnoticed that Latin America is caught up in a turbulent transition, the outcome of which will have significant repercussions for the unfolding of world history. This book examines two central and conflicting processes that are driving this transition: one is the demise of the United States as the hegemonic power in the hemisphere, and the other is the rise and renewal of socialism in Latin America.

The Pentagon apparently does have an inkling of the unstable and turbulent state of affairs in Latin America. General Douglas Fraser, the head of the US Southern Command, told the US Congress in early March 2012 that he was concerned with 'geopolitical turbulence' in Cuba, Haiti, Bolivia, and Venezuela. Haiti, he said, 'remains vulnerable to natural disasters and economic hardship,' but he saw turbulence in the other three countries as stemming from the shortcomings of their leaders and the domestic opposition. Going on to acknowledge in his congressional testimony that Central America has become the most violent region in the world, the four-star air force general painted an upbeat picture, saying 'we will focus our efforts on strengthening the security capabilities of our partners in Central America,' mentioning specifically the militaries of Guatemala, Honduras, and El Salvador.[1]

What constitutes turbulence in today's world is clearly in the eye of the beholder. In his statement, General Fraser completely failed to acknowledge the central role the United States plays in this tumultuous phase of history. It is the perspective of the authors of this book that we are entering an interregnum, a period of turbulence and transition in the world at large. The old order is breaking down with the decline of the United States as the planet's hegemonic power and the eruption of the global economic crisis in 2008 that has darkly danced from continent to continent, destabilizing countries and entire regions.

At the same time the shape of the world to come is unclear and undefined. New, anti-systemic forces appeared on the scene in 2011 with the Arab Spring, the rebellion of the *indignados* in Europe, and the Occupy Wall Street movement in the United States.[2] But these upsurges, other than rallying around the call for authentic democracy, have not defined a clear vision of the future world they are struggling for.

Latin America is part of this global upheaval. On the one hand we see the demise of the old order with the decrease of US influence in the Americas, particularly in the unraveling of the neoliberal model that was implanted more firmly in Latin America in the 1980s and 1990s than in any other region of the Global South. On the other hand, anti-systemic forces in the hemisphere began to challenge this order early on with the Zapatista rebellion in Mexico in 1994 and the rise of the indigenous movements, especially in the Andean countries of Ecuador and Bolivia. Then, in late 1999, the struggle against neoliberalism took on an inter-American character with the Battle of Seattle that shut down the conclave of the World Trade Organization. Zapatistas, indigenous groups, and trade unionists from Latin America marched alongside Teamsters, turtles (environmentalists), and farm organizations in the streets of Seattle.

In the wake of 11 September 2001, the US global offensive muted this growing opposition movement, particularly in the United States. But in much of Latin America, the left and progressive forces recovered quickly, making significant advances. Already before September 11, Hugo Chávez in 1999 had assumed the presidential office in Venezuela on an anti-neoliberal platform, and then at the turn of 2001/02, the Argentines rebelled against their neoliberal regime, sacking four presidents in the space of two weeks. As the first decade of the new millennium unfolded, the social movements in Latin America expanded. It is this popular upsurge that accounts in large part for the rise of the 'pink tide,' the left and left-of-center governments that were led by the likes of Luiz Inácio Lula da Silva in Brazil, Evo Morales in Bolivia, Rafael Correa in Ecuador, and Fernando Lugo in Paraguay.

Preoccupied with the war in the Middle East, US efforts to control events in Latin America came up short. In Venezuela in April 2002, a coup led by the head of the Venezuelan Chamber of Commerce and backed by the United States collapsed in less than forty-eight hours. Later that year, when the United States sought support from the United Nations (UN) Security Council for its war against Iraq, Brazil and Chile – then members of the Council – opposed the US war. In 2005 George W. Bush went to Buenos Aires to push the Free Trade Area of the Americas (FTAA). Bush was greeted by massive demonstrations in the streets of Buenos Aires and Mar del Plata, and his plan was overwhelmingly rejected owing to the opposition led by the governments of Argentina, Brazil, and Venezuela.

The US grip on the region also weakened as China entered Latin American markets in search of raw materials to supply its booming economy. By 2010, China had become the largest trading partner of Brazil and Chile. Chinese trade with Latin America as a whole stood at $180 billion in 2010, an eighteen-fold increase since 2000. Meanwhile, US exports to Latin America dropped from 55 percent of the region's total in 2000 to 32 percent in 2009. The global economic crisis has had only a limited impact on Latin America because of the surge in Chinese demand for Latin American commodities. The old phrase, 'when the US economy catches a cold, Latin America gets pneumonia,' is no longer true. China is also moving to displace the US dollar with the Chinese yuan in a region where the dollar once stood as the paramount currency in trade transactions.[3]

Another strand in the growing independence of Latin America is the formation of regional trade organizations. The Unión de Naciones Suramericanas (UNASUR, Union of South American Nations), launched in May 2008 as a trade and policy organization modeled on the European Common Market, proved its mettle just months later when at a special meeting held in Santiago, Chile, it endorsed the government of Evo Morales in its efforts to stop a coup attempt by the separatist opposition based in Santa Cruz, Bolivia. UNASUR is also moving to establish a customs union that would subsume two other trade blocs, the Mercado Común del Sur (MERCOSUR, Common Market of the South) and the Comunidad Andina (CAN, Community of Andean Nations).

Founded by Venezuela and Cuba in 2004, the Alternativa Bolivariana para los Pueblos de Nuestra América (ALBA, Bolivarian Alternative for the Peoples of Our Americas), encourages 'fair trade' not free trade, and promotes integration through complementarity and solidarity. Bolivia joined in 2006 and later Nicaragua, Ecuador, and five Caribbean countries. The sucre (short for *Sistema Único Compensación Regional* or Unitary System for Regional Compensation) aims to be the currency of ALBA and is used in many of its trade transactions. An ALBA Bank, with 1 percent of the currency reserves of the member countries, funds people-centered regional projects and provides support for sustainable social and economic development in its member countries.

This is the context for the ascent of twenty-first-century socialism in Latin America. The weakening of the US empire, the eruption of anti-neoliberal social movements, the rise of the new left governments and the growing integration of the region on its own terms have created a space for the rejuvenation of socialism after the dramatic setbacks of the last century.

As nearly every president in the region has highlighted, Latin America is truly undergoing a second independence. In Venezuela, this movement is referred to as *Bolivarianismo*, and it calls for fulfilling the South America Liberator Simón Bolívar's dream of a unified Latin America to fend off the new United States. Today *Bolivarianismo* stands for the expansion of democracy and national sovereignty to the fullest extent possible without necessarily going beyond capitalism. However, the rise of twenty-first-century socialism is also intertwined with this second independence movement. The socialist project builds on this foundation, striving to construct deeper, more egalitarian democratic societies by transforming the economic order. Both of these projects are continental in character; neither can advance effectively unless they are part of a broader transition and narrative in Latin America.

The rise of twenty-first-century socialism must also be located within the context of the collapse of the traditional socialist project. In rejecting authoritarianism, bureaucratic centralized planning, state capitalism, and the lack of democracy, it has distanced itself from those traits so common to the failed projects of the twentieth century. A critical attribute of twenty-first-century socialism is that it is built by social movements and by people organizing from below; it does not arise from government fiats nor from self-defined vanguard parties. By transforming circumstances, the people transform themselves. Moreover, twenty-first-century socialism is rooted in democratic processes and procedures. It is notable that the three countries that have raised the banner of socialism – Venezuela, Bolivia, and Ecuador – have all used the ballot box extensively to advance their policies and efforts to transform their societies.[4]

Drawing on the wide-ranging discussions of twenty-first-century socialism taking place in the hemisphere, social and political theorist Marta Harnecker outlines five key components of what constitutes socialism. First, socialism is 'the development of human beings,' meaning that 'the pursuit of profit' needs to be replaced by 'a logic of humanism and solidarity, aimed at satisfying human needs.' Secondly, socialism 'respects nature and opposes consumerism – our goal should not be to live "better" but to live "well,"' as the Andean indigenous cultures declare. Thirdly, borrowing from the radical economics professor Michael Lebowitz, Harnecker says, socialism establishes a new 'dialectic of production/distribution/consumption, based on: a) social ownership of the means of production, and b) social production organized by the workers in order to c) satisfy communal needs.' Fourthly, 'socialism is guided by a new concept of efficiency that both respects nature and seeks human development.' Fifthly, there is a need for the 'rational use of the available natural and human resources, thanks to a decentralized participatory planning process' that is the opposite of Soviet hyper-centralized bureaucratic planning.[5]

To fully achieve these objectives will be a long process, taking decades and generations. The tangible advances toward twenty-first-century socialism are limited. The three countries that have put twenty-first-century socialism on the agenda have had decidedly different results, as the following chapters reveal.

Moreover, the consolidation of the radical left in political power has led to the emergence of new tensions between governments and social movements, a situation further complicated by US interference in the region. And yet the quest for a socialist utopia persists in Latin America unlike any other region of the world.

The deep roots of socialism in the Latin American historical experience help explain its vitality. Socialism first appeared in the early decades of the twentieth century with the formation of socialist and communist parties around the hemisphere. Providing leadership for the trade unions and participating in coalitions and popular front governments, these parties bore the brunt of US intervention in the post-World War II era, particularly in Central America and the Caribbean.

The ideological landscape of Latin America was forever transformed with the establishment of a socialist society in Cuba less than two years after the revolutionary triumph in 1959. For the next half-century, socialism, with all its ups and downs, would be at the core of political debates and discussions of strategies for transforming societies. The Cuban revolution also touched off a chain of guerrilla movements committed to anti-imperialism and socialism that extended from Bolivia and Peru in the south to Venezuela, Guatemala, and the Dominican Republic in the north. The defeat of Che Guevara and his band of guerrillas in 1967 in Bolivia temporarily stymied the strategy of using armed struggle in the countryside to seize power.

Chileans attempted a different approach. Believing that elections and formal democratic institutions could be used to advance socialism, the Popular Unity government led by President Salvador Allende (1970–73) began implementing a socialist program that called for nationalizing the country's copper mines and expropriating the largest manufacturing enterprises. But seizing control of the 'commanding heights' of the economy and only the executive branch of the state apparatus was not sufficient to advance socialism. The Chilean military, backed by the Chilean bourgeoisie and the United States, staged a coup that toppled the only elected socialist democracy in the world.

To uproot the deeply embedded Chilean socialism, the repression was severe and bloody. The ruling class, under the dictator General Augusto Pinochet, carried out a ruthless campaign against the popular classes and the left political organizations in an effort to purge the vision of a socialist society from the popular consciousness. The Pinochet regime lasted seventeen years.

The Sandinista National Liberation Front in Nicaragua resurrected the armed strategy of the guerrilla and seized power from the Somoza family dictatorship in July 1979. The revolutionary government replaced the Somoza National Guard with its own Sandinista army and took control of key sectors of the economy. But it never proclaimed that it was attempting to construct socialism in Nicaragua. Even Fidel Castro advised the Sandinistas to go slow in their takeover of the economy. Given that Nicaragua, unlike Cuba, had porous borders through which commodities could move as well as counter-revolutionary bands (the Contras), the Sandinista government attempted to form the broadest coalition possible, including sectors of the bourgeoisie and petite bourgeoisie. However, even this approach could not stave off the counter-revolution. In February 1990, a majority of Nicaraguans voted against President Daniel Ortega and the Sandinistas largely because they recognized that there would be no end to the violence unless the US-backed candidate, Violeta Chamorro, was installed in the presidency.

The Sandinista electoral defeat coincided with the collapse of the Berlin Wall in November 1989 and the dismantling of the Soviet Union in 1991. State socialism was crumbling. Jorge Castañeda, in his 1993 book *Utopia Unarmed: The Latin American Left After the Cold War*, presented the argument that the best the left could do in Latin America would be to adopt social democratic policies.[6] Isolated and devoid of its international allies, Cuba entered a 'special period' of economic austerity. In this void neoliberalism consolidated its grip on Latin America, devastating the traditional worker and peasant social bases of left and socialist forces. The Brazilian political scientist Emir Sader, in his 2011 book *The New Mole: Paths of the Latin American Left*, argues that the setback for socialism was so severe that it is still recuperating to this day. Socialism can be part of the agenda, but the priority must be on forming governments and political coalitions to dismantle neoliberalism, even if that means accepting the broader capitalist system for the time being.[7]

This in part explains why the construction of socialism in the coming years and decades will be a diverse process – differing widely from country to country. There is no singular definition or model. However, it is widely recognized that a crucial task in the construction of twenty-first-century socialism is to break with twentieth-century state socialism by reconceptualizing the role of the state in the transition process.

A groundbreaking perspective on this theme comes from Katu Arkonada and Alejandra Santillana in their 2011 article from *Le Monde Diplomatique*, 'Ecuador and Bolivia: the state, the government and the popular camp in transition.' They assert that the state should be viewed as 'an historic aspiration of the popular organizations and the indigenous peoples, and as a space open to political dispute.'[8] In recent years the popular movements have sought to alter the state, to make it responsive to their interests and needs. With the ascent of the new left governments, the contest over who will control the state is becoming even more intense. Arkonada and Santillana assert that 'the construction of hegemony comes out of civil society,' meaning that the 'popular camp' in this period of transition is presenting its projects and interests, hoping to capture ever more space within the state. The popular forces will become hegemonic, they believe, as the state becomes an instrument of 'collective interests,' and 'a universalizing political project.' The constituent assemblies and the subsequent constitutions drafted in Bolivia and Ecuador (as well as Venezuela) are examples of how popular forces have advanced their interests and opened up new space within the state.

A related issue facing the popular forces in Latin America is the type of democracy that should be constructed. There is a growing disenchantment with traditional representative democracy. Given the power of capital, the state is manipulated by the dominant economic interests. The result is controlled democracy, in which the people are allowed to vote every few years for candidates that by and large do not question the capitalist order and the centrality of the marketplace.

The popular forces are envisioning a democracy that is more substantive, integral, and participatory, starting at the local level. Like never before, communal self-rule is being embraced in Latin America by Bolivia's indigenous communities, Mexico's Zapatistas, and the Oaxacan activists during their 2006 uprising. Hundreds of Brazilian municipalities have launched participatory budgeting to engage local communities in the allocation of city funds. Venezuelan communities have founded thousands of neighborhood-organized communal councils. And, first in Venezuela, then in Bolivia and Ecuador, constituent assemblies have drafted new constitutions that allow for greater popular participation and full citizenship for all the ethnic groups that have been marginalized in the past.

But these processes would not be in motion if not for the inspiration of movements and experiences throughout the twentieth century. As mentioned above, Cuba and Cuban socialism deserve particular credit. The revolution in its early years was particularly inspirational with its commitment to an egalitarian society with free education and healthcare for all.

However, with its roots in twentieth-century socialism, the Cuban Communist Party exercised complete control of the state and the economy, leading to the dismal results in economic performance and development that we see today. The recent reforms in housing, agriculture, and self-employment are designed to place many of the smaller enterprises and economic activities – ranging from taxis and barber shops to restaurants and small farms – in the hands of independent owners and producers. The success or failure of this economic transition will have an impact on the evolution of socialism in the rest of Latin America.

Where Cuba is not embracing the challenge of twenty-first-century socialism is in the role of the Communist Party, which is set on retaining control over the direction of the state and the political system. This differs from the emerging socialist societies in the rest of Latin America, which are committed to holding multiparty, national elections to advance their struggles.

What is important is that Cuba is now an integral part of Latin America. It is a leading member of the Comunidad de Estados Latinoamericanos y Caribeños (CELAC, Community of Latin American and Caribbean States) that was founded in Caracas, Venezuela, in December 2011. And at the Sixth Summit of the Americas held in Cartagena, Colombia, in March 2012, Barack Obama found himself isolated because the United States refused to end the half-century embargo of Cuba and to accept Cuban participation in hemispheric forums such as the summit.

The Colossus of the North is floundering – economically, militarily, and politically – but by no means will it abdicate its interventionist policies. Instead, the United States has defiantly expanded its military presence in the region. The resurrected US 4th Fleet plies the coastal waters of the Americas while the Drug Enforcement Administration disperses agents throughout the region, stirring up the drug wars and often engaging in covert and armed activities that once fell under the purview of the CIA. Other forms of intervention have also gained currency: US government entities such as the US Agency for International Development (USAID) and the National Endowment for Democracy (NED) have become powerful instruments used to fund opposition forces and promote destabilization campaigns.[9]

The June 2012 Paraguayan coup against pink tide president Fernando Lugo provided the United States with a new opportunity to bolster its declining influence in Latin America. Paraguay's location, nestled between South America's two largest economies (Argentina and Brazil) and its membership in regional integration bodies such as UNASUR and MERCOSUR, make the nation strategically important for US interests in the region. The new regime moved immediately to reopen negotiations over a new US military base that would, according to right-wing parliamentarian and head of the parliamentary defense committee José López Chávez, help Paraguay 'liberate itself from the pressures, the threats from Bolivia, and even more so the threats that are constantly emerging from the Bolivarianism of Hugo Chávez.'[10]

The ousting of Lugo was a signal to other countries that the United States and its allies would use any means available to reassert their power. It was reminiscent of the coup three years earlier in Honduras that toppled the elected government of Manuel Zelaya. Initially voting with the other governments in the Organization of American States (OAS) to oppose the coup, the United States shifted gears and backed faulty elections in late 2009 in which Porfirio Lobo won the presidency under conditions of conflict and strife. A popular movement has emerged calling for his dismissal and the convoking of a constituent assembly to refound the nation, a step that has led other nations to place socialism on the agenda.

Socialism is making an appearance in other countries through a variety of social actors. In Chile the 2011 student rebellion ignited Chilean social movements, which are now rethinking the country's socialist legacy. In Brazil the Movimento dos Trabalhadores Rurais Sem Terra (MST, Movement of Landless Rural Workers), the largest social organization in the hemisphere, continues to espouse socialism in its platform and in the daily practices of its land reform settlements. Socialism is indeed like the mole that Emir Sader describes. At times it burrows underground and is seemingly invisible, only to pop up at unpredictable times and in unforeseen locations.

There are three overarching and interrelated themes in this book: confronting US hegemony, social movements, and socialism – themes that are at the same time exciting, challenging, and perplexing.

The three chapters that follow lay out the broad sweep of political, economic, and social forces at work in the Americas that make this a turbulent period in history. In the first chapter we discuss the rise of the social movements and their resistance to neoliberalism and US-dominated globalization. Chapter 2 focuses on the challenges to US hegemony that emerged with the new left governments and imperial overstretch as the United States spent its resources on the Iraqi and Afghan wars. In Chapter 3 we look at the complex and contradictory currents at work in Latin America with the rise of twenty-first-century socialism and the reliance on extractive exports in mining, energy, and agriculture that ravage the environment and marginalize regional populations.

The next four chapters are country studies of what is happening in Venezuela, Bolivia, Ecuador, and Brazil, four of the most dynamic and turbulent countries in the Americas. They illustrate the specific processes at work that are discussed in the earlier chapters. The last country study is of Cuba, a country that is fighting to transcend its economic difficulties and the legacy of twentieth-century socialism to become a vibrant socialist society in the current century. In the Conclusion we will discuss the profoundly democratic character of twenty-first-century socialism and why it offers hope for a world afflicted by economic crises and wars.

1 Argentine *piqueteros* demonstrate in Buenos Aires during the 2001–2 financial crisis to protest neoliberal state policies and forced evictions of worker-led factory takeovers, and show solidarity with the worker occupation of the Zanon ceramic factory in southern Argentina (credit: Tim Russo).

1 | Globalization, neoliberalism, and the rise of the social movements

Nowhere else in the contemporary world have so many left-leaning governments come to power in such a short period of time: Argentina, Bolivia, Brazil, Ecuador, El Salvador, Nicaragua, Paraguay, Peru, Uruguay, and Venezuela. These governments largely owe their ascendancy to the social movements that have exploded onto the scene in the new millennium. These movements are militant and highly diverse. They originated in the 1990s or earlier, and include indigenous movements, landless peasant associations, women's and sexual rights organizations, environmental groups, radical student associations, and many others.

The call for a new socialism is embedded in the social upheaval that is sweeping the continent. Latin America is entering a new era in its history, which provides hope and inspiration in a world ravished by imperial wars and economic disasters. The press and many political commentators have focused on what is described as the 'pink tide,' the emergence of leaders such as Hugo Chávez, Evo Morales, and Rafael Correa. However, mainstream media have largely ignored the broad-based social movements over the past quarter century and how they helped lift the pink tide presidents to power.

The political definition of this turbulent period of change defies easy classification. It isn't simply the old populism of Latin America, nor is it like the revolutionary movements that gripped Latin America with the Cuban revolution. The forms of struggle and organization are many: the communal committees that formed in El Alto, Bolivia, to descend on La Paz and depose governments in 2003 and 2005, the *piqueteros*, or pickets of unemployed workers, in Buenos Aires and other parts of Argentina, the Movement of Landless Rural Workers in Brazil, the national indigenous organizations of Ecuador, Bolivia, and other countries in Latin America, and the student upheaval in Chile in 2011 calling for a radical restructuring of the country's educational system and a plebiscite for a constituent assembly.

The rise of these social movements needs to be placed in the context of the destructive impact of capitalist globalization. Over the past four decades the world economy has undergone a transition from a system of international trade centered on national economies to a globally integrated system of production under the aegis of transnational corporations. This has marked a new epoch in the history of capitalism. Neoliberalism has served as the economic doctrine for breaking down barriers to the free flow of capital around the globe.

Prior to the 1970s, the global economy had consisted of trade between many different national economies. Each country produced raw materials or finished products that were traded with other national economies, often on a limited scale. As Marxist geographer David Harvey points out, for the United States, 'The proportion of GDP growth attributable to foreign trade remained less than 10 per cent up until the 1970s.'[1] In the countries of the North, Keynesian economic policies predominated while in Latin America import substitution industrialization flourished as the state played a central role in replacing imported manufactured goods with nationally produced products by raising import tariffs and subsidizing national industries. Capital controls – greatly aided by the fixed exchange rates of the time – gave states significant power over capital to determine economic policies within a nation's borders.

During this first phase of the postwar period (1945–70), the United States dominated the capitalist world and waged a cold war against the Soviet Union. It propped up right-wing dictatorships around the globe (Iran, Indonesia, the Philippines, and in much of Latin America) and helped local elites suppress leftist governments and rebellions whenever possible (Guatemala, the Dominican Republic, Vietnam, Brazil). The US dollar served as the de facto global currency, ensuring that all countries were dependent to a certain degree on US economic policy. The United States was unchallengeable, dominating in production, technology, and military power.

However, by the early 1970s the Keynesian economic model and US supremacy increasingly came under pressure. Military expenditures, particularly in the Vietnam War, led to unsustainable deficits. The United States responded by printing more dollars, increasing inflation. For two decades, labor power and wages had been on the rise. With declining returns on their investments, capital searched for new opportunities to increase profitability. Pushed by declining gold reserves due to the expense of waging war and pulled by capital's need for greater flexibility, the United States stopped fixing its currency by the gold standard in 1971. The rest of the western world followed suit. The open fluctuation of exchange rates meant that capital was freer to flow around the globe since it was no longer tied down by the capital controls that are implied in fixed exchange rates. Trans-national corporations began expanding their production chains, as these processes became globalized.

Facilitated by new communication and transportation technologies, capital flowed around the globe in ever greater quantities. It dictated its own conditions of investment, thereby forcing countries to lower their trade and environmental regulations while gaining virtually unfettered access to a cheap labor force. As sociologist and globalization theorist William Robinson explains:

> 'Going global' allowed capital to shake off the constraints that nation-state capitalism had placed on accumulation and to break free of the class compromises and concessions that had been imposed by working and popular classes and by national governments in the preceding epoch ... Capital achieved a new found global mobility, or ability to operate across borders in new ways, which ushered in the era of global capitalism.[2]

In the previous epoch, US-headquartered transnational corporations, such as Dole in Central America, Exxon in Venezuela, or the Kenne-cott Copper corporation in Chile, had an important presence in Latin America, but they represented the old model. Countries and companies specialized in particular export commodities and corporations had to abide by internal controls and taxation policies. Today, transnational corporations engage in a far greater diversity of activities, as they search for the most efficient production locations and conditions in each step of an increasingly global integrated process.

Neoliberalism facilitated the rise of this transnational system. It began in Chile with the dictatorship of Augusto Pinochet (1973–90) and reached its formalization in the 1980s with the 'Washington Consensus' during the early Reagan administration. US-led multilateral financial institutions such as the International Monetary Fund (IMF) and the World Bank imposed neoliberal policies on the highly indebted countries of the South as a condition for further lending.

In the 1960s and 1970s, many Latin American countries had borrowed heavily to finance big, sometimes wasteful, development projects. By the close of the 1970s, in the midst of a global economic downturn, the banks began to call in their loans. Meanwhile Latin America faced rising interest rates, increased production costs, and shrinking export markets for its goods. The resulting debt crises of the 1980s and 1990s gave Latin American governments – in some cases fragile new democracies – little choice but to accept devastating conditions for debt rescheduling.

Throughout the Third World, the IMF assisted transnational capital in its efforts to free itself from national restrictions by imposing structural adjustment programs (SAPs) that countries had to implement as a condition for receiving loans. The SAPs reduced tariffs and subsidized production, cut back social spending, dismantled workplace and environmental regulations, and privatized state enterprises. Simultaneously, transnational capital engaged in capital flight and investment strikes if countries tried to impose restraints or controls on their investments. This deadly combination of the IMF and the transnational corporations ushered in the epoch of globalization in Latin America and around the world.

The effect that the transnational corporations and globalization had on Latin America can be seen by the fact that trade as a percentage of gross domestic product (GDP) nearly doubled from 10 percent in 1989 to 18 percent in 1999.[3] In another measure of Latin America's integration into the globalized production process, foreign direct investment increased from an average of $38 billion per year from 1993 to 1997, to $74 billion per year between 1998 and 2003.[4] Nevertheless, ordinary Latin American citizens did not benefit from this corporate-driven growth. SAPs prevented governments from capturing profits – through taxation and other measures – to invest in social services and development.

While the IMF and World Bank pushed neoliberalism on the Third World via its creditors' cartel (dubbed a cartel because private banks would not lend to countries unless they first had an IMF agreement), the General Agreement on Tariffs and Trade institutionalized this process by converting from a general agreement into the World Trade Organization in 1995, a fixed institution with headquarters in Geneva, Switzerland. The World Trade Organization, which has 153 member countries and represents 95 percent of world trade, became an effective tool for the implementation of neoliberalism owing to its dispute resolution process, which almost automatically gives private corporations priority over Third World governments and principles of economic sovereignty.[5]

Neoliberalism ushered in a period of deregulation and privatization as social spending was gutted. Budgets for education, healthcare, public services, and social security were cut. Water supplies in large urban areas were turned over to private companies that profited from this most fundamental human need. The cost of public transport rose dramatically in many countries, causing massive protests in countries such as Guatemala and Venezuela. As educational spending was reduced, public schools including universities declined in quality.

Families that could afford it sent their children to private for-profit educational facilities.

Large reasonably profitable state-owned corporations were placed on the trading block and sold to private interests. Telecommunications enterprises were privatized in many countries, including the largest in Argentina, Brazil, and Mexico. National economies were opened to international trade and multinational capital, boosting export sectors, particularly in agribusiness, petroleum, and mining. Finance capital sat in the driver's seat of the neoliberal system as stock markets and transnational banks determined the rise and fall of economies.

Neoliberal policies, though, gradually undermined political legitimacy in many Latin American countries because they resulted in a decoupling of economics from politics with the abdication of public control over the economy. In other words, governments not only gave up their role in helping redistribute wealth – particularly with cutbacks in social spending – but also ended up with ever fewer policy tools to lower unemployment, fight inflation, protect the environment and the workplace, or guide investment. Many of the same parties that half a century before had led nationalist struggles (including the Peronist party in Argentina and the Revolutionary Nationalist Movement in Bolivia) were now introducing neoliberal policies. Presidential candidates often ran for office in opposition to neoliberal policies, only to find that once they took power neoliberalism appeared to be the only viable option.

One of the salient examples of such a reversal was the 1988 campaign and election of Carlos Andrés Pérez in Venezuela, who ran on an explicitly anti-neoliberal platform. Merely three weeks after taking office in early 1989 he reversed completely and implemented a full IMF structural adjustment package. Similar unexpected shifts toward neoliberalism took place in Argentina under Carlos Menem (1989–99), in Peru with Alberto Fujimori (1990–2000), again in Venezuela under Rafael Caldera (1994–99), and in Brazil under Fernando Henrique Cardoso (1995–2003). These neoliberal policies did often help to lower inflation, but they also contributed to the public's general disenchantment with politics, as expressed in opinion polls. The polling organization Latinobarómetro reported in 2000 that only 37 percent of Latin Americans were satisfied with their democracies, which was 20 points less than Europeans and 10 points less than people living in sub-Saharan Africa.[6]

Another factor that contributed to this disaffection with politics was the abysmal failure of neoliberalism as an economic doctrine. According to its promoters, neoliberalism was supposed to bring about growth and economic stability. However, what it actually brought was increasing inequality and poverty, sluggish overall growth, and instability. The Gini coefficient, which measures inequality, rose in almost every Latin American country between 1990 and 1999.[7] Economic growth averaged only 0.5 percent per year between 1980 and 1999, compared with 3 percent from 1960 to 1979.[8] In agriculture, a sector expected to benefit greatly from adjustment through the correction of relative prices, there was little change in output performance from the 1970s. As sociologist Max Spoor points out, SAPs adversely affected the agrarian sector by increasing volatility and inequality.[9]

Severe economic and financial crises struck Mexico in 1994, Brazil in 1999, and Argentina in 2001/02. In every case these calamities were directly traceable to neoliberal economic policies. In short, while neoliberalism succeeded in opening countries to transnational corporations and in strengthening corporate power worldwide, it failed in its own goals of producing sustained growth and financial stability.

Feeling that their governments and politics could not resolve their problems, Latin America's poor and disenfranchised reacted spontaneously to the hardships caused by neoliberalism, protesting, rioting, and clashing with state security forces. One of the first reactionary responses to neoliberalism's harsh policies took place in Venezuela on 27 February 1989, the same day that Carlos Andrés Pérez imposed an IMF adjustment program that privatized state businesses and cut social services. Gas prices doubled and public transportation prices rose by 30 percent.[10] Residents took to the streets of Caracas. After two days of protests and riots, the Andrés Pérez government responded by sending the police and military into the poor barrios, shooting residents almost at random, killing somewhere between four hundred and a thousand people, in one of the worst human rights catastrophes of late twentieth-century Latin American history.

The *Caracazo* riot was merely one of a much larger wave of leaderless urban revolts against neoliberal policies among the poor and marginalized sectors of Latin American society. Cities across the region, including Mexico City, Santo Domingo, Guatemala City, São Paulo, Rio de Janeiro, Buenos Aires, and Santiago del Estero, Argentina, experienced similar spontaneous rebellions against unjust neoliberal policies between the mid-1980s and the mid-1990s.[11]

The challenge of the social movements

At about the same time a wave of social movements and organizations led by peasants and indigenous groups emerged in the rural areas of Latin America. By the early 1990s they had assumed the lead in challenging the neoliberal order, particularly in Ecuador, Mexico, Bolivia, and Brazil. These new organizations were generally more democratic and participatory than the class-based organizations that traditional Marxist political parties had set up in rural areas in previous decades.

In general, they came to fill the gap left by a working class that, although growing in numbers, was more fragmented, disoriented, and dispersed than ever, and therefore unable to provide any real leadership. With a broad range of interests and demands, including indigenous and environmental rights, these new social movements transcended the modernist meta-narratives of both capitalism and socialism.

The Ecuadorean indigenous movement was the first to gain both national and international prominence as a new militancy of the 'original' peoples of Latin America. Founded in 1986, the Confederación de Nacionalidades Indígenas del Ecuador (CONAIE, Confederation of Indigenous Nationalities of Ecuador) united two major indigenous organizations, one from the highlands, and the other from the Oriente – Ecuador's eastern Amazonic region where the transnational petroleum corporations were ravaging the rainforests.[12]

In 1992, the 500-year anniversary of Columbus's arrival in the Americas, a dramatic mobilization took place in Ecuador. Two thousand indigenous peoples led by CONAIE began a 250-kilometer march from the Oriente to Quito, demanding communal land titling, constitutional reforms, and an end to neoliberal policies. As the marchers passed into the Andes, numerous highland communities provided material support and joined the march. It became a national spectacle that attracted widespread solidarity as 5,000 marchers arrived in Quito, passing the country's presidential palace, surrounded by hundreds of soldiers clad in riot gear and fortified with tanks, horses, and dogs.[13]

For CONAIE and other organizations, the immediate goal was not the conquest of state power, but mobilizations based on specific demands, the opening of autonomous political spaces, the transformation of cultural values, and a critique of modernity.[14] Luis Macas, a CONAIE leader, pointed out that neoliberalism and the very process of modernization are at the root of the efforts to destroy native societies. Neoliberalism is the latest phase of capitalism and modernity, which have been inextricably linked together since the time of the conquest. 'The application of neoliberalism is quite well designed to finish with everything – the disappearance of centuries-old cultures, the disappearance of peoples, of life itself,' said Macas in a 2002 interview. 'I don't know how to interpret this term modernization. For us, modernization obviously is the changing of structures that don't currently serve to advance the economic, social, and cultural development of peoples, to try to realize at least some of the fundamental elements that are components of the humanity that we currently live.'[15]

While CONAIE and the indigenous movement were on the move in Ecuador, it was the uprising in Chiapas, Mexico, of the Ejército Zapatista de Liberación Nacional (EZLN, Zapatista National Liberation Army) on 1 January 1994 that captured broad international attention. It was clear that a new type of politics was surfacing in the hemisphere in the era of globalization. The EZLN uprising occurred on the same day that the North American Free Trade Agreement (NAFTA) went into effect, tying Canada, Mexico, and the United States into a free trade bloc, threatening local Mexican production from the start.

The EZLN sought to transcend traditional politics. 'This isn't about Chiapas – it's about NAFTA and Salinas's whole neoliberal project,' said the EZLN chief spokesperson, Subcomandante Marcos, on the first day of the uprising. Mexican president Carlos Salinas had not only pushed for NAFTA but had, in the name of the free market, altered the Mexican constitution to weaken communities' right to *ejidos*, or communally owned land, allowing them to be broken up and sold privately. The shift made campesino communities more vulnerable to business and corporate interests. The EZLN uprising was not a revolt of indigenous peoples who merely wanted to retake their lands and expel the rich who exploited them. Here was a rebellion that consciously sought to move beyond the politics of modernity, be they of past national liberation movements, or of the repressive modernization policies of the Mexican government. What distinguished the EZLN from its predecessors was that it did not seek power in Mexico City, nor did it call for state socialism. Throughout the 1990s its objective was to spark a broad-based movement of civil society in Chiapas and the rest of Mexico that would transform the country from the bottom up.[16]

From the start, the Zapatistas emphasized communication as key to their struggle. They transformed the conventional militaristic conception of revolution into one of politics and political communication. On the internet, news of the rebellion and the Zapatista communiqués spread throughout Mexico and around the world. The local Zapatista army was quickly transformed into a broad national and transnational movement of *Zapatismo*.

The new local-global politics of the Zapatistas marked a radical departure from the globalizing capitalist culture and traditional left internationalism. The Zapatista discourse and praxis challenged not only the neoliberal world order, but also conventional political wisdom across the spectrum. In Mexico and internationally, a broad-based civil society movement sprang up around the demands for democracy, social justice, and an end to neoliberal globalization.

A postmodern politics took hold throughout Latin America as movements drew on their roots and constructed their own particular form of social and political struggle. These struggles began locally. They often first sought to address direct threats to survival such as land expropriations, violent coca eradication, or water privatization. They took on global dimensions, however, as the cause of these threats was rooted in a global neoliberal model and mediated by global actors such as the IMF and the World Bank.[17]

Some observers of these indigenous and landless movements insist that they should be seen simply as class-based movements bent on continuing the project of modernization, albeit under a leftist banner. Sociologists James Petras and Henry Veltmeyer, for example, try to deny the positions staked out by indigenous leaders in Ecuador, writing that CONAIE 'has committed itself to a process of non-capitalist modernization.' They declare that the Zapatistas 'reflect class-based conditions that are grounded in a modernist project.' Petras and Veltmeyer downplay the importance of identity politics among the indigenous movements, reducing the indigenous and rural movements to class politics, asserting that 'Latin American peasants tend to see themselves as combatants in a class war.'[18]

This ignores the complexity of the struggles of the rural and indigenous movements. As Fernando Garcia Serrano, an anthropologist at the Latin American School of Social Sciences Andes, 'the identities of the actors of this movement ignore the links of exclusive class identity (be it worker, peasant or poor urban dweller) and base themselves in other principles linked to their practices and cultural values (language, ethnicity, extended familial relations, a vision of the cosmos, etc.).'[19]

In Venezuela in the 1990s, diverse and disparate community organizations sprouted up across the poor barrios of Caracas. A new union-based political party that emerged out of the industrial town of Ciudad Guayana in the 1970s, the Causa R, began to gain important support, helping to develop forms of active community participation at the level of the municipal councils that they controlled in Ciudad Guayana and Caracas. These two experiences were critical components of the Bolivarian movement that helped propel to power Hugo Chávez, a soldier who for over a decade had been building a progressive nationalist current within the armed forces.[20]

In Bolivia, the indigenous movement played a central role in a struggle that swung between the countryside and the cities. The union of coca growers, led by Evo Morales, was founded in the mid-1980s to defend the traditional rights of indigenous peoples to grow coca plants. When the United States backed a move to militarize the coca-growing region of Chapare, the union resisted, leading to frequent clashes. Sixteen coca growers died in 1988 alone. Fed up with the old political parties, in 1995 the *cocaleros*, together with a number of important indigenous and peasant movements, created their own political party, the Movimiento al Socialismo (MAS, Movement Toward Socialism), in order to fight both on the streets and inside parliament.[21]

Then, in 2000, a new popular challenge emerged in Cochabamba, Bolivia's fourth-largest city, as urban organizations waged a 'Water War,' protesting against the privatization of the city's water supply under the auspices of the San Francisco-based Bechtel Corporation. In 2003, indigenous demonstrators from the highland Bolivian city of El Alto descended on La Paz to protest against the government's neoliberal economic policies, forcing the incumbent president, Gonzalo Sánchez de Lozada, to resign. In 2005 a second rebellion erupted, leading to the resignation of Carlos Mesa and the convoking of new elections that propelled Evo Morales into the presidency in 2006.

Along with the Zapatistas, Brazil's MST became the other major Latin American movement that captured increasing international attention in the 1990s. Founded in 1984, the MST, unlike the Zapatistas or CONAIE, was more focused on the issue of land reform. Owing in part to the limited role of indigenous peoples, the MST lends itself to the class-war position staked out by Petras and Veltmeyer. At its founding national meeting in 1984, the MST delegates laid out four goals: 1) to build a broadly inclusive movement of the rural poor, 2) to achieve agrarian reform, 3) to promote the principle that the land belongs to those who work it, and 4) to help build a society that would put an end to capitalism.[22]

Given that it was founded when the Sandinista revolution flourished and socialism had not yet entered into crisis, the MST was more sympathetic to the national liberation movements, even adopting the figure of Che Guevara as an icon appearing on its red banner. This early attachment to the more classic left also stemmed in part from the repressive conditions the MST faced in its struggle for land. The military ruled Brazil from 1964 to 1985. When a civilian who was sympathetic to agrarian reform, Tancredo Neves, was elected president in 1985, he died just before taking office. His successor, José Sarney, did little to contain the armed violence that the landowners used against the MST.

However, it would be a mistake to portray the MST as a traditional rural trade union or simple land reform movement. The MST views itself as a 'mass movement' capable of attracting broad support from middle sectors and society at large.[23] Liberation theologists in Brazil worked at the grassroots to help organize the MST while the Pastoral Land Commission – set up by the Conference of Brazilian Bishops – provided sustained support. Socially-minded teachers, lawyers, and agronomists also assisted the MST, as did the newly founded Workers' Party, under the leadership of Luiz Inácio Lula da Silva.

What has distinguished the MST over the years and helped it to grow into the largest social movement in the Americas is its democratic practice combined with its discipline. Land occupations or encampments are meticulously planned and organized. The new communities practice democratic decision-making in all aspects of their existence, including the organizing of housing, education, healthcare, production, marketing, and culture. People learn to live cooperatively and with the assistance of the MST national organization they receive training in literacy, public health, farming, the administration of co-ops, and other technical skills.[24]

The social struggles and popular rebellions in Latin America proliferated as the 1990s drew to a close and the new millennium opened. A new wave of social movements emerged primarily in the cities that often overlapped with existing rural-based struggles. The urban organizations varied greatly, some with a distinct class basis and others having a multi-class composition. In Argentina, starting in 1996, unemployed workers, known as *piqueteros*, or picketers, blocked roads and major traffic arteries, demanding jobs and an end to the neoliberal privatization policies of President Menem, whose administration had destroyed national industries as imports flooded the country. Then, in December 2001, a financial crisis hit Argentina as the government could not meet its international debt payments. The government of President Fernando de la Rua froze bank account savings, including those of ordinary Argentines. The country exploded with massive multi-class protests that led to the fall of de la Rua and the installation of four presidents in ten days.

In Chile, a very different movement emerged, as largely middle-class local and international human rights organizations mounted a challenge against the remnants of the Pinochet dictatorship. He had left the presidency in 1990, but he still cast a huge repressive shadow over Chile, first as head of the army and then as Senator for Life, preventing the prosecution of human rights violators and instilling fear throughout society. Then, in October 1998, a group of human rights organizations led by Amnesty International orchestrated the arrest of Pinochet while he was in London. When he was returned to Chile in 2000 by the Blair government for alleged health reasons, local magistrates and Chilean organizations and their attorneys now felt emboldened to try Pinochet for human rights violations. Even though he was never sentenced, the public exposure of his abuses in case after case discredited him publicly and ended the pall he cast over Chilean society. He was hounded by the law until his death in 2006, and died a virtual prisoner in his house.[25]

The diversity of all these social movements and rebellions in the Americas makes it impossible to characterize them as class-based movements in the traditional Marxist sense.

'Some of the basic traditional models of political activism, class struggle, and revolutionary organization have today become outdated and useless,' write post-Marxist philosophers Michael Hardt and Antonio Negri in their 2005 book *The Multitude*. 'Such sequences of revolutionary activity are unimaginable today, and instead the experience of insurrection is being rediscovered, so to speak, in the flesh of the multitude.'

'The global recomposition of social classes, the hegemony of immaterial labor, and the forms of decision-making based on network structures all radically change the conditions of any revolutionary process,' Hardt and Negri add.[26] They mark the start of these new forms of struggle with the first generation of social movements organized largely under the rubric of identity politics in the 1970s and early 1980s. By the 1990s new forms of activism and organization had emerged, building on the earlier movements. For Hardt and Negri, the Zapatista movement in Mexico, with its national and international networking, its democratic decision-making process, its horizontal forms of organization, and its insistence on changing the world from the bottom up, reflects what they call the multitude. Whereas older Marxist theories lumped all the groups involved in global rebellion together into one group called 'the masses,' the concept of 'the multitude' recognizes the diversity of the groups involved. It also clearly differs from the classical Marxist belief that the industrial working class has to be the vanguard of any revolutionary movement.

Aside from drawing on the social movements, the multitude is also made up of rebellious individuals who do not necessarily belong to an organization or group. In Latin America, the earlier spontaneous urban upheavals of the late 1980s and early 1990s appeared to be unorganized and were virtually leaderless. They used what Hardt and Negri call 'swarm intelligence.' While they have no formal organization, they are like bees or ants, communicating horizontally and informally to mobilize against the forces that are repressing them.

By using the concepts of the multitude and swarm intelligence, we can begin to understand the new epoch in the Americas and its relationship to the pink tide governments in Latin America. Although the new organizations, groups, and movements often helped bring many of the new left governments to power, they are usually skeptical of these governments and the state in general. In Mexico, the Zapatistas will not run for any political office sanctioned by the national government. They did not back the presidential candidacy of leftist Andrés Manuel López Obrador in either 2006 or 2012 because of their belief that he would not be able to change the basic structure of the repressive state that favors the dominant economic interests. Since its founding, the MST in Brazil has set its own course, maintaining its principles and its militant actions, independent of the government. This proved critical when the Workers' Party veered to the center with Lula's presidential victory in 2002. When the Lula government wavered on its long-time campaign promises to increase land reform to small farmers, the MST quickly resumed militant occupations, actions, and protests to pressure the government to fulfill its commitments. This divergence between the left governments and the social movements accounts for much of the dynamism and tumult that characterize Latin America today.

2 From left: the presidents of Saint Vincent and the Granadines, Bolivia, Cuba, and Venezuela embrace during a 2009 ALBA summit in Cumaná, Venezuela, where the organization ratified a new regional currency, known as the sucre (credit: Michael Fox).

2 | The pink tide and the challenge to US hegemony

CELAC was founded at a historic conclave of thirty-three countries from Latin America and the Caribbean in early December 2011. The meeting in Caracas, Venezuela, excluded the United States and Canada, constituting a direct challenge to the US-promoted OAS, which had dominated hemispheric affairs for decades.

'It is clear that we need a new inter-American system,' Ecuadorean president Rafael Correa proclaimed at the gathering. 'The OAS has been captured historically by North American interests and vision, and its cumulative bias and evolution have rendered it inefficient and untrustworthy for the new era that our America is living.'

The current global economic crisis and its impact on Latin America also figured prominently in CELAC's deliberations. Bolivian president Evo Morales spoke of the 'terminal and structural crisis of capitalism' at the event.

'We have to establish the bases for a new model, for socialism, neo-socialism, living well, 21st-century socialism or whatever you want to call it,' said Morales.

Other leaders highlighted immediate concerns that could be dealt with more responsibly by CELAC. Argentine president Cristina Fernández de Kirchner criticized drug-consuming countries for not doing enough to stem demand for illegal substances. 'It seems that Latin America ends up with all the deaths and guns, and others end up with the drugs and the money,' she said.

Notably, even traditional US allies in the region ardently supported the new organization. Chile's right-wing president Sebastián Piñera agreed to join a troika along with Venezuela and Cuba to set CELAC's objectives and projects. 'Current problems cannot be resolved individually ... they require unity, collaboration and teamwork,' Piñera said at the meeting. 'The best of CELAC is yet to come.'[1]

Like the European Community, CELAC envisions integration as both an economic and a political process. On the political front, member nations believe it will create a more unified bloc of nations to resolve internal disputes and to represent the region in global forums and meetings. Economically it will push for greater integration, including coordinated trade, and fiscal and monetary policies. At the meeting, the countries agreed to a wide-ranging and detailed Plan of Action, which set the goal of establishing preferential trade tariffs, collaborating in energy and environmental projects, and ending illiteracy in every country in three years.

The Caracas summit was the latest sign that over the last decade the United States has slowly lost its historic grip on the region. Already in May 2008, a task force of the New York-based Council on Foreign Relations, comprised of former diplomats, corporate officials, and scholars, reported: 'Latin America is not Washington's to lose; nor is it Washington's to save. U.S. policy can no longer be based on the assumption that the United States is the most important outside actor in Latin America. If there was an era of U.S. hegemony in Latin America, it is over.'[2]

At the turn of the millennium, it appeared that the United States was in the driver's seat vis-à-vis Latin America. In April 2001, just months after taking office, George W. Bush called for the FTAA at a gathering of hemispheric presidents in Quebec City, Canada. The FTAA would create a giant free trade zone extending from Tierra del Fuego in South America to the Arctic Circle in the north. Only one dissident voice arose at the gathering, that of Venezuelan president Hugo Chávez, who instead raised the idea of ALBA.

Chávez was soon joined by a string of left-leaning Latin American governments that questioned the neoliberal order and refused to join the FTAA. Even before the full pantheon of left leaders had emerged, the FTAA was dealt a death knell at the Fourth Summit of the Americas in Mar del Plata, Argentina, in November 2005. Tens of thousands demonstrated in the streets while Chávez, Brazilian president Luiz Inácio Lula da Silva, Argentina president Nestor Kirchner, and others resoundingly rejected George W. Bush's call for the hemispheric free trade agreement.

Meanwhile, ALBA was becoming a reality. Venezuela and Cuba signed its founding treaty in 2004. Since then, six other Latin American and Caribbean countries have joined as full members. ALBA's objective is almost diametrically opposed to the free trade agreements, aiming instead to promote trade on the principle of solidarity instead of competition – a state-centered instead of a neoliberal approach toward integration. The exchange of Cuban medical personnel for Venezuelan oil is just one early example of the type of agreement reached under ALBA. Cuba and Venezuela have also collaborated under ALBA to provide literacy training to the peoples of other ALBA member countries, such as Bolivia. The key concept is to trade and exchange resources in those areas where each country has complementary strengths and to do so on the basis of fairness, rather than market-determined prices.

Through ALBA, member nations have also created so-called *empresas grannacionales* ('supranational enterprises') for the production of medicines and food. In contrast to transnational corporate projects these enterprises are based on serving a social need, rather than merely making a profit. The continental TV station Telesur and the regional oil company Petrocaribe are examples of supranational projects. ALBA also has a bank – with a start-up capital of 1 percent of the member countries' monetary reserves – that provides low-interest loans for agricultural and industrial development in member countries. In November 2008, ALBA agreed to develop a currency for its member countries, which would be called the sucre (Unitary System for Regional Compensation). According to the ALBA website, 'The Sucre is the first step toward a common currency of the ALBA countries, in order to liberate ourselves from the yoke of the dollar.'[3]

The pull of ALBA has had an impact on other, older regional trade blocs. MERCOSUR, founded in 1991 by Argentina, Brazil, Paraguay, and Uruguay, has been intent on establishing a common market among the countries of the southern cone. Since the arrival of left-leaning presidents in Brazil, Argentina, and Uruguay it has been much more active in promoting democratic politics as well as trade among its members than CAN, which was founded in 1969 with strong link to the United States. Venezuela withdrew from CAN in 2006 because of differences with Colombia and sought to join MERCOSUR. Approval for Venezuela's full entry into the bloc was stymied by the right-wing-controlled Paraguayan Senate, which had veto power over all new entrants. Ironically, the congressional coup against Lugo led to Paraguay's suspension from MERCOSUR and enabled the other three countries to approve Venezuela's full incorporation in July 2012. Venezuela's entry is a further boost to regional trading, as MERCOSUR now represents the equivalent of the fifth-largest economy in the world (after the United States, China, Germany, and Japan). The bloc has also encouraged associate members such as Bolivia and Ecuador to seek full membership.[4]

The drive for greater regional collaboration and integration took a decisive turn in May 2008 with the establishment of UNASUR. Along with the goal of integrating their economies, the twelve member countries agreed to maintain a headquarters in Quito, Ecuador, and set up a parliament in Cochabamba, Bolivia. They also called for the establishment of a common defense council. With annual summits, UNASUR's presidency rotates on a yearly basis between the presidents of the member countries. Other projects include the founding of the Banco del Sur (BANCOSUR, Bank of the South) with $20 billion in capital in 2009, establishing a single market by 2019, creating a common passport and a common currency.

Prior to the crisis in Europe, many South American leaders looked to the European Union for inspiration for their process of unification. In other words, a substantial part of the basic principles underlying the process is rooted in free trade and capitalism. Venezuela, Ecuador, and Bolivia, though, clearly have a different vision, which is more politically and socially oriented.[5] As long as the integration and unification process has remained on a political level, there haven't been any major issues of dissent. However, as soon as the countries have moved toward economic integration, conflicts have emerged. The discord over the BANCOSUR is a good example. The formation of the bank was delayed several times because the participating UNASUR countries could not agree on basic issues such as whether the initiative would serve as a development bank or also as a monetary stabilization fund, whether all countries would have an equal vote in bank decisions or whether voting would be proportional to contributions, and whether the bank would raise funds only from members or also from international capital markets. The difference of opinion on these issues has tended to be marked by how anti-capitalist the member countries' governments are, with Venezuela, Ecuador, and Bolivia staking out more leftist positions and Brazil and Argentina taking up more pro-capitalist positions.[6]

Countries will differ over the speed and degree of integration, but the fact remains that with the rise of the 'New Continentalism,' the integration of the region has advanced in the past decade far more rapidly than at any time since Simón Bolívar dreamed of a united Latin America roughly two centuries ago. The reasons for this renewed effort are manifold, but directly related to the rise of the Latin American left, which believes in unification as essential for achieving true independence from the United States and the neoliberal order.

Underlying the rise of the social movements and the New Continentalism is a growing international consciousness and networking fomented by regional meetings such as the World Social Forum (WSF), which held its first gathering in Porto Alegre, Brazil, in January 2001. The WSF was initially convened as an alternative to the World Economic Forum of the globe's ruling elites held in Davos, Switzerland. A decade later, it has brought together a vast array of social movements, civil society organizations, political leaders, academics, and others under the banner of 'Another World Is Possible.' The tremendous diversity of the participants facilitated wide-ranging debates about tactics, strategies, and visions for a counter-hegemonic world. Many working alliances, campaigns, and calls to action have been launched at the WSF around issues such as indigenous and ethnic rights, water as a fundamental human right, biodiversity and opposition to genetically modified organisms, debt cancellation for the world's poorest countries, and opposition to US bases and militarism in Latin America. While the WSF as a whole does not endorse any particular agenda, its apex as a vital political platform came at the 2009 Forum in Belém, Brazil, with the attendance of five South American presidents: Hugo Chávez, Luiz Inácio Lula da Silva, Evo Morales, Rafael Correa, and Fernando Lugo.

This wide-ranging challenge comes as US influence in Latin America has declined over the twenty-first century, owing largely to 'imperial overstretch.' Since 2001, the United States has become embroiled in two costly wars (the war in Afghanistan is now the longest in US history). The skyrocketing military budgets have sucked up capital and commodity production, creating enormous budgetary and trade deficits, and causing the United States to lose its prominence in the global economy. Latin America has reacted by beginning to take matters into its own hands.

A definitive sign of the region's consolidated independence from US dictates occurred in March 2008 when a meeting of OAS foreign ministers condemned a Colombian military incursion into Ecuador to bomb a Fuerzas Armadas Revolucionarias de Colombia (FARC, Revolutionary Armed Forces of Colombia) guerrilla camp. The raid killed twenty-five people on Ecuadorean soil. The OAS unanimously passed a resolution, which, among other points, rejected 'the incursion of military and police forces of Colombia in the territory of Ecuador,' calling it a 'clear violation' of the OAS charter. Despite US resistance and 'reservations,' the United States agreed to the resolution.

UNASUR disputed US influence in the region just months after it was founded. In September 2008, the US-funded right-wing opposition in the eastern lowland departments of Bolivia rebelled against the government of Evo Morales, occupying and burning government offices. In response, Chilean president Michelle Bachelet convened an emergency meeting of the new organization in Santiago. On 15 September, the twelve UNASUR governments signed the 'Declaration of La Moneda,' denouncing the genocidal atrocities committed in the eastern department of Pando, and decrying any attempt to undermine the Bolivian government and the country's territorial integrity.

'For the first time in South America's history, the countries of our region are deciding how to resolve our problems, without the presence of the United States,' said Evo Morales at the gathering, thanking UNASUR for its support.[7]

Another major blow to US regional hegemony occurred in May 2009, when OAS members unanimously passed a resolution that reversed the 1962 decree expelling Cuba from the OAS. Secretary of State Hillary Clinton unsuccessfully tried to tie the resolution to placing political demands on Cuba. Subsequently, Cuba declined the offer to rejoin the organization. But the episode served as a powerful sign that the region was emancipating itself from US dominance. The United States had effectively lost control over the hemispheric organization it had used since the beginning of the Cold War to impose its will on Latin America.

Only a month later, in late June 2009, the democratically elected Honduran president Manuel Zelaya was toppled by the country's entrenched business and political interests. Zelaya had taken office in 2006 on a neoliberal platform, but midway through his term he had changed course, expanding social spending, aligning himself with Chávez, and joining ALBA. In response to the coup, an array of Latin American governments and organizations demanded that Zelaya be restored to office, including ALBA, MERCOSUR, and UNASUR. The OAS, under the sway of new left governments, convened an emergency session, and compelled even the United States to support a unanimous resolution calling upon the coup leaders to restore Zelaya to power.

The Obama administration backed away slowly but solidly from its outright opposition to the coup. When questionable elections were held on 29 November 2009, under repressive conditions, special interests and lobbyists in the United States aligned with the Honduran elite persuaded Secretary of State Hillary Clinton to recognize the results. The State Department increasingly came to view Zelaya as part of the so-called 'bad left,' led by Chávez, that was directly challenging US interests in the region. But even the 'good left' wasn't following the US lead. Along with Chávez, Lula proved to be one of the most vocal critics of this shift in US policy on Honduras. Together with a majority of Latin American nations, they refused to recognize the legitimacy of the election of Porfirio Lobo as the new president of Honduras.

Globalization and nation-state autonomy

The constellation of forces at play in Latin America reveals that while the hemisphere is part of the globalization process in which the transnational corporations have gained the upper hand vis-à-vis national capital, Latin American governments none the less continue to display a great degree of autonomy in taking on the US empire. We disagree with William I. Robinson, who views even post-neoliberal capitalist states and their rulers largely as transmission belts for the integration and the interests of transnational capital. The reality is that many of the larger states in the Global South, along with those in the North, still project 'national interests' on the international stage, often jockeying intensely with one another in order to carve out larger roles for their respective nation-states in the economic and geopolitical realms.

The lynchpin of Robinson's analysis begins with America's imperial wars in the twenty-first century. He asserts that the George W. Bush administration moved into the Persian Gulf mainly to make the world safe for global capitalism: 'When the U.S. state invaded Iraq and imposed a property regime that gave free rein to transnational capital in the occupied country and promoted integration into global capitalism, it was internalizing in the occupied country global capitalist relations.'[8]

While it is certainly true that the United States sought to advance capitalism in Iraq, the cabal of neoconservatives who advocated and pursued the war were principally concerned with any and all challenges to US supremacy. In an increasingly multipolar world, they sought to rectify this situation by invading Iraq, gaining control of its petroleum resources and turning it into a platform for warding off other powers in the Middle East, including Russia, China, and even France and Germany. 'Imperial overstretch' was the historic dynamic driving the Bush administration to undertake the war. Like empires past, the United States sought to compensate for its declining economic and strategic position by undertaking military adventures.[9]

Latin America is part of this broader global thrust of the United States to deal with the loss of hegemony by adopting a belligerent stance. As defined by Giovanni Arrighi, who draws on Antonio Gramsci, hegemony is the ability of a government or a state to dominate largely through consensual agreements and arrangements with those under its rule; force is resorted to only when rebellious elements get out of hand.[10] This has largely characterized US domination of Latin America since the end of the nineteenth century. Even with the Cuban revolution and the guerrilla insurgencies of the 1960s, and then the Sandinista revolutionary government in Nicaragua in the 1980s, the United States – with the acquiescence and support of the Latin American elites – was able to contain these conflicts and reassert its hegemonic position.

Today the challenge to the US empire in the hemisphere may be less dramatic, but it is broader and more complex with the rise of the social movements and new left governments on the one hand, and the faltering US economic dominance on the other. China is also challenging the United States in the region, as a powerful commercial competitor. The total trade balance between China and Latin America increased from $10 billion in 2000 to $180 billion in 2010. China shipped mainly manufactured goods while Latin America exported soybeans, petroleum, copper, iron ore, and timber.[11] Chile signed a free trade agreement with China in 2005, and by 2009 Chile was exporting more copper and agricultural commodities to China than any other country. In 2009, China surpassed the United States as Brazil's leading trade partner.[12] China has also concluded major petroleum supply and investment agreements with Argentina, Brazil, Ecuador, and Venezuela.

At the 2009 Summit of the Americas in Trinidad and Tobago, Barack Obama acknowledged 'past errors' and called for an 'equal partnership.' But while the United States may pay lip-service to the growing independence of Latin America, the Obama administration is following in the footsteps of the Bush administration as it boosts the US military presence in Latin America in tandem with the promotion of free trade agreements. In his first year in office, Obama moved to establish seven military bases in Colombia, and augmented the activities of the 4th Fleet, which George Bush had pulled out of mothballs and assigned the mission of plying the oceanic waters off Latin America. The logic of a new militarism in the region also explains why, in the aftermath of the Haitian earthquake, the Pentagon took control of Haiti, and dispatched 6,500 soldiers, placing the military in charge of the largest humanitarian crisis in hemispheric history.

With the Merida Initiative and Plan Colombia, the United States is bent on militarizing a corridor running from Mexico through Central America to Colombia. Spending billions on arming and training local militaries and police forces under the auspices of the Pentagon, the United States is in fact carrying out the Latin America version of Global Counterinsurgency. Allegedly there is a 'fusion' of terrorists, guerrillas, drug dealers, and criminals that requires the United States to work with local allies to 'clear, hold and build' in this security corridor.[13] NAFTA and the US–Central American Free Trade Agreement are the overlapping economic components of the corridor. Obama reneged on his campaign promises to revisit the already signed trade agreements, even lobbying the US Congress to extend the free trade network to Colombia and Panama. Indeed, in its immediate backyard – Mexico, Central America, and parts of the Caribbean – the United States still exercises much of its historic muscle, as we see with the growing military intervention in the name of fighting the drug wars.

In Latin America at large, transnational capital may be ascendant over national capital, but US trade and investments are in a position of relative decline and many of the countries in the southern hemisphere have an amalgam of political and economic interests that cause them to oppose US imperial initiatives. Lula, for instance, facilitated the advance of transnational capital during his eight years as Brazilian president, but he also established a series of policies that are independent of the United States. He helped foster the axis of BRICS nations – Brazil, Russia, India, China, and South Africa – which has questioned, and even challenged, the United States in political and economic forums. Lula also reached out to Iran, signing commercial agreements and inviting President Mahmoud Ahmadinejad to Brazil. Perhaps most importantly he often allied Brazil with Venezuela under Chávez, backing the construction of a transnational oil pipeline and bringing Venezuela into the fold of MERCOSUR. When Colombian president Álvaro Uribe signed the agreement with the United States for seven military bases, Lula and Chávez demanded that he reveal the exact terms of the agreement. (These bases were ultimately blocked by the Colombian Constitutional Court.) Lula also made it clear that the new, very deep petroleum deposits discovered off the coast of Rio de Janeiro will be under the direct control of the state. Brazil will dictate the terms of any explorations, relegating transnational petroleum corporations to an auxiliary role as the state seeks to capture the bulk of the revenue.

Reform left and radical left in power in Latin America

Analyzing the complexity of these state relations, it would be premature to believe that transnational corporations have fully eclipsed national interests in Latin America. We may be witnessing the beginning of that process, but each country is configured differently, with its own historic national tensions and traditions. Taking this into consideration, what have the varying composition of forces between government and capital meant for the different governments' policies in the region? How best can these diverse policies be characterized?

First, it has become common to divide Latin American left governments into two categories. At times it makes sense to repeat this inadequate dualism.[14] However, it is also important to note that it probably makes more sense to see these governments as residing on different points on a political spectrum. It is up to the political analysts to draw the line that divides one group of governments from another.

To complicate matters even further, it is also important to note that the different Latin American lefts have very different origins.[15] Bolivia's government has its roots in the country's indigenous majority, Venezuela's is rooted in an urban and military progressive nationalism, and Ecuador's in an urban citizens' movement. Brazil's government comes out of the union movement, Argentina's derives from left Peronism, and Uruguay's from the Tupamaro guerrilla movement and the leftist Frente Amplio (Broad Front) political coalition of the 1970s.

Despite these complexities, in order to determine which countries have developed policies that are actually moving in a more radical direction, it is important to identify criteria for making such an evaluation. André Gorz, a radical social theorist, has provided a relatively simple criterion for this purpose, which he identifies as the difference between policies that are 'reformist reforms' and those that are 'non-reformist reforms.'[16] Reformist reforms are those that merely appease immediate social needs, but leave the population or the movement that pushed for them demobilized and less empowered than prior to the reform. This means, in effect, that the political or economic system has been stabilized and conserved. Non-reformist reform, or transformative reform, on the other hand, also addresses social needs, but leaves the population and the movement that pushed for these more empowered and mobilized than before. As a result, future progressive social change becomes more likely.

If we examine policies this way, we propose that the governments of Cuba, Venezuela, Bolivia, and Ecuador have, on balance, implemented important transformative reforms. The other left-leaning governments in the region, such as Brazil, Argentina, and Uruguay, are committed to stabilizing the existent economic system and have implemented mostly reformist reforms.

3 Bolivia begins testing to exploit the world's largest reserve of lithium on the Uyuni salt flats in November 2009 (credit: Noah Friedman-Rudovsky).

3 | Between neo-extractivism and twenty-first-century socialism

On 30 January 2005, Hugo Chávez addressed the fifth annual gathering of the WSF. 'It is necessary to transcend capitalism,' he said, 'through socialism, true socialism with equality and justice.'[1] He went on to tell the roaring crowd of 15,000 at the Gigantinho stadium in Porto Alegre, Brazil: 'We have to re-invent socialism. It can't be the kind of socialism that we saw in the Soviet Union, but it will emerge as we develop new systems that are built on cooperation, not competition.' This marked what many came to refer to as the inception of 'twenty-first-century socialism.'

Four years later at the 2009 WSF gathering in Belém, Brazil, Ecuadorean president Rafael Correa, noting that the world was in the midst of an economic calamity, stated: 'Let us take advantage of this crisis, of this current weakness of capitalism, and use the opportunity to create something new and better – a 21st century socialism.'[2] With Chávez and presidents Evo Morales of Bolivia and Fernando Lugo of Paraguay at his side at the Hangar auditorium on the evening of 29 January, Correa declared that the new socialism, unlike 'traditional socialism,' would push for gender justice and ethnic equality and defend 'the life and the social value of ecosystems like the Amazon rainforest.'[3]

Morales told the gathering: 'The world is being shaken by many crises: of finance, energy, climate, food, and institutions. But all of these crises are part of one big crisis experienced by the capitalist system. If we, the peoples of the world, are not able to bury capitalism, then capitalism will bury our planet ... This crisis presents us with a great opportunity to build a different world, as long as we are willing to employ an alternative model.'[4]

These declarations, however, did not mean that socialism was about to take the hemisphere by storm. As Bolivian vice-president Álvaro García Linera declared two and a half years later, 'The continent may be living its most progressive – and, to a certain point, its most revolutionary moment of the last fifty years.' We are witnessing 'the rise of progressive, left, revolutionary governments on the continent, but governments that are not necessarily socialist.'[5]

A real anti-capitalist challenge?

Can any of these governments be said to have truly embarked on the construction of a post-neoliberal society, let alone a radical anti-capitalist one embedded in historic socialism? Are we just witnessing a neo-developmentalist twenty-first-century version of the failed import substitution industrialization project of the 1960s and 1970s, or have any of these governments begun to break with the logic of capital? Put simply, how real is the specter of twenty-first-century socialism in Latin America?

None of the new left governments has taken office as a result of revolutionary upheavals like those that occurred in Cuba in 1959 and Nicaragua in 1979. Elected via the ballot box, they control only a portion of state power. The militaries were not defeated or reconstituted, and none of their electoral platforms called for a frontal assault on the reign of capital.

There are several reasons why the contemporary left in Latin America has been so reluctant to call for a socialist economy based on public ownership of the means of production. First, as in the rest of the world, the collapse of the Soviet bloc and 'actually existing socialism' decimated and discredited the socialist model, making it difficult to create an alternative that enjoyed popular appeal. Moreover, the singular hemispheric experience in advancing workers' power and economic democracy via a peaceful transition – Salvador Allende's Popular Unity government (1970–73) – was by and large viewed as a failure. Most of the left in Chile, as well as the rest of Latin America, came to believe that the Chilean quest for socialism had contributed to the destabilization and overthrow of the Allende government.

Another critical factor in the decline of socialism is the fragmentation and smashing of traditional working-class organizations. The neoliberal offensive in the 1980s and 1990s shifted the balance of social forces in many countries, dramatically weakening the trade unions and allied political parties. Social movements often stepped into this void, but they have been notably more hesitant to take on the issue of socialism, instead focusing more on ethnic and identity politics.

Given this historic backdrop, none of the pink tide governments entered office on a platform promising a transition to socialism. While lambasting the neoliberal model, they largely accepted the capitalist economy as a given. As Uruguayan ecologist Eduardo Gudynas argues in his 2010 article 'The new extractivism of the 21st century: ten urgent theses about extractivism in relation to current South American progressivism' that neo-extractivism became the de facto economic and trade policy of the new governments.[6] Countries such as Venezuela, Bolivia, Ecuador, Brazil, Argentina, and Uruguay are 'very different from each other,' he acknowledges, but they are similar in that they engage in 'neo-extractivism.' Over 90 percent of the exports of Venezuela, Bolivia, and Ecuador comprise hydrocarbons, minerals, and agricultural commodities. Even Brazil, with a substantial industrial sector, derives over 50 percent of its export revenue from primary commodities.

Gudynas recognizes that the pink tide governments are promoting a model of development in which the state plays a central role. Rejecting the minimalist state of neoliberalism, the new left in power is determined to capture a much larger portion of the revenues generated by the extractive sector. In Bolivia the government has renegotiated the contracts of all the multinational corporations involved in the export of hydrocarbons so the state receives over half of the revenue. The Argentine government of Cristina Fernández de Kirchner has re-nationalized Yacimientos Petrolíferos Fiscales (YPF), the country's largest oil and gas company, and enraged the agribusiness sector with export taxes on soybean exports. Correa has expanded the role of the Ecuadorean state in the petroleum sector and is prosecuting multinational corporations that have ravaged the environment in the past.

Gudynas writes, however, that none of the pink tide governments has 'substantially modified the extractive sector,' nor are they 'ameliorating the social and environmental impacts through a transition to another kind of development which does not depend on the exportation of primary materials such as copper and petroleum.' Instead, continued dependency on extractive activities and agricultural commodities means that these economies remain subordinated to the needs of the international market.

Bolivian vice-president García Linera does not deny that the continent is reliant on extractive exports, but he argues that Latin America has created a 'regional space' that goes beyond neo-extractivism.

'We are exporting more gas, more minerals, and the prices have risen ... But at the same time, today, 80% of the wealth stays in Bolivian hands: before this 80% remained in foreign hands,' García Linera told Chile's bi-weekly magazine *Punto Fijo* in 2011. 'Bolivia has bet on exports and the internal market as a model of economic development, a way of distributing wealth, and a way of satisfying more peoples' needs. This is the major difference with the neoliberal model. The country grows at a high rate, but the appropriation of wealth is collective.'

For García Linera, the continent rests on a new economic tripod:

the diversification of international markets, greater regional economic ties, and a strong internal market.[7] This shift has been beneficial to many Latin American countries.

'Why have the Latin American economies not been so affected by the global economic crisis, in 2008 and even now?' asks García Linera. 'Because they have diversified their exports to various markets, and because countries like Brazil, Argentina, Venezuela, and Bolivia have bet on their internal markets'.

The conundrum of the state

Under the pink tide governments, the state has been used to regulate multinational and national corporate interests, to secure the best terms possible for new investments, and to expand the role of state enterprises. Coupled with this comes a commitment to use some of the new revenues for social expenditures and anti-poverty programs. This differentiates these countries not only from previous neoliberal regimes, but also current conservative governments such as those in Mexico and Panama.[8]

Nevertheless, Gudynas contends that the increased dependency on extractive activities to fund social programs has fed a circular dynamic whereby these same governments, using the social legitimacy won as a result of their social programs, justify continued and expanded extractivist practices as essential to the continuation of such programs. He adds that while these programs dampen social discontent by alleviating the worst excesses of neoliberalism, the extractivist model – with the limited industrialization and employment generation that accompany it, combined with high environmental costs – falls short of providing a systemic alternative to neoliberalism.

Other critics of the pink tide governments question the usefulness of holding even a portion of state power. John Holloway, author of the influential and widely debated book *Change the World Without Taking Power*, asserts that the poverty-alleviation focus of the pink tide does not offer a genuine alternative that empowers the popular classes from the bottom up. The state subordinates social conflict to the dynamic of capital, separating the leaders from the led. The state may be able to bring about change on behalf of the people, but it cannot be the organizational form of change by the people, and that is what a real break with the current system of domination requires.[9]

Holloway, even more than Gudynas, insists that the focus on poverty reduction of these new left governments inherently leads to a reliance on state-oriented policies and the pursuit of economic progress above all else, regardless of its consequences. This approach stands in glaring contrast to many of the social movements in Latin America, particularly the ecological and indigenous movements that, Holloway writes, 'are very explicitly opposed to the destruction that Progress entails.' (For Holloway, Progress is the destructive drive of capitalism.) Thus these two left positions stand in direct opposition to each other: one enthusiastically embraces the state while the other remains independent.[10]

In his 2010 book on social movements and states in Latin America, *Dancing With Dynamite*, Benjamin Dangl takes a more nuanced position. He recognizes the importance of government-created initiatives aimed at empowering local communities and believes that some of the region's governments are building alternatives to capitalism, but he is also clear that the state is 'by its nature, a hegemonic force that generally aims to subsume, weaken, or eliminate other movements and political forces that contest its power.'[11]

The result is a multifaceted dance between the autonomous movements and the leftist governments. As Dangl highlights, some governments have continued to work closely with movements, while others have ignored, co-opted, manipulated, or even repressed grassroots sectors. For their part, some movements have turned to defending themselves from the state crackdown, while others have had more symbiotic relations with the ruling party, backing political candidates and pressuring the government for concessions. Alternatives are being built both within and outside the state.

The radical left in government

The subsequent chapters will deal in more detail with the issues raised above with a focus on Venezuela, Bolivia, Ecuador, Brazil, and Cuba. Of particular interest are the domestic, regional, and international alliances that these governments have made in order to shift the balance of power away from US hegemony and in favor of the popular movements.

Over and above the discussions of extractivism and the state, Venezuela, Bolivia, and Ecuador share certain similarities that place them at the more radical end of the political spectrum. All three Andean nations are characterized by an extreme class polarization and a crisis of legitimacy of the old regimes. Popular mobilizations, led mainly by the indigenous movements, toppled governments in Bolivia and Ecuador, while in Venezuela an urban insurrection discredited the Punto Fijo system that divided the rule of the country between two political parties for roughly forty years. Morales, Correa, and Chávez rode these systemic crises to power, adopting the demands of the social movements and the dispossessed as their own. Many of the traditional parties virtually collapsed once the new movements and leaders took power.

The rewriting of new constitutions via democratically elected constituent assemblies was another common characteristic of these three governments during their early years in office. The constitutions helped shift the institutional rules of the game, which had always been stacked against the poor majority. Despite the ambiguous capitalist elements that are retained in a number of articles in the new constitutions, and notwithstanding some of the criticisms raised by social movements, the traditionally excluded and marginalized have won gains in an important range of cultural, economic, and social rights. The new constitutions also enshrine a greater role for state intervention in the economy and control over natural resources – fundamental demands of the social movements.

Perhaps more importantly, the process of elaborating the constitutions played a vital role in invigorating organizations from below. Along with the elected delegates to the assemblies, activists and concerned citizens participated in round tables and drafted articles for the new constitutions on women's rights, basic services, environmental issues, and questions of indigenous self-determination. Many of the social movements view these new constitutions as weapons in their struggles not just against the old elites but also in some cases against the very same politicians who had supported the calls for the constituent assemblies.

While the constitutions advanced numerous rights and guarantees, they also collided with the old state apparatus inherited by the new governments. Years of neoliberalism had strengthened states' repressive arms – the military, security forces, and the police – and dismantled governments' social welfare functions, as well as their regulatory powers, particularly over transnational capital. The state bureaucracies themselves – often run and staffed on the basis of favoritism and political affiliation – also weakened the new governments. These bureaucracies had no interest in implementing some of the promised social reforms or capacity to do so. The progressive forces began to realize that winning control of the government and exercising power were not the same thing.

In order to alter this balance of power, the new left governments have expanded state control over strategic industries such as petroleum, gas, mining, and telecommunications, through renegotiating contracts or outright expropriation. At each step of the way they confronted counter-revolutionary forces that have attempted to destabilize and overthrow these governments. In Venezuela, as the government moved to take control of the state oil company Petróleos de Venezuela SA (PDVSA, Petroleum of Venezuela SA), pro-capitalist managers attempted to shut down the industry in order to cripple the country's economy and force Chávez from power. Instead, the combined mobilization of workers, communities, and soldiers broke the bosses' lockout. The economy contracted by roughly 25 percent in the first quarter of 2003, but the government, now with PDVSA firmly under control, was able to resuscitate the economy and begin to fund some of the initial social missions aimed at providing education and healthcare for the most needy.

The defeated lockout, as well as the April 2002 military coup attempt against Chávez, and similar violent reactions by local oligarchies in Bolivia in September 2008 and a police rebellion in Ecuador in September 2010, demonstrate the old elite's fierce resistance to the new progressive administrations. Social movements have remained mobilized. This time, however, instead of fighting neoliberal policies, they have responded to the right-wing attacks by defending what many view as 'their' governments.

Finally, all three have been the only governments to talk up socialism as an alternative to capitalism and have spearheaded the most radical process of regional integration under way – ALBA.

Concluding perspectives on the left in power

Other interesting perspectives have been put forth on the new social movements and the pink tide in Latin America. Cuban analyst Roberto Regalado notes that in Uruguay and Brazil, the left political parties came to power after decades of building political momentum as the influence of the right declined. Electoral victories in Venezuela and Bolivia, on the other hand, were more directly linked to the rise of social movements and the profound crisis of the traditional political system. In all cases, the margin of maneuver and the ability to use governmental power to halt, or reverse, neoliberalism are marginal. For Regalado, the 'priority of the left' cannot be to simply carve out a permanent space within the existing political system 'but rather, to politically accumulate power with a view to the future revolutionary transformation of society.'[12]

Marta Harnecker, a leading theorist of socialism, postulates that each of the new left governments emerged from very different economic, cultural, and social conditions, and have, at best, won only governmental power. They have not conquered state power, something that the left traditionally saw as indispensable for bringing about transformational change.

'Rather than classifying Latin American governments according to some kind of typology as many analyst have done,' Harnecker writes, we should 'try to evaluate their performance by keeping in mind the balance of forces with which they have to operate. Therefore, we should not look as much at the pace with which they proceed as the direction in which they are going.'[13]

Argentine Marxist Claudio Katz argues that the previous revolutions in Latin America – Mexico, 1910, Bolivia, 1952, Cuba, 1959, and Nicaragua, 1979 – were won through military confrontations and resulted in the dismantling of the former armies. What we have today are not revolutions but rebellions whose three common planks are opposition to neoliberalism, imperialism, and authoritarianism.[14] Three types of governments exist in Latin America today: conservative, center-left, and radical nationalists. Governments may oscillate between the center-left and radical nationalist positions on different issues, blurring the line between one classification and the other. However, according to Katz, radical nationalists such as those in power in Bolivia, Ecuador, and Venezuela differentiate themselves through their 'confrontation with imperialism, conflicts with local capitalists and encouragement of popular mobilizations.' None, however, has initiated a socialist course like that of Cuba in the 1960s.

Raúl Zibechi, in *Dispersing Power: Social Movements as Anti-State Forces*, presents an intriguing interpretation of the role of the social movements. While focusing on the community of El Alto, Bolivia, which was largely responsible for the overthrow of two presidents, Zibechi argues that societies in movement cause cracks in the 'mechanisms of domination,' ripping at the 'fabric of social control.' The dispersal of power at the base through horizontal grassroots decision-making, as in El Alto, constitutes a direct challenge to the power of the state and to US imperial designs on the region.

'For those of us who struggle for emancipation, the central and critical challenges are not from above but from below,' writes Zibechi. 'There is no point in blaming the governments or issuing calls of "betrayal." It is a daily task for all of us committed to creating a new world to care for the people's power as the sacred fire of the movement.'[15]

In this discourse on the social movements and the advance of the pink tide governments, the role of Cuba needs to be addressed: the island nation that withstood the collapse of the Soviet Union continues to defy the United States and remains deeply committed to socialism. With a fresh breeze blowing from the south, Cuba's role has been twofold in constructing a new socialism. On the one hand, its internationalism – as embodied by the 'export' of doctors and teachers to help combat poverty in the region – has been vital for advancing social programs initiated by the ALBA governments. In Venezuela it is almost impossible to imagine the social missions in health and education without acknowledging the contribution of Cuba.

But this is only one side of the equation. Cuba has served as a historic laboratory for the rise of twenty-first-century socialism. Other countries have learned from its economic shortcomings, as well its social policies in the areas of health and education. And now Cuba with its own massive economic restructuring is entering a new period in its efforts to renovate socialism. We are witnessing a new synergy in Latin America as each of the left governments borrows from others to advance the reforms and transformations that are best suited to its own national history and identity.

4 Hundreds of thousands of supporters of Venezuelan president Hugo Chávez flood Bolívar avenue in Caracas for a campaign rally in support of Chávez's 2006 re-election (credit: Sílvia Leindecker).

4 | Venezuela's twenty-first-century socialism

The rise of twenty-first-century socialism is linked to Venezuelan president Hugo Chávez more than any other figure. In the early years of this century, with the world focused on the US wars in Iraq and Afghanistan, socialism appeared moribund, a political relic of the past relegated, in the Americas, to the island of Cuba. This changed abruptly in January 2005, when Chávez announced at the WSF in Porto Alegre, Brazil, that it was time to reclaim the socialist dream:

> It is impossible within the framework of the capitalist system to solve the grave problems of poverty of the majority of the world's population. We must transcend capitalism. But we cannot resort to state capitalism, which would be the same perversion as the Soviet Union. We must reclaim socialism as a thesis, a project, and a path ... a new type of socialism, a humanist one, that puts humans and not machines or the state ahead of everything.[1]

Chávez's call to construct a new socialism for the twenty-first century marked a turning point in progressive history. Before this moment, even sectors of the left believed that the collapse of the Soviet Union had heralded the death of socialism. Yet here was a president willing to reclaim the word 'socialism,' placing it back on the public agenda. These were not just the words and aspirations of a single figure; they reflected the growing anti-capitalist consciousness of a popular democratic movement that was directly challenging US hegemony in the region. Socialism could be achieved with 'democracy,' insisted Chávez, 'but not the type of democracy being imposed from Washington.'[2]

Since then, through numerous extensive speeches, Chávez has consistently sought to build support for his socialist vision. And according to numerous polls, a majority of Venezuelans have come to view this dream as a viable alternative to capitalism. Chávez has attempted to enunciate some guiding principles for twenty-first-century socialism. By 2007, he had formulated a vision of what he called the 'elementary triangle of socialism,' based on the concepts of social property, social production, and social distribution. For Chávez, twenty-first-century socialism required social ownership over the means of production in order to ensure that social wealth remained in the hands of society as a whole. Social needs, and not profit, had to drive production, with communities actively participating in deciding what was produced and for whom. Democracy in the workplace was vital for ensuring an end to the exploitation of labor and to allow for the free and full development of workers' creativity. Socialism required democratic participation in all spheres. This alone would guarantee 'integral human development,' an explicit goal that had been set out earlier in Venezuela's new constitution.[3]

Over half a dozen years after Chávez's first official proclamation of the socialist character of the Bolivarian revolution, an intense debate continues over how serious a challenge Venezuela's twenty-first-century socialism represents to capitalism. While important strides have been made, there are tensions, contradictions, and weaknesses. Socialism's ability to advance in Venezuela will continue to be impacted by ongoing US intervention, the process of regional integration, the intensifying class struggle at home, and the political fate and health of Chávez.

Revolution in an unlikely country

For many on the left, Venezuela hardly registered on the radar during the period of rising anti-neoliberal mobilizations throughout the 1990s. While anti-globalization activists were drawing inspiration from the struggles of the *piqueteros* and neighborhood assemblies in Argentina, indigenous organizations in Bolivia and Ecuador, and the MST in Brazil, Venezuela appeared to be a regional backwater in terms of powerful social movements.

Venezuelans, however, can claim credit for the first major anti-neoliberal uprising to occur in Latin America. Triggered by the imposition of an IMF austerity package that saw fuel prices skyrocket overnight, a massive uprising shook Caracas for four days in February 1989, extending outwards to several other cities and towns. A brutal massacre by state security forces finally quelled the revolt. Despite the massive repression, the *Caracazo* marked a point of no return for a society reeling from a deep economic slump and a crisis of the state and the political system.

Similar scenarios of economic and political crises resonated across the continent. However, in Venezuela, the turbulence took on a specific configuration because of the country's petroleum-rich history.

The rise of oil production in the 1920s fueled a dramatic transformation in Venezuela's economy. Agricultural production, until then the main pillar of the economy, slumped as capital shifted to the oil sector, with local elites preferring to rely on imports to satisfy the domestic market. As oil's contribution to state revenues rapidly rose, business elites became increasingly dependent on their connections with the state to accumulate wealth. This process helped to fuse power and wealth within the state, creating a parasitic capitalist class that sought to enrich itself by appropriating government resources.[4] This reality underpinned the emergence of a pervasive culture of clientelism and corruption. Venezuelan society came to be dominated by what the late Venezuelan scholar Fernando Coronil termed a 'social system and political culture deeply implicated in legitimating and consolidating the vast set of formal and informal mechanisms through which oil is produced and oil money is appropriated.'[5]

Venezuela's thorough dependency on the international market for both income and imports meant it was heavily impacted by the economic crises and the gyration of petroleum prices that hit the world economy from the 1970s onwards.[6] Despite Venezuela's nationalization of petroleum in 1976, the private appropriation of public resources by Venezuela's elite continued unabated, while US-based corporations – the destination of most of Venezuela's oil exports – extracted the largest share of the country's resources. The five-year-old state oil company PDVSA handed over 71 percent of its gross income to the government in 1981. By 2000 this had dropped to 39 percent.[7] As a result, fiscal income experienced a steep decline, falling from $1,500 per person in 1975 to $350 per person in 1999 (in 1998 US dollars).[8]

These developments also shaped the formation of Venezuela's popular classes, as people fled the countryside en masse, flocking to the cities in pursuit of their share of the oil rent. Confronted with rising unemployment, aided by a wave of privatizations in telecommunications and basic industries, they came to create a massive belt of barrios along the hillsides of Caracas, where informal workers attempted to eke out an existence. By the end of the twentieth century, informal workers made up the majority of Venezuela's workforce. Poverty rose as real wages (in 1998 US dollars) declined from $5,200 in 1978 to $2,000 in 1999.[9]

Venezuelans responded by holding over seven thousand protests throughout the 1990s, with almost three-quarters of them considered 'confrontational' or 'violent,' according to a study done by Venezuelan academic Margarita López Maya.[10] New dynamic forms of organization began to emerge as the stream of demands leveled at government authorities became a progressively unstoppable wave.[11]

'Given the central role of the state in accumulation of capital through appropriation of international rents' rather than extracting surplus value, and the small presence of a formal working class, Daniel Hellinger, a US professor specializing in Venezuelan politics, argues, 'most Venezuelan movements over the last twenty years have focused their energies on the state.'[12] Control over oil rents would come to be the flashpoint in the early years of the Chávez government.

While this spontaneous and incoherent ferment from below failed to immediately impact the policies of the neoliberal government, it accelerated the plans for a military rebellion by a group of dissident officials in the armed forces. During the 1980s, discontent among sectors of the military had led to the creation of numerous clandestine organizations, including the Movimiento Bolivariano Revolucionario 200 (MBR-200, Bolivarian Revolutionary Movement 200), led by a young lieutenant colonel by the name of Hugo Rafael Chávez Frías. Although this group initially planned to organize a coup in 2000 that would pave the way for a transitional government, the *Caracazo* pushed Chávez and his followers to pre-emptively launch their military rebellion in February 1992.

The plot failed in its immediate goals, but the events propelled Chávez as a political leader into the collective imagination of the poor majority. Imprisoned after the rebellion, Chávez emerged two years later resolved to stand in the 1998 presidential elections. He began campaigning across the country, arguing that the only way to achieve real independence and eradicate poverty was by giving power to the people. He focused his campaign on three key issues – national sovereignty, poverty eradication, and participatory democracy – which would remain the key concerns of the Chávez government over the next decade.

Reclaiming control over the military and oil

Chávez's message enabled him to tap into the deep discontent among Venezuela's popular classes and unify the various strands of the political left behind his platform for independence, justice, and equality. The result was an overwhelming victory. On 6 December 1998, Chávez garnered 56.2 percent of the vote. He was inaugurated as president two months later.

However, from the beginning the new government was conscious that its mass popularity was not rooted in existing social organizations. The dispersed and unorganized nature of *chavismo*, as Chávez's support base came to be identified, meant the center of gravity lay within the executive power. As such, the pace and course of reforms would tend to be driven almost exclusively by the initiatives taken from above. Critically, with each advance, Chávez sought to organize and consolidate the social base.

The first move was the drafting of a new, popularly approved constitution that helped shift the institutional rules of a game set up to benefit the elites. In opposition to the 'representative' democracy during the period (1958–98) known as *puntofijismo* – dominated by Venezuela's two traditional parties that had negotiated a power-sharing pact to maintain their stranglehold on power – the Bolivarian revolution proposed a new 'participatory and protagonist' democracy. The new constitution, approved in 1999, gave this concept a legal backing, stating that 'the participation of the people in forming, carrying out, and controlling the management of public affairs is the necessary way of achieving their involvement to ensure their complete development, both individual and collective.'[13] The challenge was now to turn this novel idea into reality.

Chávez decided to use the right granted by the new constitution to ask parliament to allow him to rule by decree for a short period of time, thereby accelerating the pace of change. In November 2001, he issued forty-nine decrees covering such areas as the oil sector, land reform, cooperatives, and oil wealth redistribution. The laws asserted the government's willingness to shift away from neoliberalism and take Venezuela down a very different path.[14] The decrees were far from socialist measures, but powerful domestic sectors understood the package of laws to represent a direct challenge to their interests. This put him on an inevitable collision course with the traditional elites.

The response by the capitalist class was immediate. In December 2001, Fedecámaras, Venezuela's largest and most important business federation, together with the corrupt right-wing leadership of the Confederación de Trabajadores de Venezuela (CTV, Confederation of Venezuelan Workers) organized a largely successful general strike. Wealthy landowners declared their opposition to the new land decree, which sought to redistribute idle lands to peasants, by publicly burning copies of the law. The new hydrocarbon law, which reasserted state control over the country's oil reserves, and Chávez's subsequent decision to appoint a new board of directors at PDVSA, further infuriated those that historically had accumulated their wealth by appropriating the country's oil rent. With a showdown inevitable, Chávez began to organize his support base into *círculos bolivarianos* (Bolivarian circles), formed to encourage people to collectively discuss the country's new constitution and promote the dozens of reforms.

Over the next three years, these two competing blocs would face off three times. Each time, *chavismo* came out victorious, in doing so consolidating its military, economic, and political hegemony.

The first major showdown occurred on 11 April 2002, when a Fedecámaras and CTV rally against Chávez's changes to PDVSA morphed into a mobilization aimed at toppling the Venezuelan president. Following days of agitation by the anti-Chávez media, rally organizers ignored the previously established march route for the 11 April protest and directed the angry crowd toward Miraflores, the presidential palace. There, snipers were in position to ensure civilian deaths among the anti-*chavista* protestors and those that had gathered outside Miraflores to defend their president.

Once chaos and violence ensued, dissident elements in the military took Chávez hostage, blaming him for the bloodshed, and claiming that he had resigned. In his place, the coup plotters anointed Fedecámaras president Pedro Carmona as the country's new president. Carmona immediately dissolved the National Assembly, the courts, and the new constitution. Within hours the Bush administration announced Washington's willingness to work with the 'new government,' asserting that the 'undemocratic actions committed or encouraged by the Chávez administration provoked [the] crisis.'[15]

As repression escalated in the streets, spontaneous protests erupted across the country demanding the return of Chávez. Thousands marched to the Fuerte Tiuna military barrack in Caracas, calling on their brothers and sisters in uniform to oppose the coup. As divisions developed among the coup plotters, high-ranking military officers began to voice their opposition to the coup, calling on the people and soldiers to rise up. Demonstrations around Miraflores grew. More military battalions came out in support of Chávez. The coup plot began to unravel and within forty-seven hours Chávez had returned to power.

The defeat of the coup attempt by a civic–military uprising was critical in consolidating Chávez's hegemony within the armed forces. The events helped publicly expose the counter-revolutionary elements in the military, allowing the government to subsequently purge hundreds of rebellious officers. The civic–military alliance forged through this process provided the revolution with a vital weapon for defeating the second major attempt to bring down Chávez.

At the end of the year, PDVSA management, capitalist elites, corporate media, and corrupt trade union officials united forces once again. This time the strategy was to strangle the country's economy by halting production in the strategic petroleum sector. They hoped that the ensuing crisis would turn the people against Chávez, forcing him from power.

The PDVSA lockout did temporarily bring the Venezuelan economy to a halt, yet, like the coup, this destabilization attempt also backfired. For two months, loyal PDVSA workers, soldiers, and community activists mobilized to restart production. The Venezuelan government quickly fired all PDVSA managers and employees involved in the lockout, allowing the state to purge the existing right-wing bureaucracy, and placing the company firmly in the hands of the revolution.

For the first time in history, Venezuela's oil wealth was under the control of a government intent on using oil revenue to tackle social inequality and transform the economy. Chávez could also count on the support of a mobilized population. The impact of this two-month-long battle, which directly pitted the old capitalist elites against an alliance of workers, urban poor, and the military, had a profound radicalizing effect on the consciousness and organizing capacity of the people. Within only a few months, in April 2003, workers sympathetic to the revolution created the trade union confederation the Unión Nacional de Trabajadores (UNETE, National Union of Workers).

The qualitative leaps in worker and community organization proved crucial to defeating the third major offensive by the opposition. Using the expanded democratic rights available under the new constitution, the opposition set about collecting signatures to invoke a recall referendum against Chávez. The months leading up to the August 2004 referendum were dominated by constant mobilizations both for and against the Venezuelan president. In order to organize his base, Chávez called on the people to form *patrullas* (patrols). Each was composed of ten people, tasked to campaign for Chávez in their neighborhood. These patrols were coordinated by *Unidades de Batalla Electoral* (UBE, Units for Electoral Battle), which were organized to cover each voting center.

The grassroots strategy of relying on the people and not electoral machines paid off: Chávez won with a record number of votes, almost five million (58 percent of votes cast). Turnout was also historically high, at 70 percent. This third powerful defeat for the opposition in less than three years allowed Chávez to consolidate his democratic credentials within and outside Venezuela.

It also sent the opposition into a state of terminal decline. Divided, in November 2004 they were almost completely wiped off the electoral map in regional elections for governors and mayors. In December 2005, they committed political suicide, boycotting National Assembly elections and handing legislative control to pro-Chávez forces. Running on a platform that stressed the need to deepen the revolution and move toward socialism, Chávez was re-elected president a year later with over seven million votes.

Challenging US hegemony

Early in his first administration Chávez moved to cement relations with the United States' historic enemy – Cuba. Given an official welcome when he visited Cuba shortly after being released from prison in 1994, Chávez chose this country as his first port of call after winning the 1998 elections. The move infuriated the US government, given the propensity for Venezuelan presidents to first travel to Washington upon being elected. When Chávez finally arrived in Washington a few days after visiting Fidel Castro, he was afforded only a brief and rather informal meeting with then president Bill Clinton. Over the next few years, the deepening of the Venezuela–Cuba alliance was to be matched by Washington's increasingly hostile attitude toward the Bolivarian revolution.

Early in his presidency, Chávez further irked the United States by moving to strengthen the Organization of the Petroleum Exporting Countries (OPEC), in order to ensure that oil-producing countries received a greater share of oil wealth. Venezuela's diplomatic moves drove global oil prices to more than double between 1998 and 2000.[16]

Chávez strongly opposed US president George W. Bush's decision to invade Afghanistan in 2001 following the September 11 attacks. He condemned the Bush administration for 'fighting terror with terror.'[17]

As the political process radicalized throughout 2002/03, Venezuela came to play a bigger role in the region, working to put bilateral and regional relations on a new footing. Under the Cuba–Venezuela Agreement signed in October 2000, the two countries began shifting toward a solidarity-based trade arrangement in which Cuba provided Venezuela with teachers and doctors to help tackle the nation's huge pedagogical and medical needs. In turn, Venezuela provided the Caribbean island with much-needed access to cheap oil, helping to undermine the impact of the fifty-year-long US blockade of the island. This relationship was further cemented in 2004 when the two countries founded ALBA.

Over the next few years, ALBA progressively developed from a solidarity-based trade agreement toward a political bloc involving eight countries that coordinated their intervention in regional and international summits. This shift was reflected in the 2009 decision to modify its name to the Alianza Bolivariana de los Pueblos de Nuestra Américas (Bolivarian Alliance of the Peoples of Our Americas).

Venezuela played a fundamental role in the development of other regional initiatives, such as the formation of the regional TV station Telesur, the creation of Petrocaribe to provide cheap oil for Central American and Caribbean nations, and proposals for the establishment of various other initiatives, such as the BANCOSUR. In February 2010, Cuba and Venezuela carried out the first transaction involving the new regional currency known as the sucre. Proposed by the ALBA bloc as an alternative to trading in US dollars, the sucre has since been used for trade with Ecuador and Bolivia.

On the international stage, Venezuela has worked to strengthen links with non-traditional trading partners, such as China, Russia, and Iran, in an attempt to break the nation's economic dependency on the United States. Chávez's appearances at international forums, such as the United Nations, have also represented a continuous thorn in the side of the US empire. During his 2006 UN speech in which he referred to Bush as 'the devil,' he also recommended Noam Chomsky's book *Hegemony or Survival.* The book briefly became a bestseller on Amazon and in US bookstores. Eduardo Galeano's *Open Veins of Latin America* received a similar response when Chávez handed US president Barack Obama a copy during the 2010 Summit of the Americas in Trinidad and Tobago.

These two events symbolized the growing hearing that the Bolivarian revolution and Chávez were getting among people in the United States and around the world. Along with strengthening relations with the leaders of other countries, Venezuela worked to forge greater links between peoples and social movements. In 2005 Venezuela hosted an international festival of progressive youth, and the following year the WSF was held in Caracas. Chávez has promoted the creation of a Council of Social Movements of ALBA and declared that the Council should also include those movements in Latin American countries not currently members of the bloc. A key supporter of this initiative is Brazil's MST.

In 2009 Chávez launched perhaps his most ambitious initiative yet, calling on left parties from around the world to help form a new Fifth International, in the tradition of the internationals forged previously by Marx, Lenin, and Trotsky. For now, though, the initiative has yet to become a reality, owing largely to the reluctance of more conservative forces, including the Brazilian Workers' Party and numerous communist parties internationally, to support the proposal.

Each step toward building greater regional unity and forging new international alliances has been met by increased US hostility and international campaigns aimed at isolating Venezuela. This has included repeated accusations linking Venezuela to everything from drugs and terrorism to child trafficking.

Through Colombia, its main proxy in the region, the United States has worked to increase tensions between the neighboring countries, which at times has threatened to spill over into open conflict. In 2009, Colombia approved a proposal to establish seven new US military bases on its soil. While this plan was blocked by a Colombian Constitutional Court decision that ruled the agreement unconstitutional, the United States has continued to stage military maneuvers in the region and patrol regional waters with its recently reactivated 4th Fleet.

The United States has not been the only country to wage a campaign against the Bolivarian revolution. In 2002, the Spanish government of then president José María Aznar was quick to praise the brief military ouster of Chávez and worked to cobble together diplomatic support for the coup regime.[18] The Netherlands has aided the US government in militarily surrounding Venezuela by providing access to military bases in the neighboring Dutch Caribbean islands of Aruba and Curaçao, located only 15 and 24 miles off the coast of Venezuela, respectively.[19] Over twenty transnational and foreign-owned companies affected by the Chávez government's nationalization policies have also waged intense ongoing battles in international courts to force Venezuela to pay compensation.[20]

However, by the time Chávez began his new term in 2007, he was surrounded by a rising sea of pink tide governments across the region. This growing alliance of progressive and left governments provided a favorable scenario for greater regional cooperation and integration, a key objective of the Bolivarian revolution.

Eradicating poverty by giving power to the people

By this time Chávez was also facing favorable conditions at home. The new economic, military, and political framework arising out of the intense battles of 2002/03 provided the Chávez government with a chance to overcome some of the weaknesses of the revolution. There was a pressing need to rapidly improve the living standard of workers, the urban poor, and the lower middle class in order to weaken the opposition's support in these sectors. It was also vital to shift critical areas of the economy, such as agriculture and basic services, away from capitalist control. If not, the opposition could capitalize on these failings to bring down the government.

Convinced that the only way to eradicate poverty was to give power to the people, the government continued to push forward by applying the Bolivarian constitution. This document contained the seeds of a radical alternative to the failed projects of representative democracy and neoliberalism: 'participatory and protagonist democracy' in the political and economic realms, and the creation of a human-focused and solidarity-based 'social economy.'

To this end, in 2003 the government began taking its first steps toward creating what it called a 'new productive model,' aimed at diversifying Venezuela's economy and breaking its dependency on oil. It focused on three key areas: land reform, the promotion of cooperatives, and the reactivation of closed factories under workers' *cogestión* (co-management).[21] The government's most important program, however, was the *misiones sociales* (social missions), aimed at expanding access to education and healthcare. As a result of these government-sponsored initiatives aimed at promoting citizen's participation, a whole series of new social actors – cooperativistas, community activists, and workers – came to play an increasingly greater role as protagonists within the process. These social forces were critical in securing Chávez's landslide re-election on 3 December 2006.

The government was able to count on the financial resources of PDVSA to help with its aim of massively reducing poverty. [22] Rising international oil prices facilitated the government's massive expansion in social spending, much of which went to funding these new parallel state institutions. Between 1999 and 2006, government social spending as a percentage of GDP increased from 9.4 to 13.6 percent. PDVSA itself began to directly fund some of the social missions, designating $13.3 million, or 7.3 percent of overall GDP, toward social spending in 2006 alone. The same year, social spending was equal to nearly 21 percent of GDP, a phenomenal increase of 314 percent in real per capita social spending compared to 1998.[23]

Combined with minimum wage increases and price controls on essential food items, the impact of this massive redistribution of oil wealth via social spending was remarkable. Poverty levels dropped by 24.5 percent between 2003 and 2006, and the number of households in extreme poverty fell by 16 percent during the same period.[24] A report by the Venezuelan American Chamber of Commerce and Industry revealed that between 2004 and 2006, the real income of the poorest 58 percent of the population increased by 130 percent, even after adjusting for inflation.[25]

Newly emergent community organizations were also critical to poverty reduction, particularly through their role in facilitating the creation of the social missions. With the help of the Cuban government, Chávez launched *Misión Barrio Adentro* (Mission Inside the Neighborhood) in April 2003, sending Cuban doctors into poor communities. There, pre-existing local health committees worked with the Cuban doctors to run awareness campaigns about the new services, carry out local censuses in order to identify key community health concerns, and suggest where doctors should go. Where such committees did not exist, promoters from the Chávez government encouraged the community to organize them. According to a 2009 report from the Washington-based Center for Economic and Policy Research, 'from 1999 to 2007, the number of primary care physicians in the public sector increased more than twelve times, from 1,628 to 19,571,' providing healthcare to millions of poor Venezuelans who previously had no access.[26]

The health committees also helped to identify the educational needs of communities, which were addressed in subsequent educational missions. In July 2003, the government launched *Misión Robinson*, which focused on combating illiteracy. *Misión Robinson II* was later founded, providing free primary-school-level education to the graduates of *Robinson I*. *Misión Ribas* and *Misión Sucre* were established to address the needs of those who had been traditionally excluded from high school and university-level education. The new education missions led to increased participation rates at all levels of education from pre-school to university. In 2005, UNESCO declared Venezuela to be a 'territory free of illiteracy' after 1.5 million people learned how to read and write. Net enrollment at primary, secondary, and university-level education rose by 8.6, 14.7 and 86 percent, respectively.[27]

Important networks of both experienced and new activists began to emerge. They became the heart and soul of these initial missions, which developed into parallel structures to an inherited state bureaucracy that remained both paralyzed and dominated by powerful economic and political interests. The result was the creation of what key Chávez collaborator the late Alberto Müller Rojas defined as an 'adhocracy,' based on ad hoc and more flexible state institutions that could help overcome the inertia of the existing state bureaucracy.[28]

The social missions also increased citizen participation in administering public affairs. An extensive investigation of popular participation carried out in mid-2005 found that a 'general understanding of the participatory and protagonist concept' existed among Venezuelan citizens. However, it also noted that social organizations continued to be 'characterized by fragility and incipient development.' The report's authors concluded that the government's 'social policies [had played] an important role in creating sustainable organizational and social networks to advance in the democratization of society.'[29]

The government's land reform program and cooperative drive also lowered unemployment and led to modest gains in land distribution and food production. In December 2003, Chávez launched *Misión Zamora*. The mission redistributed large idle landholdings to peasant farmers, while providing technical and financial support, and promoting collective organization and labor. The government also hoped to incorporate urban poor sectors into the emergent rural cooperative sector through *Misión Vuelvan Caras* (Mission About Face), created in March 2004. Fifty percent of the scholarships offered to participants in the new mission were for training in the agricultural sector.[30]

These programs faced various obstacles: the powerful resistance of large landowners, a poorly organized campesino movement, and the nascent nature of the state institutions entrusted with implementing the mission. Land redistribution was thus initially limited to idle, and largely poor-quality, land already in public hands. Attempts to occupy land often faced violent resistance from landowners (responsible for the assassination of over 250 peasants by 2011) and repression by the National Guard. With strong ties to local elites, many of the regional authorities and core military personnel remained unsympathetic to Chávez's radical program for the nation.[31]

Two million hectares of state-owned land had been redistributed by the end of 2004; however, according to Ministry of Agriculture figures, by 2005, of the 6 million hectares identified as *latifundios* (large, idle landholdings), less than 650,000 hectares had been recuperated. Cultivated land increased from 1.6 million hectares in 1998 to more than two million in 2006, but remained below 1980s levels. Despite dramatic increases in agricultural funding, production in the countryside was unable to keep up with sharply rising consumption levels. Moreover, the combination of price and currency controls acted as a disincentive for local production as it was cheaper to import than produce locally.

Similar results were also registered in the attempts to stimulate new economic enterprises based on cooperative labor. Between 1998 and 2005 the number of cooperatives rose from fewer than one thousand to more than seventy thousand.[32]

'More than a spontaneous process from below, [the rise in cooperative number] has in large part been the result of public policies that have fostered their growth,' wrote Cuban investigator Camila Piñeiro Harnecker in a 2008 article in the Venezuelan magazine *Cayapa*.[33]

While pointing to the importance of the 2001 law on cooperatives that facilitated the creation of cooperatives and obliged the state to protect them, Harnecker highlighted the fact that co-op numbers really took off in 2004. The boom was stimulated by government programs that provided technical-professional training, preferential loans to co-operatives by financial institutions, the obligation of state companies to prioritize contracting cooperatives, and, most importantly, the creation of *Misión Vuelvan Caras*.

The promotion of cooperatives was an important factor in the 9.3 percent drop in unemployment experienced between 2003 and 2007. Yet these figures can be misleading. Independent investigations suggested that despite 184,000 cooperatives being registered by early 2007, only about 30,000, or 15 percent, were active.[34] By the end of 2008, only 201,773 people were employed in the cooperative sector.[35]

In 2005, Chávez encouraged workers to occupy their factories, and run them cooperatively or in *cogestión* with the state. UNETE leaders asserted that they planned to occupy 800 abandoned factories. However, by the end of 2006, recuperated or cooperatively run factories, or factories under *cogestión*, numbered fewer than forty.[36] Serious problems emerged in the state-owned companies, which had been working toward *cogestión*. At the aluminum company Alcasa, workers had begun to oppose co-management as disputes over pay and conditions took precedence. Elsewhere, in the state-owned electricity company CADAFE, management succeeded in severely limiting worker participation until the issue was all but dropped. Throughout PDVSA, where the experience of worker control had flourished during the 2002/03 management lockout, union leaders had reverted to the deeply rooted practice of political clientelism, using their positions of power to sell lucrative jobs in one of the highest paying industries in the country.[37] The weaknesses and divisions that pervaded the workers' movement only strengthened the hand of those opposed to worker participation.

Building a parallel Venezuela

By the end of its first term, the government was facing other important challenges, questioning the viability of its strategy to create parallel institutions and a new 'social economy' alongside the country's existing capitalist structures. As experiments in the social economy stumbled forward and the new institutions remained incipient, attempts to diversify the economy were seemingly faltering. The dramatic rise in private consumption, which largely explains the high economic growth experienced during this period, was not matched by

TABLE 4.1 Distribution of income by quintiles (1998–2006)

Year	Poorest 20%	Middle 20%	Richest 20%
1998	4.06	13.20	53.36
1999	4.36	13.22	51.90
2000	3.95	13.53	52.28
2001	4.45	13.07	49.55
2002	4.40	12.64	54.13
2003	4.01	12.96	52.83
2004	3.53	12.94	54.77
2005	4.63	15.87	52.36
2006	4.80	14.30	49.80

a similar rise in domestic production. Installed production capacity remained low and concentrated in a few hands, with 571 companies accounting for 80 percent of domestic production in 2007.[38] As a result, imports more than doubled, from just under $14.3 million in 1998 to over $30.5 million in 2006. Many saw this as proof that Venezuela's economy was indeed becoming more, not less, dependent on external markets.

Furthermore, falling investment, a failure to expand installed capacity, and the allure of cheap imports due to an overvalued local currency meant growth in the manufacturing sector was minimal and limited largely to the reactivation of existing companies.[39] Agriculture experienced growth but saw its share of GDP fall from 14 to 12 percent between 1998 and 2006.[40] Most growth occurred in the tertiary sector (finance, insurance, and communications) and in construction, the result of massive government spending on infrastructure projects.[41]

TABLE 4.2 Gini index of income distribution (1998–2006)

Year	Gini index
1998	0.4865
1999	0.4693
2000	0.4772
2001	0.4573
2002	0.4938
2003	0.4811
2004	0.4559
2005	0.4748
2006	0.4422

Moreover, while government policies had led to important strides in increasing the wealth of the lower classes, this had not been accompanied by a similar shift in the overall redistribution of wealth. Statistics show only a mild redistribution of wealth toward the poorest sector, as Tables 4.1 and 4.2 demonstrate.[42]

Although the poor had clearly benefited as a result of the government's economic policies, so had the rich. Overall, advances toward decreasing inequality had been minimal (0.04 points in terms of Gini) and Venezuela's elites had demonstrated their ability to utilize periods of crisis and convulsion, such as the period from 2002 to 2004, to further their own economic interests.

Former minister of basic industry Victor Álvarez argued that the reactivation of the economy experienced during this period represented a reinvigoration of the capitalist economy in which 'the owners of capital have improved [their situation] much more than the workers.'[43] Without a fundamental and radical transformation of the economy, capital could and would continue to reproduce itself at the expense of the workers.

The challenges faced in expanding popular power were another area of concern. The social missions, experiments in co-management, and the cooperative sector faced two recurring problems: 1) State initiatives stimulated participation, but also tended to reproduce and reinforce vices such as corruption and clientelism that were deeply embedded in society as a result of the culture created by Venezuela's rent-based economy of the previous century; 2) Moves to expand popular participation faced resistance from both the pro-capitalist state bureaucracy and pro-Chávez sectors within the state apparatus that were unwilling to give up their posts of influence and control. Increasingly, these sectors relied on the cultivation of a cult of personality around Chávez to further their own positions of economic and political power. Claiming to represent 'the leader,' these sectors deemed that those opposing them were counter-revolutionaries.

In sum, by 2006 the Venezuelan government had clearly advanced internationally, forging greater regional links, aided by the arrival of new progressive-leaning countries. Solidarity with the Bolivarian revolution was also growing among the social movements in Latin America and elsewhere. All of this was critical to undermining US influence in the region. Domestically, initiatives to create parallel state institutions and economic enterprises had begun to tackle poverty while simultaneously increasing the organizational capacity of masses. At the same time, the revolution seemed unable to definitively break the resistance of capital and the inherited capitalist state, which acted to undermine the process while attempting to reassert their power. Analyzing the situation, Chávez constantly repeated Italian Marxist Antonio Gramsci's idea that 'the crisis consists precisely in the fact that the old is dying and the new is yet to be born.'

Radicalization and the advance of socialism

To turn this situation around, the Chávez government once again went on the offensive after his 2006 re-election, announcing a radicalization of the process. Chávez concluded that a frontal attack on capitalism was necessary. This, he said, required advancing simultaneously on three fronts: increasing social ownership over the means of production, encouraging greater workplace democracy, and directing production toward social needs. These were the three sides of what Chávez came to call the 'elementary triangle of socialism.'

To achieve this agenda, Chávez called for the formation of a united party of the revolution and the launch of 'the five motors of the revolution.' These included: 1) enacting an enabling law to give Chávez the power to rule by decree over certain policy areas as a way of speeding up legislative reform; 2) modifying the constitution to remove some of the pro-capitalist elements it contained; 3) expanding communal power; 4) restructuring Venezuela's political and geographic territories to attend to previously marginalized regions; and 5) promoting socialist education throughout Venezuelan society.

At his 8 January inauguration ceremony, Chávez explained that his election victory represented a new point of departure for the revolution, and that the goal of this new term was to 'transfer political, social, and economic power' to the people. To do so it was vital to dismantle the old capitalist state that was undermining the revolution, and tackle the two problems that Chávez increasingly warned could strangle the revolution: corruption and bureaucratism. As a sign of the new direction, Chávez took the opportunity to announce a round of nationalizations in the oil, electricity, and telecommunications sectors. Chávez also reaffirmed his decision not to renew the broadcasting license of the private TV station RCTV, which had supported the 2002 coup.

This series of announcements and actions immediately increased class polarization both between the opposition and pro- Chávez sectors and within the Bolivarian process itself. Internationally, the US government stepped up its campaign of disinformation and attacks on the Venezuelan government.[44] Through vehicles such as USAID, Washington increased funding to opposition forces within Venezuela. Internally, right-wing parties began to decry the installation of a 'communist dictatorship' that was threatening to take away people's homes and even their children. A new opposition force erupted on the streets, as the outcry over RCTV's imminent closure provoked protests among students predominantly from the country's opposition-controlled private and autonomous universities, such as the Universidad Central de Venezuela and Universidad Católica Andrés Bello. Supermarket shelves became increasingly bare as powerful companies fought government price controls by provoking shortages. Rising concerns over spiraling inflation and crime became central issues for citizens, who felt that the revolution was not doing enough to address these serious issues. The opposition-dominated corporate media incessantly harped on these issues, creating the sensation of a country descending into chaos.

The reverberations of this new phase were most keenly felt by the political forces that, until then, had supported the revolution. Expressing its opposition to joining the Partido Socialista Unido de Venezuela (PSUV, United Socialist Party of Venezuela), the social democratic Por la Democracia Social (PODEMOS, For Social Democracy) party broke with the Chávez government in mid-2007. Later that year, it joined the opposition and campaigned against Chávez's proposed constitutional reform. Among the proposed reforms that were put to a popular referendum in December 2007 were: a reduction in the working day to just six hours, direct government control over the Central Bank of Venezuela, inclusion of the militia as part of the armed forces, granting the government the power to nationalize companies without waiting for a court order, the outlawing of *latifundios*, and a significant increase in the power of institutions such as the communal councils and social missions.

Two other integral parties in the National Assembly's pro-Chávez alliance, Patria Para Todos (PPT, Homeland For All) and the Partido Comunista de Venezuela (PCV, Communist Party of Venezuela) also announced they would not join the PSUV, although they maintained that they would continue to support Chávez. General Raúl Baduel, a former defense minister and a key figure in Chávez's return to power during the April 2002 coup, also came out against Chávez's proposed constitutional reforms. He called on the armed forces to 'profoundly analyze' the proposed changes, which he argued amounted to a 'constitutional coup.'[45] Within the workers' movement, divisions deepened in the UNETE, with a small faction announcing its decision to oppose the proposed reforms. A number of intellectuals who had been supportive of the process became progressively more critical of the government, claiming it was moving away from its original project of a participatory and protagonist democracy.

The process of founding the PSUV also faced substantial internal hurdles. Chávez's decision to dissolve the Movimiento V República (MVR, Movement for a Fifth Republic), an electoral machine that had come to be dominated by power blocs tied to figures in national and regional government posts, created new struggles for control over the nascent party. Four and a half million people joined the PSUV in its initial recruitment drive, a clear sign of support for the initiative. However, local activists complained of being excluded from the local party committees, called *batallones* (battalions), in favor of paid government functionaries, leading many to decide against participating in the new party. More broadly, many *chavistas* began to question the inaction of the state in tackling key problems such as food shortages.

All these issues came to a head on 2 December 2007, when the pro-revolutionary forces suffered their first defeat at the ballot box since Chávez was elected to power nine years before. Chávez's proposed constitutional reform was voted down by the narrowest of margins, effectively blocking at least two of the 'five motors': the constitutional reform and the new geometry of power, which was largely dependent on some of the proposed constitutional changes. As Chávez's program for socialist education, *Moral y Luces* (Morals and Enlightenment), also failed to ever really get off the ground, it appeared that the radicalization of the process had perhaps reached its limits.

Chavistas responded to the referendum defeat by engaging in a nationwide debate on a scale never before seen. Uncertainty hung over the future of the revolutionary project. Increasingly, dissident factions began to appear. Although still too weak and lacking sufficient effective coordination to win control of the PSUV, their presence was strongly felt at the founding congress of the party in the first months of 2008. Chávez requested that the contentious congress finish early in order for the party to quickly come out with a united front and kick-start its campaign for the regional elections later in the year.

During the regional elections on 23 November 2008, the opposition increased the number of governorships under its control from two to five of the twenty-two up for grabs, including the three most populated states. An opposition candidate, Antonio Ledezma, was also elected mayor of Greater Caracas. Discussions and discontent once more erupted within *chavismo*. Again, Chávez intervened to maintain unity among the competing forces. To do so, he launched an ultimately successful initiative to amend the constitution by popular referendum and permit elected officials to stand for re-election indefinitely. The move was critical to ensuring his chances of re-election in 2012.

Further problems emerged in 2008. With the global economic crisis, government revenue fell along with international oil prices. By the first quarter of 2009, the country's economy had gone into recession, with GDP shrinking by 3.3 percent.[46] While the oil sector shrank by 7.2 percent in 2009, manufacturing contracted by 6.4 percent after five years of sustained growth. This sector was also hit by a climate-induced energy crisis. Throughout 2009, a severe drought led to water levels at Venezuela's Guri hydroelectric dam – the source of more than 70 percent of the country's electricity – becoming dangerously low. Blackouts rolled across the country as the government imposed rationing of electricity. Meanwhile, inflation regularly exceeded 20 percent each year.

To confront this complex situation, the government unleashed a second wave of nationalizations. While the first wave in 2007 had targeted basic services, this one was intended to give the state greater control over strategic productive industries such as agriculture and manufacturing. The state carried out this round in accordance with the government's overall economic plan. Private capital would not be eliminated, but the government made clear that it had to operate within the stated goals of the state or face possible expropriation.

In agriculture, the government announced a wave of land takeovers. By the end of 2011, more than 3.6 million hectares had been expropriated.[47] In early 2008, the government nationalized Lacteos Los Andes, which controlled 35 percent of the distribution and commercialization of milk and derivative products in Venezuela. It also nationalized a number of slaughterhouses, sugar refineries, and refrigeration and storage companies. Over the next few years the government extended its control over the agro-industrial sector through the nationalizations of coffee processing plants, sugar mills, flour processing factories, and two private supermarket chains.

One of the government's most important moves in this area was taken in October 2010 when Chávez announced the nationalization of the Venezuelan-owned Fertinitro and Spanish-owned Agroisleña companies.[48] The former is one of the world's largest producers of nitrogen fertilizer, while the latter had until then maintained an almost complete monopoly over the commercialization of seeds and other agricultural supplies, with outlets across the country. Agroisleña also controlled about a third of the country's grain storage capacity.

In 2008, the government acquired 90 percent of the country's cement industry and announced its intention to nationalize the massive Sidor steel processing plant, privatized in the late 1990s. Sidor's return to state hands was announced in April 2008 following a long dispute by workers for a fair collective contract.[49] In 2009, the Chávez government seized control of Gold Reserve's Brisas project, located in the southeastern state of Bolivar and one of the largest gold mines in Latin America. In 2011, it nationalized all of Venezuela's gold mines.[50] The following year, Industrias Venoco, the country's largest independent auto lubricants company, was nationalized after it was accused of overpricing.[51] With this move, the government also gained control of all of Venoco's subsidiaries, including Nacional de Grasas Lubricantes and Aditivos de Orinoco.

In July 2008, Chávez also announced plans to nationalize the Spanish-owned Banco de Venezuela, doubling the state's control of the financial sector from its previous 10 percent. The government intervened in Banco Federal in June 2010 following allegations of fraud and liquidity problems.[52] Further problems in the banking sector led to the government's decision to close down a dozen small banks. A majority of these banks were subsequently nationalized and merged as part of the creation of the new state-owned Banco Bicentenario. The state now controlled 25 percent of the banking sector, making it the biggest player in the industry.[53] A number of brokerage firms were also shut down, and some of their managers were jailed or placed under investigation for their involvement in illegal activities. Chávez warned other financial institutions that they too would be nationalized if found to be involved in destabilizing the financial sector or failing to comply with strict government regulations.

Between 2005 and 2009, the government expropriated 762 factories and idle farms.[54] The state now had either full command or enough weight across all the strategic sectors of the economy to be able to dictate production goals, with the threat of expropriation looming for those that refused to cooperate. These moves represented a clear reassertion of sovereignty over the nation's economy.

Bureaucracy, corruption, and popular power

But what about worker and community participation? As Chávez himself had stated, twenty-first-century socialism was not about repeating the errors of twentieth-century socialist experiences. Fundamental to this was ensuring direct worker participation in the management of the economy and community participation in distribution.

Nevertheless, the spate of nationalizations clearly came from government initiatives aimed at responding to the needs of the poor and not some workers' struggle from below, where fragmentation predominated within the workers' movement. One year after Sidor's nationalization in 2008, however, it appeared this was beginning to change.

Venezuela's state-owned steel, aluminum, and bauxite companies faced growing problems as a result of falling production and enforced energy rationing due to the electricity crisis. The future of these companies, the government decided, largely depended on the political and organizational capacity of the working class to begin taking control of the management. The government initiated a discussion among workers from the industrial region of Guayana, located in the southeastern state of Bolivar.

Addressing a May 2009 workshop that had brought together roughly four hundred workers from across Guayana to discuss the 'socialist transformation of basic industry,' Chávez noted, 'I can see, sense and feel the roar of the working class. When the working class roars, the capitalists tremble.' Chávez went on to announce a series of radical measures largely drawn from the proposals coming from workers' discussions. These included the nationalization of six iron briquette, ceramics, and steel companies and the introduction of workers' control along 'the entire productive chain.' To facilitate this, workers would elect state company managers as part of an all-out struggle against the 'mafias' rife in the management of state companies.[55]

Over the next weeks, workers across the basic industry sector met in round tables to draft the *Plan Guayana Socialista*.[56] The plan, delivered to Chávez on 9 June, proposed 'converting the current structural crisis of capitalism' into an 'opportunity' for workers to proceed in 'the construction of socialism, by directly assuming control over production of the basic companies in the region.' The workers proposed several measures including the election of managers, management restructuring, collective decision-making by workers and local communities, the creation of workers' councils, and the opening of companies' books. The workers hoped to acquire 'direct control of production without mediation by a bureaucratic structure.'

Almost a year later, and with the electricity sector in crisis, Chávez sat down to listen to 600 electrical workers from around the country. Representatives from twelve workers' round tables read proposals, again including the introduction of workers' control and co-management, measures to eradicate corruption and bureaucratism, and ideological and technical education. They also demanded that contract workers be converted into permanent employees and the fusion of the various existing electricity companies into one state corporation to facilitate the creation of a truly socialist electricity company.[57] Chávez responded by declaring, 'The electricity revolution has begun!' and urged them to push forward with their proposals as part of the transformation of the electrical sector.

As was the case with the radicalization push of 2007, internal tensions within the process were exacerbated by the combined push for nationalization and workers' control. Each time the Bolivarian revolution advanced, it was increasingly forced to face its own demons. The nationalizations began to expose the interests of pro-Chávez sectors that had come to be popularly referred to as the *boliburguesía* (bolibourgeoisie, or Bolivarian bourgeoisie, a new capitalist class that had emerged within the revolution) or *la derecha endógena* (the endogenous right wing). Current planning minister Jorge Giordani described them as 'a singular or collective grouping, which, during [the time of this government], has concerned itself with amassing immense fortunes in the name of the revolution.'[58] Denouncing them as white-collar criminals disguised in *rojo-rojito* (reddish-red) T-shirts, Giordani noted their impunity from prosecution. The traditional pattern of using the state in order to enrich oneself seemed to be reproducing itself.

During the banking crisis of late 2009, a number of the bankers prosecuted and jailed had been closely aligned with the government. Ricardo Fernández Barrueco, a relatively unknown entrepreneur in the food sector, had risen up the ranks of the business elite to own four banks and twenty-nine Venezuelan companies. Much of this meteoric rise was due to generous contracts he was given to supply government-subsidized Mercal food stores, earning Fernández the nickname 'the Czar of Mercal.' The arrest of another banker, Arné Chacón, over corruption allegations, led to the resignation of his brother Jessie Chacón as Chávez's science minister. Many believe these actions have only touched the surface of the corruption and illegal enrichment that continue to infect the state.

The moves to transfer greater power to workers also faced mounting resistance from within the existing bureaucracy. Sensing the danger that the *Plan Guayana Socialista* represented to their business interests, bureaucratic sectors within the revolutionary movement moved quickly to try to block the proposal. During June and July 2010, these bureaucratic sectors stoked up dissatisfaction among workers at the management's lack of attention to their demands regarding back pay owed to them, provoking a wave of strikes and protests in Guayana. Among protest organizers were union leaders and PSUV parliamentarians. They were supported by the local PSUV governor, Francisco Rangel Gómez, who called on the national government to negotiate directly with local unions. Together, this bloc hoped not only to stifle the radical proposals from the 21 May workshop, but also to depose the then minister of basic industry Rodolfo Sanz, who, in the process of placing his own people in management positions at the Corporación Venezolana de Guayana (CVG, Venezuelan Corporation of Guayana), had removed those whom the current governor had appointed during his term as CVG president. As negotiations began between union leaders and Sanz, it seemed the more radical proposals of the worker round tables had been pushed aside. The previous failed attempts to introduce co-management in CADAFE were also a harbinger of things to come in the electrical sector.

The government's promotion of communal councils was also confronting similar problems. In order to give greater power to communities, in late 2005 Chávez began calling on citizens to form communal councils.[59] The Law of Communal Councils was approved in April 2006, defining these councils as 'instances for participation, articulation, and integration between the diverse community-based organizations, social groups and citizens, that allow the organized people to directly exercise the management of public policies and projects.'[60]

These councils – elected from between 200 and 400 families in urban areas and twenty to fifty families in the countryside – were aimed at building upon the various forms of existing community organizations (such as water, health, and urban land committees). Collectively, the communal councils were charged with diagnosing the main problems facing their communities and creating a plan to resolve them. All major decisions were made in citizens' assemblies.

Importantly, funding for these projects came from the state, with the communal councils becoming mechanisms for the democratic distribution of oil rent among the poor. While state financing carried with it the dangers of dependency and clientistic relations, the head of an investigation team established to observe the communal councils by the Centro Gumilla (which has been critical of the Chávez government) noted:

> According to the data obtained, we cannot affirm that the type of participation in the communal councils reinforces patterns of political conduct such as *asistencialismo* [passive presence] or paternalism; on the contrary, the data indicates that there is a progressive process of protagonism and popular responsibility in the construction of collective responses in the search for a better life.[61]

While the actual number of communal councils fell short of the government's overly ambitious goal of 100,000 by March 2008, some 36,143 communal councils had been registered or were awaiting registration.[62] This new form of organization came to involve an unparalleled number of citizens in community organizing, and by 2007 was increasingly seen as a fundamental building block of the new state.[63]

In 2009 the government took a further step, promoting the creation of *comunas* (communes). In essence, communes were to encompass several communal councils within a self-defined community so they could collectively tackle problems on a larger scale. However, together with the persistent problems of corruption and clientelism, community activists increasingly complained that state officials manipulated or divided communities for their own interests. Some argued that government policies appeared to be reviving the 'dying' capitalist state rather than promoting new forms of the communal state. Without resolving these issues, the idea of community control over production seems a distant dream.

Rising crime rates have impacted on government support and directly undermined community organizing. In some areas, gangs and drug leaders infiltrated communal councils in order to use them for their own ends. In others, activists who campaigned against the presence of gangs became the targets of selective assassinations. Government attempts to tackle the biggest factor in rising crime – the existence of over 150 different municipal and regional police forces, all infested with criminal elements and corruption – have encountered great difficulty in turning this situation around. The state has continued to focus on creating a new national police force to replace the existing ones, though again the government faces the twin problems of dealing with the old elements while simultaneously shielding the new police force from being infected by long-standing corruption.

Twenty-first-century socialism without Chávez?

The September 2010 National Assembly elections gave an insight into the state of class struggle in Venezuela. Out of 165 seats, the PSUV won 98. The opposition parties grouped in the Mesa de Unidad Democrática (MUD, Democratic Unity Round Table) won 65 seats, while the PPT, which presented itself as a 'third option,' went from 6 to 2 seats. Although the PSUV won a clear majority, it fell short of its goal of controlling two-thirds of parliament. Without this, the PSUV has been forced to seek the support of the opposition in order to pass 'organic' (entirely new) laws.

Of greater concern, though, was the overall popular vote nationwide, where the difference between the *chavista* and opposition support base was just over 100,000 votes. Broken down area by area, it was apparent that the opposition had made important headway, including in traditional *chavista* strongholds. The opposition increased its votes in the states bordering Colombia (Zulia and Táchira). While the PSUV won more seats than the MUD in the opposition-controlled Carabobo state, and tied in Miranda, the opposition actually won the popular vote across both states. The opposition also once again narrowly won the popular vote in Greater Caracas. These opposition gains were largely due to an increase in voter participation by middle-class sectors and a parallel drop in voter turnout in traditional *chavista* strongholds. In some cases, such as the barrios in Petare in eastern Caracas, electoral support for the opposition rose substantially, with opposition candidate Carlos Oscariz winning the position of mayor in the local area.

One factor, though, stands out: despite all the problems and massive US-funded corporate media campaign against the revolution, more than 5.4 million people voted for openly socialist candidates. They did so despite the threat of war, the impact of the global economic crisis, food shortages, and an energy crisis. The revolution clearly continued to maintain a powerful social base with which to further deepen the revolution.

After these elections the government once again shifted gears, in preparation for the 2012 presidential elections. Appearing to enter a new phase of the revolution, the government hoped that by using its control over strategic industries, it could dramatically expand production in agriculture and manufacturing. Two new *Grandes Misiones* (Grand Missions) were announced in the area of housing and agriculture. Both intended to carry out a census of all agricultural producers and citizens without adequate housing, in order to identify the most pressing needs in these areas. Once they were completed, the state shifted massive resources into agricultural production and the construction of housing.

Intricately tied to the success of these measures is the ability of workers and communities to assert themselves in the struggle against internal sabotage and corruption. Positive signs emerged following the 2010 National Assembly elections, which pointed to a revitalization and greater coordination of worker, peasant, and urban poor organizations. The Frente Nacional Campesino Ezequiel Zamora (FNCEZ, National Peasant Front Ezequiel Zamora) and UNETE organized separate mass mobilizations in November 2010 and March 2011.[64] Along with raising sector-specific demands, both protests were permeated by the need to deepen the fight against capitalism and bureaucratism. These two organizations, together with a range of other social organizations, in particular housing activists, also joined forces to take to the streets again in June 2011.[65]

In Guayana, close to a thousand workers from around the country met in April 2011 to discuss how to reignite the struggle for workers' control in the face of bureaucratic opposition.[66] Their efforts received an important boost in June 2011 with the arrest of a number of key figures involved in corruption in industrial companies in Guayana.

The year 2011 also began with renewed discussions among party militants about the future of the PSUV. Speaking to a PSUV mass assembly in Caracas on 28 March 2011, Chávez attacked the vices that continued to plague the party, warning 'the old way of doing politics is devouring us, the corruption of politics is devouring us ... the old capitalist values have infiltrated us from all sides.' The Soviet Union failed, Chávez said, because its leaders 'forgot their principles, they were corrupted.' The party needed to return to its principles to 're-charge and refresh' itself, added Chávez, otherwise the PSUV would go down the same road as the previous party of government (the MVR) and be dissolved.[67] Perhaps in recognition of the continued problems facing the PSUV, Chávez launched the *Gran Polo Patriótico* (GPP, Great Patriotic Pole)[68] in October 2011, calling on all pro-revolution social movements and parties to unite in order to ensure a decisive victory in the 2012 presidential elections.[69]

At the same time, *la derecha endógena* appeared to be reasserting its power within *chavismo*, exemplifying the fact that the Bolivarian process continues to be just that – an ongoing process whose fate will be determined by class struggle. In February 2012, the alliance of corrupt government officials, bureaucratic union leaders, and foreign capital seemed to have partially reimposed itself within the companies in Guayana.[70] By sacking pro-worker-control presidents selected by workers to run companies, and pushing aside the workers' round tables that had been created to deepen the process of worker management, control of these companies was seemingly once again in the hands of these powerful forces. Numerous social movements have also publicly voiced their concerns that after a promising start to the GPP, traditional faction leaders within the PSUV had progressively excluded them from any further active participation.

Today Venezuela's revolution faces three main challenges. The first is the United States and the Venezuelan opposition it continues to support in order to oust Chávez. The second is the revolution's ability to deal with the twin problems of corruption and bureaucratism. Overcoming these obstacles will require greater popular participation through initiatives such as the *comunas* and the push for workers' control. The success of the Great Patriotic Pole can also help lead the way.

The third challenge, which has become ever more apparent in the wake of Chávez's diagnosis of cancer, is the necessity of a collective leadership. History will record that the Bolivarian revolution succeeded in rolling back neoliberalism and laying the foundations for a transition to twenty-first-century socialism. The dynamic relationship that has existed to date between Chávez and the masses has been a key factor in ensuring this.

While many have criticized Chávez's predominant role in the Venezuelan revolution, his leadership must be placed within the historic context previously outlined: one of a Venezuela marked by intense ferment from below but with varying organizational strength among the social movements. At each step, Chávez has launched initiatives to encourage the self-organization of the people. Through this process the Venezuelan people have increasingly taken the destiny of their country into their own hands.

It is none the less true that his role as the key figure in the revolution and the trust placed in him by the poor majority make Chávez, for now, irreplaceable. His re-election to the presidency on 7 October 2012, in the face of a reinvigorated opposition, demonstrated once again that most Venezuelans believe he is the sole figure capable of leading the country forward. Yet the future of the process will depend on increasing the self-organization of the masses and the development of a collective leadership that can support, and eventually substitute for, Chávez's singular role.

Explaining this phenomenon, Gonzalo Gomez, a co-founder of the Aporrea website, explained in an interview published on *Kaos en la Red*:

> Today, Chávez is a unifying figure including for those that don't like everything he does. The people recognize him as a force for unity. Now, if we are unable to construct the communes, the communal cities and other organizations of the movements in Venezuela, the future of the revolutionary process will remain uncertain. For me that is the most important thing. The post-Chávez era will not depend on individual figures, but rather on our capacity to continue developing, deepening and advancing the Bolivarian revolution once that leadership is no longer there.[71]

5 Thousands of Bolivian *campesinos* and indigenous farmers raise their hands during a people's assembly in La Paz, Bolivia, in 2005, in support of making a recently passed hydrocarbons law even tougher on multinational companies (credit: Noah Friedman-Rudovsky).

5 | Bolivia's communitarian socialism

The inauguration of Evo Morales in January 2006 marked a watershed in Bolivian history. Winning the presidency with an unprecedented 53.7 percent of the popular vote, he became the country's first indigenous head of state. His victory also marked the ascent of Bolivia's social movements and reflected the wider aspirations of Bolivians to bring to an end two decades of economic and social devastation levied on the country by neoliberalism. As legendary Peruvian indigenous activist Hugo Blanco noted, it represented 'an important step in the path of the organized Bolivian people in their struggle to take power into their own hands.'[1]

Morales's election to the presidency marked a new phase in the anti-neoliberal struggle that began in 2000 with the 'water war' against water privatization and which subsequently saw Bolivia's diverse and dispersed social movements rise up and depose two presidents, first in October 2003, and then in June 2005.

The strategy behind the 2005 presidential victory had emerged a decade before in the humid Chapare region of central Bolivia. There, the *cocaleros*, led by Evo Morales, collaborated with the Bolivian indigenous campesino movement to create a new 'political instrument,' the Instrumento Político por la Soberanía de los Pueblos (IPSP, Political Instrument for the Sovereignty of the People), commonly referred to as the MAS. Under Morales's leadership, the MAS-IPSP would combine street mobilizations with election campaigning in its quest to construct the necessary alliances and balance of social forces that would make a victory possible in the December 2005 presidential elections.

The rise of Morales and the MAS-IPSP reflected the fact that the party encapsulated and built upon Bolivians' historic memory of struggle: the *long memory* of indigenous resistance to colonialism and the *short memory* of revolutionary nationalism, best exemplified by the 1952 National Revolution when armed miners and campesinos marched on La Paz to demand the nationalization of the mines and a radical redistribution of land.[2] The result of this fusion of collective memories was a new 'indigenous nationalism' in which indigenous pride came to be viewed as synonymous with the creation of a new dignified Bolivia.[3]

Communitarian socialism became the vision of a new society that embodied these social forces. Vice-President Álvaro García Linera, the leading theorist of the new Bolivian revolution, proclaimed: 'Communitarian socialism is the struggle for a distinct, harmonious, respectful and non-exploitative society.' According to García Linera, there are two sources of Bolivian socialism: 'one is the working class, science and technology, the other, communitarianism.' Regarding the latter, García Linera explains that, in Bolivia, 'campesino agrarian structures exist that mean that our struggle for socialism has the particularity of communitarian socialism.'[4]

In the current stage, García Linera sees 'the integral state as the bridge between capitalism and socialism,' and asserts that 'the integral state is a government of the social movements, of rural and urban dwellers, of campesinos, of barrio residents, of students, intellectuals and academics.'[5] In the economic sphere Luis Alberto Arce Catacora, who has served as minister of economy and public finance since 2006, proclaims that the government 'does not pretend to immediately change the capitalist mode of production, but instead to lay the foundations for the transition toward a new socialist mode of production.'[6]

Economic roots of social revolution

The backdrop to the new vision and the dramatic rise of Bolivia's social movements is the devastating impact that neoliberalism had upon South America's poorest country. In a 17 May 2006 US embassy cable made public by WikiLeaks, embassy officials outlined the role neoliberalism played in 'undermin[ing] the faith of many Bolivians in the old economic and political order.'[7] The failure of neoliberalism was pinpointed by David M. Robinson, the US Deputy Chief of Mission in La Paz, as the 'economic roots of Bolivia's social revolution.'

The impact of neoliberalism in Bolivia is clearly described in Benjamin Kohl and Linda Farthing's insightful 2005 book *Impasse in Bolivia: Neoliberal Hegemony and Popular Resistance*. Kohl and Farthing recount how between 1980 and 2005, successive neoliberal governments implemented a program of handing over Bolivia's state-owned companies to transnational corporations, debilitating working-class organizations, dismantling the Bolivian state, and concentrating decision-making among an ever smaller political elite.

The first target of the neoliberal onslaught was the mining sector, home to the historic backbone of Bolivia's radical trade union movement. Through the process of 'capitalization' – the euphemism utilized to describe privatization – 20,000 jobs were shed and with them the power of the miners' union. In the hydrocarbon sector, which accounted for 50 percent of government revenue, privatization was accompanied by a drop in the royalties companies had to pay the state from 50 to 18 percent. The process of dismembering the state hydrocarbon company, Yacimientos Petrolíferos Fiscales Bolivianos (YPFB, Bolivian state oil company), similarly resulted in a workforce reduction from more than 9,000 in 1985 to 600 by 2002.[8]

As a result, the Bolivian state increasingly depended on foreign governments and their transnational corporations and institutions to cover falling government revenue. During the neoliberal era, international loans and aid covered 'roughly half of Bolivia's public investment.' Each budget deficit resulted in further IMF-imposed SAPs. The removal of state subsidies directed toward Bolivia's small industrial sector – which was critical to job creation in the formal economy and for Bolivia's value-added exports – led to some 35,000 jobs disappearing in the manufacturing sector alone. By 1988, the informal sector had ballooned to 70 percent of Bolivia's urban workforce, and the few jobs created in the formal sector were subject to labor flexibilization practices. These measures seriously weakened the Central Obrera Boliviana (COB, Bolivian Workers Central), the country's main federation of workers' unions that was founded with the Bolivian revolution in 1952.[9]

Bolivia's traditional parties established power-sharing pacts, while successive governments imposed restrictions on the registration of new, alternative parties. Both moves enabled Bolivia's political class to maintain a 'government majority capable of effectively isolating the opposition and marginalizing the legislature from policy-making.'[10] The distribution of quotas of power among these parties was extended to the appointment of judicial authorities, facilitating their subordination to the executive power.

By the beginning of the twenty-first century, Bolivia was rocked by explosive mass uprisings and mobilizations that succeeded in halting the advance of the neoliberal project and created the possibility of a fundamental political and social transformation. In 2005, the social movements that had led the rebellions of the previous five years succeeded in electing Morales to power. Since then his government has presided over a self-proclaimed 'Democratic and Cultural Revolution' that has focused on two key tasks: nationalizing Bolivia's economy and decolonizing the state.

Nationalizing the economy

'After hearing the reports from the transition commissions, I have seen how the state does not control the state and its institutions. There is a total dependency,' said Morales on 22 January 2006, the day he was sworn in as president.[11] He described Bolivia as 'a transnationalized country' and noted that, under the pretext of capitalization, 'the country has been decapitalized.'

'I want this to end,' said Morales, and he argued that it was therefore necessary 'to nationalize our natural resources and put in march a new economic model.'[12]

Morales's new economic model seeks to roll back neoliberalism by: 1) reasserting state sovereignty over the economy and particularly over Bolivia's natural resources; 2) breaking out of Bolivia's traditional position as an exporter of primary materials by industrializing these resources; 3) promoting productive sectors such as manufacturing and agriculture; 4) redistributing the nation's wealth in order to tackle poverty; and 5) strengthening the organizational capacity of proletarian and communitarian forces as the two essential pillars of the transition to socialism in Bolivia.

According to Arce, Bolivia's New Economic, Social, Communitarian, and Productive Model has replaced the neoliberal model. Under the old model transnational capital appropriated rent via the extraction of natural resources. The Bolivian state arbitrated the rules, but received little return. Under this new model, the government now prioritizes stimulating the internal market in order to reduce dependency on foreign capital and demand. As the introduction to Arce's article outlines, the state today is endowed with functions 'such as planning the economy, administering public enterprises, investing in the productive sector, taking on the role of a banker and regulator and, among other things, redistributing the surplus.'[13]

To break free from underdevelopment and industrialize Bolivia's economy, the state aims to coordinate its actions with private, communitarian, and cooperative sectors, 'whose integration configures a clearly plural model, that is, a Plural economy.'[14] According to Arce, this model of a plural economy with four actors – of which the state is the most important – has two mainstays: the strategic sector that generates rent and the productive sector that generate profits and employment. Among the first group are hydrocarbons, mining, and electricity, while the second includes manufacturing, tourism, housing, agriculture, and others 'that have yet to be invigorated.'

In order to develop the economy of this small, landlocked Andean country and break with the traditional model that has relegated Bolivia to the role of raw materials exporter, Arce proposes transferring the rent and profits generated from the mining, hydrocarbon, and electricity sectors toward this second group, with an emphasis on promoting communitarian, cooperative, and family-based enterprises. Since Morales came to office in 2006, this revenue has also been funneled into increased social spending

This new economic model, says Arce, does not claim to move directly to a change in the capitalist mode of production. Rather it seeks to lay the basis for the transition towards socialism by 'gradually resolving many social problems and consolidating the economic base through an adequate distribution of economic surpluses.' He adds a provocative historical insight:

At no time have we thought of building socialism in the here and now; Karl Marx himself, when speaking of the Paris Commune, and Lenin, provided elements that explain why there cannot be a mechanical transition from capitalism to socialism. There is an intermediate period in which ... we begin to construct a society of transition from the capitalist system by generating conditions for a socialist society.[15]

In a February 2012 interview with the Mexican daily *La Jornada*, García Linera further outlines how these economic measures are components of a comprehensive strategy that is not only 'post-neoliberal' but constitutes steps toward a 'post-capitalist transition.'[16] He said:

Led by the indigenous movement, [the government plan] has involved regaining control of natural resources that were in foreign hands (gas, oil, some minerals, water, electricity) and putting them in state hands, while other resources such as government lands, large estates, and forests have come under the community control of indigenous peoples and farmers.

Today the state is the main wealth generator in the country. That wealth is not valorized as capital; it is redistributed throughout society through bonuses, rents, direct social benefits to the population, the freezing of utility rates and basic fuel prices, and subsidies to agricultural production. We try to prioritize wealth as use value over exchange value. In this regard, the state does not behave as a collective capitalist in the state-capitalist sense, but acts as a redistributor of collective wealth among the working classes and as a facilitator of the material, technical and associative capacities of farmer, community, and urban craft production modes. We place our hope of moving beyond capitalism in this expansion of agrarian and urban communitarianism, knowing that this is a universal task, not just that of a single country.

So how has the Morales government done in terms of turning these novel ideas into reality? A key component of this new economic model is the nationalization of the crucial hydrocarbon sector. Initiated less than four months after Morales took office, the 1 May 2006 nationalization decree represented a complete overhaul of the rules of the game and brought immediate benefits to the Bolivian people.

Prior to nationalization, transnational capital appropriated 82 percent of the wealth generated by gas royalties. Under the new system the state retains between 80 and 90 percent of gas rent. This means that the total amount of gas revenue received by the Bolivian government during Morales's first six years was roughly seven times greater than that obtained during the previous five years. In 2011 alone, the state received almost as much revenue from the hydrocarbon sector as it did from 1996 to 2005.[17]

Under the Morales government the Bolivian state decides what happens to every single drop of Bolivian gas produced. While transnationals technically extract most of Bolivia's gas, they do so as contractors hired by the state to operate according to the country's terms. When they have failed to comply with their contracts, the government has not been afraid to nationalize them. In the meantime, the MAS government has sought to rebuild YPBF, starting with the renationalization of those sections of the company that were privatized.

The Morales government has also taken steps to industrialize gas, in order to turn around a situation in which for decades transnational corporations have extracted and exported Bolivia's gas and then shipped it back as high-cost fuels. This includes having begun construction on two gas processing plants. When completed, these plants will supply all of Bolivia's gasoline and liquefied petroleum gas needs.[18] The Bolivian government is also carrying out studies for the construction of a third plant that would enable the country to become self-sufficient in diesel.

The state has also tried to exert greater control over the mining sector, starting with the 2006 nationalizations of the Posokoni tin deposit in the Huanuni mine and the Vinto tin smelter the following year. Difficulties have emerged, however. During the neoliberal era some of the biggest mining enterprises were broken up into smaller operations, many of which became cooperatives while others remained private. Rising mineral prices have underpinned the escalating number of mine occupations by local campesino communities seeking to grab their share of the wealth. Intra-class conflicts have erupted between private mineworkers, co-op miners and local communities over profits and markets. Within this complex scenario, transnationals have worked to stoke up tensions in order to maintain their privileged positions.

Government calls to nationalize some of these mines have on a number of occasions met with opposition from private mineworkers and cooperatives.[19] However, a series of conflicts in early 2012 forced the government to initiate dialogue among these different forces, culminating in the rescinding of contracts with transnational mining corporations operating the Colquiri and Mallku Khota mines.

Other nationalizations have allowed the state to become the biggest player in the telecommunications and electricity sectors.[20] Unlike transnational capital, whose motivation was purely to make profit, the state has redirected efforts in these sectors toward ensuring that ordinary Bolivians have greater access to basic services. As a result, the number of households with gas connections has increased by 835 percent, the percentage of rural households with access to electricity has jumped to 50 percent from 20 percent, and the number of municipalities with telecommunications coverage has gone from 110 to 324 (of a total of 339).[21]

The redirection of wealth toward promoting other productive sectors led to the creation of 485,574 new jobs between 2006 and 2010, a key contributing factor to the fall in unemployment, from 8.2 percent in 2005 to 5.7 percent in 2010.[22] The government has also embarked on a number of experiments with small state-owned enterprises in the area of food processing (Empresa Boliviana de Almendras, Lácteosbol, la Planta de Cítricos y la Empresa de Palmitos), gold (la Empresa Boliviana del Oro) and cardboard production (Cartónbol). The plan is for these companies to be handed over to local communities to run as part of fostering the communitarian sector.[23]

Agrarian reform has been put on the front burner in a country where most of the indigenous population work in agriculture. Between 2006 and 2010, over 35 million hectares of land was handed over to peasant communities as communitarian property or placed under the direct control of the original indigenous inhabitants.[24] A further 21 million hectares, previously occupied illegally by large landowners, were declared public lands, and largely converted into protected forest areas. The creation of the Empresa de Apoyo a la Producción de Alimentos (EMAPA, Food Production Support Company) in 2007 has ensured that the small agricultural producers have preferential access to equipment, supplies, interest-free loans, and state-subsided markets.[25] The result has been an increase in the area of land under cultivation and in the levels of food production.[26]

Viewed as a whole, the measures taken to recover sovereignty over Bolivia's economy have meant that the state has become the central player in the national economy. Today, more of Bolivia's wealth stays in Bolivia and is used to expand the internal market, promote industrialization, and stimulate the communitarian sector.

Increased revenue has also led to increased social spending.[27] The result of this spending was clearly evident by 2010, with the level of poverty having fallen from 60 to 49.6 percent, while extreme poverty dropped from 38 to 25 percent. The gap between the richest 10 percent and the poorest 10 percent has shrunk from 128 times more wealth to 60 times more.[28]

'Refounding' the state

These advances in the economic sphere have been accompanied by important changes in the political arena directed at empowering Bolivia's indigenous popular classes. Like never before, Bolivia's previously excluded indigenous, campesino, and working-class sectors have moved into elected positions. In 2011 five of the country's nine governors were of indigenous or campesino origins, while 90 of the 166 elected representatives in the Plurinational Legislative Assembly came directly from the ranks of Bolivia's social movements.[29]

While the Bolivian government continues to function within a deeply entrenched capitalist culture and capitalist social relations, a combination of successful electoral and insurrectional battles have enabled the indigenous-popular forces to take control of important positions of power within the state.[30] From these positions they have used the increased revenue to begin nationalizing the state, i.e. breaking its dependency on international funding. Strategically, this has empowered the government to dismantle army units that have been funded and trained by the US military and to dismiss high-ranking military figures with ties to the US embassy.[31] This strong economic position has also allowed those running the Bolivian state to dictate their own domestic and foreign policy, free at last from impositions set in the neoliberal era in return for loans by international agencies.

Unsurprisingly, each of these moves has been met with disapproval from Washington and international financial institutions. The United States responded to the Morales government's 2006 announcement that it would not grant immunity to US soldiers or officers by slashing military aid by 96 percent.[32] The World Bank, on being told in 2006 by the then planning minister, Carlos Villegas, that it would not be part of the process of elaborating the government's economic plan, halved Bolivia's annual budget, and the IMF stopped lending money to the country.[33]

The sacking of US and IMF officials in developing government policy has led to a greater participation of Bolivia's social movements. To facilitate this process, in January 2007 the government initiated the Coordinadora Nacional por el Cambio (CONALCAM, National Coalition for Change). Its role is to bring together Bolivia's main indigenous and popular organizations with their representatives in the executive and legislative branch of the state in order to coordinate and debate strategies. This process was critical to strengthening the necessary alliance between the government and social movements required to overcome the resistance of the right-wing opposition. It was also essential to ensuring the implementation of one of the most important steps taken by the Morales government – the convening of a constituent assembly.

Envisaged as a space in which to rewrite Bolivia's constitution, the goal of the constituent assembly was to create a new 'plurinational' state that for the first time in Bolivia's history would recognize the previously excluded indigenous 'nations' and provide them with an important weapon to advance their struggles and demands. Beginning in early 2006, the Pacto de Unidad (PU, Unity Pact), comprising Bolivia's five main rural indigenous campesino organizations, began collectively constructing its proposals for the constituent assembly.[34] The PU's proposed constitution became a central reference point for the debates within the constituent assembly.

Notwithstanding some important deficiencies, the final version of the constitution is generally viewed as a significant achievement of the social movements that enshrined their three key demands: plurinationalism, indigenous autonomies, and reclaiming control over natural resources. The overwhelming support for the new constitution was verified in the January 2009 referendum, with more than 60 percent of voters supporting this new charter for Bolivia. Since its approval, the process of 'decolonizing' the state has continued to advance, most recently in October 2010, with the holding of Bolivia's first popular elections to elect judicial authorities. A record number of women (50 percent) and indigenous people (40 percent) flooded into the judicial branch of the state, as a result of the elections. They have been entrusted with the task of implementing popular justice.

Resisting US imperialism and the rise of an indigenous-popular hegemony

The Morales government also initiated a significant shift in Bolivia's foreign policy, leaving behind the country's traditional subservient position toward the United States. In its place, the Morales government has established a new relationship based on 'sovereignty, dignity and reciprocity.'[35] Key policy shifts are the rejection of the US-proposed FTAA, the naming of ministers and military officials without seeking US embassy consent, the campaign to bring former president Gonzalo Sánchez de Lozada back to Bolivia to face trial (for murdering demonstrators), and the expulsion of the US Drug Enforcement Administration (DEA) from Bolivian soil.

At the same time, the Morales government is establishing trade and political relationships with new allies. A constant concern for Washington is Bolivia's close relationship with Cuba and Venezuela, formalized with its integration into the ALBA bloc in 2006. On joining ALBA, Bolivia brought to the table the proposal to establish *Tratados de Comercio del Pueblo* (TCPs, Peoples' Trade Agreements). While ALBA had come to represent an alternative to the FTAA, the TCPs were posited as an alternative to the United States' promotion of an FTAA-lite through the signing of bilateral free trade agreements (FTAs or TLCs in Spanish). The focus of TCPs was to develop bilateral 'trade based on complementarity, solidarity and cooperation.'[36]

As part of its leading role in the formation of UNASUR, Bolivia is today home to the Centro de Estudios Estratégicos de la Defensa (CEED, Center for Strategic Defense Studies), a training ground for South American military officers – considered an alternative to the US-run School of the Americas. Addressing the inauguration of the center in May 2011, García Linera argued for the creation of a 'regional state' that would allow South American countries to take common international positions on issues such as natural resources, military defense, and economic policies.

'We are a region with important natural resources, with 400 million inhabitants and a Gross Domestic Product that represents almost 7% of the world GDP,' he said. 'This obliges us to unite, to articulate a project for integration ... and to think of UNASUR as a Regional State.'[37]

The Morales government has also led two important international campaigns in close collaboration with social movements from around the globe. It has spearheaded the global fight against climate change, raising real solutions based on climate justice and the defense of the rights of *Pachamama*, or Mother Earth.

'We send a message to the world to reflect deeply and to the presidents of the capitalist system to change their economic model which is destroying the environment and planet earth,' Morales said at the United Nations conference on climate change in Copenhagen in December 2009. 'Capitalism and imperialism are forms of industrial development without limits.'[38]

He argued for drastic reductions in global carbon emissions and demanded that rich nations repay their 'climate debt' through the transfer of technology and funds to underdeveloped countries. The Morales government played a central role in strengthening the burgeoning global climate justice movement by hosting the World's People Summit on Climate Change, in Bolivia, in April 2010. The summit ratified a radical program for change, the Cochabamba Declaration, which called for an end to capitalism.[39]

The other important international campaign waged by the Morales government has been for the decriminalization of coca. Under the pretence of waging a 'war on drugs,' the United States has consistently tried to undermine Bolivia's sovereignty. In response, Bolivia's Aymara and Quechua indigenous peoples have pointed out that coca is part of their millenarian culture and can be used as well to produce useful derivatives such as tea, soap, and toothpaste.[40] Resisting US intervention during the 1990s, the *cocaleros* converted the coca leaf into a symbol of the struggle to defend national sovereignty and Bolivia's indigenous cultures. The Morales government has sought to remove coca from the list of criminalized drugs in the 1961 UN Single Convention on Narcotic Drugs, a major impediment to Bolivia's sovereign right to grow and industrialize coca as an asset to human health.

Class showdown

The Morales government's overall strategy has the overwhelming support of Bolivia's working classes, and not just at election time. Each attempt by the social movements to advance this agenda – both before and after the 2005 elections – has met with strong resistance from the United States and Bolivia's traditional elites. This intervention in turn has stimulated mobilizations by these same social movements.

The signs of imperial and elite resistance were present long before Morales won the presidency in 2005. Three years earlier, Gonzalo Sánchez de Lozada narrowly defeated Morales in the country's 2002 presidential election, owing in large part to the corporate media's anti-Evo campaign run with the support of the US embassy. Declassified documents from 2002 asserted that the US government was involved in attempts to foster 'moderate, pro-democracy political parties that can serve as a counter-weight to the radical MAS.'[41]

In the run-up to the 2005 elections, a separatist movement emerged in Santa Cruz, Bolivia's second-largest city. While those who had held power during the neoliberal era sensed their grip on power loosening over the Andean, western part of Bolivia – where the strength of the social movements and MAS seemed almost impenetrable – this predominantly eastern-based elite, backed by transnational gas and agribusiness interests, began to retreat to their territorial trenches in early 2005, demanding greater 'regional autonomy.' These right-wing separatist forces, with their base in the urban centers among the whiter population, won elections for the governorships in Bolivia's four eastern departments – Santa Cruz, Pando, Beni, and Tarija – collectively known as the *media luna* (half-moon) owing to the crescent-shaped nature of the bloc.

The US government channeled funds to these groups, primarily through USAID, to support their pursuit of regional autonomy. Between 2002 and 2007, USAID directed more than $97 million toward opposition parties, as well as 'decentralization' and 'regional autonomy' projects.[42] By 2007, USAID was working closely with right-wing opposition prefects to 'develop sub-national, de-concentrated' models of government with the objective of establishing the political, economic, and territorial autonomy of the region from the national government. That same year, over $1 million was allocated to opposition parties for 'training for members of political parties on current political and electoral processes, including the constituent assembly and the referendum on autonomy.' The US government also targeted funding toward indigenous communities, particularly those based in the east, in hopes of demonstrating 'that the US is a friend to Bolivia and the indigenous people.'

As in Venezuela under Hugo Chávez, the advance of the MAS government in implementing its mandate meant a showdown was inevitable. Pro- and anti-government forces carried out numerous street mobilizations and confrontations throughout 2006 and 2007, with the decisive battle played out in August and September 2008. Failing to remove Morales at the ballot box through the July 2008 recall referendum, the right-wing opposition (in coordination with the US embassy) initiated a campaign of violence, looting and seizures of government buildings. Opposition prefects began to speak openly of 'regional independence.' The mayor of Santa Cruz, Percy Fernandez, publicly stated 'that the armed forces should overthrow the useless national government.'[43] The right-wing opposition hoped that the military would be forced to react, causing deaths and Morales's resignation, or creating the justification for some kind of United Nations intervention to restore stability.[44]

On 5 September, US embassy officials met with Bolivian military figures.[45] The aim was to convince them not to act against the coup plot. When the government ordered the top commander of the armed forces, General Luis Trigo – with known links to the Santa Cruz oligarchy – to move into Pando and take back control, he responded that he would do nothing until a presidential decree had been signed. This would ensure that full responsibility for any blood spilt lay with Morales. Trigo then ordered his troops to remain in their barracks and turned off his phone. Others in the military high command followed suit.

In response, an emergency meeting of social movements was held in Cochabamba on 10 September. The groups resolved to march on Santa Cruz and crush the coup-plotting offensive. The same day, Morales expelled the US ambassador, Philip Goldberg, for his leading role in the coup plot. With the attention of the social movements focused on Santa Cruz, the coup plotters moved to create a crisis in Pando. There, paramilitary forces ambushed and fired on unarmed peasants travelling to a meeting of their regional union federation called to organize resistance to the rebellion. At least thirteen people were killed.

A wave of revulsion reverberated throughout society. The killings even outraged middle-class sectors in the *media luna* that the opposition had hoped to mobilize. As the social movements stepped up plans to encircle Santa Cruz, campesinos in the rural areas of the department cut off all access to the city. Important pockets of resistance also emerged within the city of Santa Cruz as neighborhood groups in the impoverished barrio of Plan 3000 fought off attacks by armed youth gangs. Demands for action swept through the military as soldiers requested they be deployed to the east to defend their indigenous brothers and sisters. Under direct orders from Morales, new troops were sent to Pando, and, after beating back armed paramilitaries at the airport, moved in to restore order in the capital city of Cobija. An emergency UNASUR summit held in Santiago, Chile, declared its support for the Morales government and opposition to any attempts to break up Bolivia.

Lacking international support, and with their plan unraveling, the prefects quickly called for a return to dialogue. The right-wing gangs began to lift their roadblocks and the government regained control of public buildings. With the balance of forces shifting decisively in favor of the government, the right-wing opposition was forced to surrender. The coup plot had failed.

The subsequent popular approval of the new constitution, Morales's re-election in 2009 with a historic 64 percent vote, and the extension of MAS control over two-thirds of the regional governorships further ratified the powerful presence of indigenous-popular forces within the state. With the absence of any political alternative to the MAS project, either to its left or right, the task, it seemed, was to deepen the process of transformation under way.

'Creative tensions' on the path to communitarian socialism

The emergence of an indigenous-popular hegemony, with a new constitution in hand, represented a new phase for generating and redistributing the country's wealth while unleashing the creative capacities of the social movements by opening spaces for their participation in decision-making. However, the Morales government has confronted powerful obstacles, especially an inherited capitalist state apparatus that remains largely intact and ill equipped to implement progressive reforms. As in Venezuela, much of Bolivian society is 'characterized by a rentist mentality that sees in the state one of the few spaces for social ascendancy,' notes Argentine sociologist Pablo Stefanoni.[46] Many social movement activists view the MAS more as a 'political instrument' for gaining access to the state (including through corruption) than one aimed at achieving 'peoples' sovereignty'. Commenting on this phenomenon, Morales said:

I worry that, at the moment, we have leaders that are more concerned with their own personal ambitions than social issues. This is the old mentality ... Previously, the union used to be the state, the ayllu [a traditional form of indigenous community organization] was the state, the community was the state. Now that we have strengthened the position of the party, that we have won elections, I ask myself: are we losing the union-state, the ayllu-state, the community-state. Why does this worry me? Because previously, the union, the ayllu and the community resolved everything. The colonial state never appeared ... Now when there is a problem over roads, the people place demands on the mayor, the governor ... Logically, we are discussing this, but the union, the ayllu, the community cannot disappear.[47]

Moreover, the seemingly untouchable MAS government encountered unexpected challenges in the form of a series of protest movements in 2010/11. These included protests in May 2010 by the COB for higher wage increases, a July 2010 march for greater indigenous autonomy organized by the Confederación de Pueblos Indígenas de Bolivia (CIDOB, Confederation of Indigenous Peoples of Bolivia), an August 2010 rebellion in Potosi over the perceived failure of the government to meet local demands, and, perhaps most significantly, the December 2010 *gasolinazo*, when growing protests among the government's own ranks forced it to back down on a proposal to remove subsidies on gas.[48] An unparalleled number of protests, more than any government has faced since the 1970s, was accompanied by the emergence of increasingly critical voices, many of them former government officials or MAS militants.[49]

'The large majority of our people basically find themselves in the same situation of poverty, precariousness and anguish in which they have always been,' proclaimed a group of former MAS militants and ex-government officials in their *Manifiesto Colectivo* (Collective Manifesto), issued in June 2011. 'It would seem that those who have improved are those that had always been well off: the bankers, transnational oil and mining companies, the smugglers, and the narco-traffickers.'[50]

The dispute that garnered the most international attention was over the government's proposal to build a highway through the Territorio Indígena y Parque Nacional Isiboro Sécure (TIPNIS, Isiboro-Secure National Park and Indigenous Territory). In response to the government, leaders of the TIPNIS Subcentral (the main organization uniting indigenous communities within TIPNIS) initiated a 500-kilometer protest march on La Paz, in July 2011. On their way they were violently repressed by the police – an action denounced by Morales himself. After arriving in the capital, the protestors finally forced the government to back down, igniting extensive debate about the nature of Bolivia's first indigenous-led government.[51]

A number of features stand out in attempting to grasp the underlying dynamics common to all these disputes. Strikingly, the source of all the discontent and protests originated from within the ranks of the MAS social base and not the traditional right. Unlike in the period between 2000 and 2009, when Bolivia's social movements were united in opposition to transnational capital and its local allies in the Bolivian elites, these protests have mainly involved specific social movements and revolved around particular issues and demands. In some cases the demands have been contradictory: the 2011 anti-road march was characterized by some as a movement against 'developmentalism' and a Brazilian-financed highway to benefit 'Brazilian sub-imperialism,' yet those that had taken to the streets of Potosí the year before had been demanding more 'development,' in the form of factories, airports, and the completion of two highways, both part of the same Brazilian regional integration project as the TIPNIS highway. This also led to many conflicts pitting the interests of different social movements against each other: cooperative miners versus mineworkers, campesinos versus local indigenous communities, etc.

Moreover, none of these protest movements put forth any serious proposals or a program that posed a political alternative to the MAS government. Disagreements instead focused on how to best implement the MAS project, itself the collective result of the previous period of struggle. As such, most conflicts tended to be resolved through a process of dialogue involving the differently affected groups.

The social conflicts over turning the revolutionary project into reality have led to the emergence of what García Linera defines as 'creative tensions.'[52] He argues that the constellation of social forces since the victory in the 2008 confrontations has opened a new period in Bolivia's revolutionary epoch 'that is now characterized not by the presence of contradictions between antagonistic power blocs, between irreconcilable societal projects,' as hitherto, but one that 'will be marked by the presence of contradictions within the national-popular bloc, that is, by tensions between the very sectors that are leading the Process of Change.' These contradictions, he says, 'are not simply secondary but are *creative* because they have the potential to help drive forward the course of the revolution itself [his emphasis].'[53]

These creative tensions, García Linera argues, have emerged in various ways. One has to do with the relationship between the state and the social movements, between the government's tendency to concentrate decision-making in administration and the social movements' affinity for 'full and ongoing socialization of deliberations and decisions around matters of common concern.' This is 'a creative, dialectical, productive and necessary tension,' he adds.

A second creative tension, says García Linera, is between the revolution's need to incorporate broader sectors and 'the need to guarantee indigenous, campesino, worker and popular leadership' in this process.[54] A third involves the tension 'between the general interest of the society as a whole and the particular interest of an individual segment ... between the common, communitarian, communist struggle and the search for individual, sectoral, particular and private interest.'[55]

While this tension was not as evident during the previous period when the primary struggle was waged against transnational capital and its governments, the defeat of this historic enemy has opened up space for these internal tensions to resurface. He adds that this tension

> is precisely what we have been experiencing since 2010. A victory of the universalist will of the indigenist-worker-popular bloc will allow for the expansive and hegemonic consolidation of the revolutionary process. If on the contrary, a corporatist and trade-unionist particularism triumphs, this will be the beginning of a degenerative process in the revolution, the starting point for the conservative restoration of the business bloc that is the people's adversary.[56]

Finally, García Linera points to a fourth tension, between the need to develop and industrialize Bolivia's economy and the need to respect the rights of Mother Earth.[57] The starting point for resolving this tension, he argues, must be ensuring people's access to basic services while protecting the environment.

The emergence of these 'contradictions within the people,' as García Linera describes them, has demonstrated the need for greater collective debates over the future of the revolutionary process. One challenge in all this is to avoid the possibility that these tensions might lead to outright confrontations, particularly in the context of constant and ongoing imperialist attempts to penetrate and divide Bolivia's social movements. One example is the close attention that the US embassy and USAID have paid to indigenous leaders from the east, including through regular meetings and funding training programs.[58] However, far from discouraging or attempting to repress these tensions – the general response taken by the socialist regimes of the twentieth century – today's revolutionary processes, he notes, must be driven forward by these conflicts, tensions, and debates.

'The struggle is our nourishment, our peace, not our fear,' explained García Linera in a speech delivered in Mexico in February 2012. 'Absolute tranquility makes us scared. The opposition believes that the struggle will tire us out; instead, it nourishes us.'[59]

Bolivian political scientist Helen Argirakis Jordan argues that social conflict, rather than being a negative factor for the government, 'constitutes a manner in which to know the concerns and demands of social society – in real time.' The idea, explains Argirakis, is that through this process, the MAS government interiorizes these conflicts, processes the demands of civil society, and converts them into laws or government policies.[60]

For now, the unity of Bolivia's diverse laboring classes has in large part relied on the central role played by Evo Morales, a figure capable of encompassing the broad base of the revolution, with all its internal contradictions. In his role as mediator, standing above the clash of interests, Morales's political intuition has been key to the continued advance of the revolution given the continued close bond he maintains with union leaders and the grassroots (facilitated by the constant national, regional, and local assemblies he attends). For this reason, criticism from the social movements has overwhelmingly been directed at ministers and others in his close circle, but rarely at Morales himself.

Perhaps the greatest challenge facing the revolution is to go beyond relying on Morales, and in the process alter the MAS-IPSP – an amorphous conglomerate of indigenous popular organizations more focused on gaining employment than strategic alternatives. The party needs to be transformed into an organizational space that can house these tensions and debates while charting a common path forward. That is, MAS itself ought to become an agile and consolidated 'political instrument' at the service of worker and communitarian forces that are committed to advancing twenty-first-century socialism.

6 An indigenous Ecuadoran blows a conch shell at the opening march for the June 2010 Meeting of Original Peoples and Nations of Abya Yala in Quito, Ecuador (credit: Marc Becker).

6 | Ecuador's *buen vivir* socialism

MARC BECKER[1]

On the morning of 30 September 2010, discontented police officers and military troops plunged Ecuador into a political crisis as they took President Rafael Correa hostage, seized Quito's international airport, and stormed the National Assembly building. A new public service law that raised salaries but curtailed bonuses had triggered the revolt. The protesting officers attacked Correa when he unexpectedly arrived at the police barracks to explain the law's intent. When an exploding tear gas canister injured the president, the police brought Correa to a police hospital where they held him captive. Although the police made no moves to assassinate him, they did forcefully repel a march of his supporters on the hospital. Ten hours later, an elite military squad stormed the hospital to free the president. As they fled the hospital, snipers fired on the president's armored sport-utility vehicle, killing one of the rescuers. Upon his return to the presidential palace, Correa gave a fiery speech to his gathered supporters in which he accused his political opponents of plotting his overthrow and assassination.[2]

The events of 30-S (as they came to be known) pointed to the contradictions, complications, and conflicts inherent in Ecuador's turn to the left. Correa came to power on the strength of his denunciation of neoliberal economic policies, but yet as president his opponents accused him that in cutting bonuses he was implementing some of the same austerity measures he had pledged to defeat. Furthermore, despite assuming strong anti-imperialist positions, Correa also seemed too willing to compromise on key socialist positions. At play were debates over what political and economic direction Ecuador should take, and whose interests those developments would benefit.

A young and charismatic economics professor, Correa first won Ecuador's presidency in November 2006. He had successfully campaigned on a platform of leaving the long, dark night of neoliberalism behind. In its place, Correa proposed to construct a government based on five revolutions: an economic revolution that re-established the government's redistributive role; a social revolution that favored equality for Ecuador's different social sectors and ethnic groups; a political revolution to reverse the privatization of state structures and enhance participatory democracy; a revolution for Latin American integration that would create new organisms to replace mercantilist structures; and an ethical revolution to combat corruption. In 2010, two more revolutions were added, one in favor of the environment and the other for judicial reform.[3] In line with other South American governments that accompanied Ecuador's turn to the left, Correa promised to fundamentally remake the country's governing structures.

Correa spoke openly of twenty-first-century socialism, and positioned himself as part of Latin America's leftward drift that pledged to open up more participatory governing structures.[4] 'Personally, I am not a communist, I am a socialist,' said Correa in an interview with Radio Netherlands Wereldomroep, 'but a socialism for the 21st century is a socialism of *buen vivir*,' in reference to the indigenous perspective of an alternative to development based on the concept of the good life.[5] Correa acknowledged that 'almost no one can define' twenty-first-century socialism, even while it was urgent to move in that direction. He commonly defined his perceptions in terms of what twenty-first-century socialism was not.[6] Soon after taking office, Correa said that this new form of socialism 'differs totally from the idea of state control over the means of production and traditional socialism.'[7] Correa later summarized that twenty-first-century socialism can be defined by one word: justice.[8] Other than ambiguous comments about curtailing the power of congress, depoliticizing the judiciary, expanding government control over natural resources, and democratizing the media, advocates generally lacked concrete proposals as to what it would do.[9] This led Brazilian sociologist Boaventura de Sousa Santos to define twenty-first-century socialism succinctly as 'a metaphor for something to which one aspires but does not know exactly what it is.'[10] Correa, along with other leaders, was searching for new solutions to persistent problems of poverty and inequality.

Correa notes that current ideas on socialism needed to be situated in a pluralistic tradition of many different kinds of socialism: classic, orthodox, traditional, scientific, utopian, agrarian, Christian, and even the Andean socialism of José Carlos Mariátegui. When asked what flavor of socialism he belonged to, Correa responded that his was the Ecuadorean version. Even though this new socialism shared similar values with the classic socialism of social justice and placing human needs over capital, Correa said that in the twenty-first century a class struggle or government control over the means of production were no longer necessary. Instead, it was more important to democratize the means of production, speak of Latin American integration rather than anti-imperialism, and fight for sovereignty in the face of the attempts of international finance institutions to recolonize Latin America. Finally, this new socialism should not be dogmatic, and it should think in terms of principles rather than models.[11]

During a January 2009 trip to Cuba, Correa rejected the 'dogmas history has defeated,' including 'the class struggle, dialectical materialism, the nationalization of all property, the refusal to recognize the market.'[12] Discarding these key elements traditionally associated with socialism while failing to identify alternative visions raised questions as to what exactly Correa meant by twenty-first-century socialism. Furthermore, even as Correa distanced himself from traditional state-centered models of socialism, he still relied on government structures as a tool to advance a socialist agenda.

Citizens' revolution

In office, Correa followed a playbook that his Venezuelan counterpart Hugo Chávez had pioneered on how to use electoral contests to consolidate his grasp on power. Beginning with the presidential race, Correa won a succession of six elections over the course of less than five years. In April 2007, 80 percent of the Ecuadorean electorate approved a referendum to convoke an assembly to rewrite the constitution. In September 2007, Correa's new political party, Alianza País (AP, Country Alliance), won a majority of seats in the constituent assembly. A year later, almost two-thirds of the voters approved the new constitution that had been drafted largely under Correa's control. As was the case with Venezuela's 1999 constitution, Ecuador's new Magna Carta so fundamentally remapped Ecuador's political structures that it required new elections. Correa also dominated these contests, including winning the 2009 presidential election with 52 percent of the vote.

The significance of Correa's re-election under the new constitution should not be understated. Most South American presidential campaigns are highly fragmented multiparty races that require either a runoff election between the top two vote-getters or a congressional decision to select the victor. For a candidate to win a high enough percentage of the vote to avert a runoff election, particularly in the crowded field of eight candidates that Correa faced in 2009, was unprecedented in Ecuador, and historically almost unheard of anywhere in South America. Having consolidated his political position, Correa appeared situated to win re-election in four years, as permitted under the new constitution, and to remain in power until 2017. Not only did

Correa's presidency appear to transcend Ecuador's stormy history of frequent and extra-constitutional changes of government, but it also seemed to be an unequivocal victory for Latin America's rising left tide.

Correa repeatedly rallied against the *partidocracia*, the traditional party system in which the oligarchy controlled the government through their dominance of all aspects of a corrupt state, including congress, the Supreme Court, and various 'autonomous' agencies. Even Michel Camdessus, the former director of the IMF, commented that 'an incestuous relation between bankers, political-financial pressure groups and corrupt government officials' characterized Ecuador's governing system.[13] The oligarchy had consolidated their economic and political control during the 1970s oil boom. With the rise of the Washington Consensus in the 1980s, the *partidocracia* adopted a neoliberal agenda of cutting social programs and privatizing government-owned enterprises. Correa's electoral victories broke the back of the oligarchy's control over an antiquated and dysfunctional political system.

In office, Correa quickly implemented policies that shifted resources to poor and marginalized peoples. Initial economic indicators were positive, as increased government spending on healthcare and other social programs led to reductions in unemployment and poverty. A study from the Center for Economic and Policy Research revealed that Latin America's 'left-populist' governments of Venezuela, Bolivia, and Ecuador were making significant progress in reducing inequality, while the more moderate 'social democratic' governments of Brazil, Chile, and Uruguay had made less progress on this front.[14] Despite these positive indicators, Correa repeatedly clashed with many on the traditional left and other members of Ecuador's strong and well-organized social movements. His agrarian policies favored large-scale economic development and minimized aid for small farmers, alienating rural communities that formed the basis of Ecuador's powerful Indigenous movements that had repeatedly pulled down previous neoliberal governments that ruled in favor of the oligarchy's interests. In contrast, Correa proposed a citizens' revolution that leftist critics complained was based on liberal, individualistic notions of governance rather than mass mobilizations that addressed structural issues. While his economic and social policies led to dramatic reductions in poverty and inequality, these gains were largely limited to urban areas that provided the base of his electoral support. While urban poverty rates in 2011 had fallen to 17 percent, in rural areas they continued to linger above 50 percent, and remained disproportionately higher in Indigenous and Afro-Ecuadorean communities.[15] When criticized for not making more rapid and radical changes, proponents of Correa's project argued that it was impossible to solve in five years problems that were a result of five centuries of exploitation and oppression.

Correa did not emerge out of either Ecuador's political left or out of powerful social movements that had repeatedly challenged the traditional conservative oligarchy's hold on power. Instead, he had a Catholic education that gave him a strong concern for social justice but did not provide him with as sophisticated an understanding of Marxism as his counterparts, who were products of the public school system. Because he emerged out of a Catholic left, his positions on such hot-button social issues as abortion and gay marriage were also not the same as those of leftist feminists. Furthermore, environmentalists opposed his state-centered development projects, leading to significant tensions over mining, petroleum, and other extractive industry policies. Correa's agrarian policies favored large-scale economic development and minimized aid for small farmers, alienating rural communities that formed the basis of Ecuador's powerful Indigenous movements.

Rather than building on the legacy of powerful Indigenous and social movements that had removed previous presidents from power, much of Correa's electoral base came out of the urban lower classes and small business owners. Many of those who took positions in his government were from academia and non-governmental organizations which felt squeezed by previous governments' neoliberal policies.[16] Activists accused Correa of engaging in clientelistic programs of strategic handouts designed primarily to solidify his electoral support, rather than addressing structural issues of oppression and exploitation.[17] From the beginning, it was apparent that his would not be a government of the traditional left, nor of social movements that had repeatedly played the role of kingmaker over the previous decades, but of urban dwellers who responded well to populist styles of governance.

Economic policies

As is common in Latin America, Ecuador had long faced the burdens of an export-oriented dependent economy. As with the rest of the Andes, Ecuador was historically divided between inward-focused domestic highland agricultural production and an outwardly oriented coastal export economy. During the twentieth century, Ecuador enjoyed three export booms that corresponded with periods of unusual political stability in which a sequence of presidents were able to complete their terms in office and peacefully pass power on to an opposing politician. The first boom came with a growth in cocoa exports at the beginning of the century and the second with bananas at mid-century. The third and longest export boom began with the 1970s oil boom, this time based in the eastern Amazon basin rather than the coastal plain. In the 1980s, cut-flower production in the highlands led a turn toward non-traditional exports. In addition, mining, particularly of gold in the southern part of the country, remained ever present.

Neoliberal economic policies in the 1990s, including raising transportation and cooking gas prices, and replacing the local currency with the US dollar, reintroduced extreme political instability into Ecuador. Correa's moves against the conservative oligarchy that implemented these policies earned him broad popular acclaim among the masses. For example, in July 2008 the president expropriated 195 companies belonging to the Isaías Group in order to recover some of the assets that customers had lost when corporate corruption led to the collapse of their bank Filanbanco in 1998. Correa gained further support when in December 2008 he defaulted on more than $3 billion in foreign bonds. Although the treasury did have the means to make payments, not doing so was a political statement in defense of the country's sovereignty. Correa labeled the debt that previous governments had contracted to benefit the upper classes as 'illegal, illegitimate, and corrupt.' He argued that Ecuador should sacrifice debt payments rather than cut social investments.[18]

Correa implemented a series of financial reforms intended to subjugate private property to the public good. The president blamed the Central Bank for sacrificing the country to foreign and neoliberal interests, and he moved to eliminate its autonomy. He taxed windfall oil profits, raised taxes on the wealthy and implemented mechanisms for more effective revenue collection. These reforms provided funding sources to increase social services, including tripling spending on education and healthcare, providing subsidies to poor people to lower their utility costs, and expanding access to credit.[19] The president's social policies played very well with Ecuador's impoverished majority. These policies formed part of a nationalistic economic platform that included criticism of foreign oil corporations for extracting the majority of petroleum rents out of the country. 'Now the oil is everyone's,' Correa declared.[20] He stopped short, though, of nationalizing control over any natural resources, which raised questions of whether his policies were more of a social democratic flavor than those of a radical socialist.

Anti-imperialism

Popular movements in Ecuador had long criticized previous governments for sacrificing national sovereignty in pursuing policies that benefited the interests of the oligarchy. In 1999, former president Jamil Mahuad granted the United States the rights to use a military base at Manta rent-free for a forward operating location in its war against drug trafficking and guerrilla insurgents in neighboring Colombia. Opponents complained that the federal legislature had not properly approved the lease agreement, that the law was a violation of Ecuador's sovereignty, and that the agreement needlessly dragged the country into social conflicts in Colombia. Social movements had repeatedly pressed for the termination of the ten-year lease, and as a presidential candidate Correa announced that he would not renew the agreement when it expired in 2009. Correa declared that the United States could keep their base at Manta if in exchange Ecuador could maintain a base in Miami. If the United States saw no problem with foreign bases, then granting Ecuador such access would seem to comprise a fair and reciprocal agreement. A provision against foreign military bases was written directly into the 2008 constitution with the declaration that 'Ecuador is a land of peace.'[21] Correa followed through with his campaign promises not to renew the lease, and in September 2009 the United States formally withdrew its troops. Nevertheless, even with the military forces gone from Manta, the Correa government championed its drug interdiction efforts and pledged to continue its collaboration with the United States.[22]

Correa's response to Colombia's 1 March 2008 military assault on a guerrilla base in Ecuadorean territory further underscored his anti-imperialist credentials. Correa broke diplomatic relations with Álvaro Uribe's conservative government when his cross-border attack on the FARC threatened to trigger a regional crisis. Not until November 2010 and after Juan Manuel Santos replaced Uribe in office did the two countries fully restore relations. Correa's actions pointed to a principled stance against the militarization of social conflicts.

In June 2011, Ecuador was the only holdout when the OAS voted to readmit Honduras which had been evicted after a 2009 military-backed coup that removed president Manuel Zelaya from office. Correa stated that Ecuador would recognize the Porfirio Lobo administration only if those involved in the coup were punished. Even the Venezuelan and Bolivian governments consented to a normalization of relations with Honduras, seemingly positioning Ecuador to their left. Only four days before the Honduran coup Correa had joined ALBA. The coup underscored in Correa's mind the importance of international allies in the context of a polarized domestic environment.

Similarly, in April 2012, Ecuador was the only country to boycott the sixth Summit of the Americas in Colombia because of Cuba's exclusion from the meeting. Then, in June, Correa took another step against US meddling when he ended Ecuadorean participation in a US-sponsored military program – commonly referred to as the 'School of the Americas' – that has trained thousands of Latin American military officials over the years, many of whom led or participated in coups against civilian elected governments.

The Correa government played a leading role in new regional organizations such as UNASUR, even providing it with a home for a permanent secretariat in Quito. Correa is a vocal proponent of CELAC, a new move toward hemispheric integration that explicitly excluded Canada and the United States, as a replacement for the OAS, which he criticized as being dominated by the powers to the north. Even as social movements pressured Correa to move leftward, in terms of international policies his administration seemed to be staking out the most leftist position of any American government.

Correa's most dramatic stance against the big powers came with the granting of asylum to Julian Assange – the founder of WikiLeaks – in the Ecuadorean embassy in London in August 2012. When the British government threatened to invade the embassy, Correa, in an address to the Ecuadorean people, said, 'I don't know who they think I am or what they think our government is. But how could they expect us to yield to their threats or cower before them? My friends, they don't know who they are dealing with.' He added: 'They haven't found out that the Americas are free and sovereign and that we don't accept meddling and colonialism of any kind.'

South America rallied behind him. The UNASUR foreign ministers met in Guayaquil, expressing 'solidarity' with Correa, while ALBA warned of 'grave consequences' if Britain breached the territorial integrity of the Ecuadorean embassy.

Extractive enterprises

Correa maintained that extractive economic activities would boost the economy, provide more employment, contribute to spending for social programs, and that all of this could be accomplished without negative environmental ramifications. The president sought to promote responsible mining endeavors that benefited both the government and local communities. He favored socially responsible large-scale mining operations governed by strong state control to protect the environment and workers' rights, and contended that poorly regulated artisanal mining was more damaging to the environment. He emphasized the necessity of access to the revenues that mining and petroleum production would generate to fund important social programs.

In December 2007, Correa rejoined OPEC, joining Venezuela as one of two South American members. Ecuador originally enrolled in the cartel in 1973 but left in 1992 under the mandate of conservative president Sixto Duran-Ballen, who complained about the $2 million membership fee and limits on production quotas.[23] Although Ecuador was OPEC's smallest producer, the effort to regain control over the productive output of the country and build international alliances was a significant gesture. Correa also began to renegotiate contracts with private petroleum companies in order to keep more profits in the country. The state-owned oil company Petroecuador, which dated to 1972, did not operate with the same level of autonomy that plagued Chávez in Venezuela before he brought that country's state oil company, PDVSA, under his control in 2003. Nevertheless, Correa did engage in pitched battles with Petroecuador administrators for what he criticized as their inefficient and laissez-faire attitudes toward managing the company. In August 2011, Correa threatened to follow a neoliberal approach and privatize Petroecuador unless the company adopted new technologies to increase production. At the same time, he announced the restructuring of state companies in order to rid them of inefficient bureaucracies and increase profits.[24]

In pursuing these policies, Correa once again could be seen as taking a cue from Chávez's experience in Venezuela. In what some commentators derisively termed petro populism, both governments sought to use petroleum rents to fund social programs. Extractive-industry-driven growth policies, however, commonly run into local opposition, and Ecuador was no exception. Correa's arguments failed to persuade many opponents, who remained unconvinced of the likelihood of the materialization of the promised benefits of mining. Although Ecuador's new 2008 constitution codified much of what popular movements and others on the political left had long demanded, including reasserting government control over oil, mining, transport, telecommunications, and other economic sectors that previous governments had privatized, Correa's concrete policy objectives of expanding and developing mining industries and other extractive enterprises led to growing tensions with rural communities. These communities agitated for prior and informed consent before mining activities could proceed on their lands, while

Correa wanted the federal government to retain the right to decide when and where mining operations could take place.[25] The constitution conceded that communities had the right to consultation, but extractive endeavors would not be subject to their consent or veto power. This decision was a major blow to the power of social movements.

Anti-mining activist Carlos Zorrilla argued that exporting raw materials and importing finished projects back into the country continued patterns of economic dependency that could be traced back to the colonial period. Furthermore, he contended that 'there is no way that large-scale mining in Ecuador can avoid grossly violating the rights of nature as guaranteed in the country's Constitution.'[26] Ivonne Ramos, president of the environmental group Acción Ecológica, argued that the constitution's failure to protect the rights of local communities meant that the country had not broken from a reliance on the exploitation of natural resources to provide its primary source of income, with all of the resulting liabilities and complications that this position implied.[27] Given the dirty legacy of petroleum extraction in the Amazon, environmentalists readily recognized that those who bore the brunt of ecological impacts of extractive enterprises rarely realized its economic benefits.

While rural communities criticized Correa for pursuing policies that flowed against their interests, some of the strongest denunciations of the president's policies came from former allies. Economist Pablo Dávalos, who worked with Correa in the Ministry of Finance under the previous Alfredo Palacio government, complained that 'the new political system is more vertical, more hierarchical, and more dependent on the president than before.' Dávalos argued that Correa's 'government is far from a leftist government and corresponds more closely to the interests of powerful groups that are emerging with the new mining and agro-fuels sectors.'[28] The economist Alberto Acosta, former minister of mines and president of the 2008 constituent assembly and originally one of Correa's closest allies, also broke with the president in part over a contention that extractive enterprises were not consistent with the new constitution's emphasis on the *sumak kawsay*, a Quechua concept that privileged human needs over those of capital. Many critics did not call for an end to mineral extraction, but they were opposed to new large-scale mining plans that continued pre-existing extractivist paradigms. 'We are obligated to optimize the extraction of petroleum without causing environmental and social damage,' Acosta argued. Ecuador needed to realize the highest possible social benefit from each barrel of oil extracted, instead of focusing only on maximizing production. 'We have to learn,' he continued, 'exporting natural resources has not led to development.' Rather, 'the principal factor in production and development is the human being.' Ecuador had to change, Acosta insisted, 'that vision that condemns our countries to be producers and exporters of raw materials' which historically had underdeveloped economies in the developing world.[29] Embracing the *sumak kawsay* necessitated a move beyond rhetoric and vague platitudes to a pursuit of alternative development models. Underlying these conflicts were different concepts of the state, and in particular the role of social participation in decisions over public policy.

In response to grassroots pressure, Correa attempted to negotiate an end to oil exploration in the biologically sensitive and diverse Yasuní National Park in exchange for international debt relief and development aid. Yasuní was home to the Huaorani, who had gained little from the petroleum economy. In November 2007, a simmering dispute at Yasuní boiled to the surface. In the town of Dayuma, local inhabitants protesting against oil exploitation seized control of several oil wells. They demanded support for economic development and environmental protections for Indigenous communities. Correa responded with a heavy hand, deploying the military to stop the dissidents and accusing the protestors of being unpatriotic saboteurs. The government arrested forty-five people and charged them with terrorism for attempting to disrupt petroleum extraction.[30] Correa appeared determined to destroy any independent social movement organizing that could potentially raise opposition to his government.

In the midst of these conflicts, the president complained about 'infantile environmentalists' creating obstacles to economic development. He dismissed groups that opposed him as part of an 'infantile left' comprised of 'fundamentalists' who had joined forces with political conservatives in an attempt to undermine his government. 'We are not allied with the right,' Humberto Cholango, president of the militant Indigenous organization Ecuarunari, retorted. Instead, Indigenous activists challenged Correa from the left and pressed him to make a clean break with Ecuador's neoliberal past. Cholango pledged to keep fighting until the neoliberal model was destroyed. 'We will not allow this process of change to be truncated, stopped, or remain half completed,' Cholango declared.[31]

Correa's critiques of environmentalists and Indigenous movements were not that different from those of right-wing neoliberal governments, including his counterpart Alan García in Peru, who framed opposition to extractive models as an attack on modernity and denounced those who opposed him as lazy and irrational people who were controlled by outside interests. Furthermore, his repressive responses to resistance also seemed little different from those of previous governments, and for Indigenous and environmental activists committed to sustainable development Correa's actions ultimately revealed his true colors. Opponents criticized Correa for betraying 'signs of subscribing to the most radical proposals of colonial territoriality in recent years.'[32] This included his desire to open spaces to mining and increase petroleum extraction. In response, Correa called on his opponents to respect the law. 'No more strikes, no more violence,' he said. 'Everything through dialogue, nothing by force.'[33] He indicated that he would not be swayed by social movement pressure.[34] The president contended that the pro-testors did not have any significant support, and that their leaders lacked genuine representation. 'Three or four people are enough to make a lot of noise,' he claimed, 'but, quite sincerely, they don't have the popular backing.' Rather, he claimed that he enjoyed broad public support for his extractive policies, and that this translated into electoral endorsement of his government.[35] Nevertheless, Correa's efforts to restrict the actions of social movements led to charges that he was attempting to criminalize political protest. More than any other issue, the conflicts over mining illustrated the wide, growing, and seemingly insurmountable gap between Correa and social movements.

Social movement challenges to Correa's government also surfaced in protests against alleged water privatization plans. Opponents com-plained that a proposed water bill would allow transnational mining corporations, bottling firms, and large landholders engaged in the export of agricultural commodities such as cut flowers and bananas to appropriate water reserves in violation of the 2008 constitution. The water bill was part of what activists interpreted as broader gov-ernmental moves to privatize the country's natural resources, with a particular emphasis on oil extraction and large-scale mining projects. The cut-flower and mining industries in particular required access to large amounts of water that came at a cost to local communities. Correa retorted that charges of water privatization were based on lies, and that his proposal had no such intent. He continued to insist that the proposed legislation prohibited the privatization of water, but rather was needed to regulate water supplies. Social movements, he contended, were trying to destabilize his government, and they had become 'useful idiots' for the extreme right. He accused intransigent radical groups of playing into the hands of conservative interests, and undermining the positive gains that his citizens' revolution promised the country.[36] The demonstrations grew more intense in September 2009 as the Shuar and Achuar in eastern Ecuador blocked highways with barbed wire. In an echo of protests in June in the Peruvian Amazon that resulted in dozens of fatalities, the Ecuadorean demonstration also grew deadly with the shooting of Shuar schoolteacher Bosco Wisum while dozens more were injured. The death of Wisum seemed to shock Correa, who called for the violence to stop.[37]

Further alienating environmentalists, in January 2010 Correa back-pedaled on a proposal to halt petroleum exploration in the Yasuní National Park in exchange for international funding for development programs. Experts estimated that the Ishpingo Tiputini Tambococha (ITT) oilfields could generate $7 billion a year. Extracting the crude, however, would threaten the park's biodiversity, release 400 million tons of carbon dioxide into the atmosphere, and place two Indigenous groups in the park, the Tagaeri and Taromenane, in danger from exposure to the outside world. Several European countries agreed to provide half of the value of the petroleum over a period of ten years to support healthcare, education, and other social programs if the government left the oil in the ground. While environmental groups and Indigenous allies applauded the proposal as a brave and innovative step, foreign governments were not immediately forthcoming with the cash needed to make the program viable. Despite promising talks, the conservative German government of Angela Merkel withdrew from the proposal because of Ecuador's alliances with objectionable governments. Meanwhile, Correa, who had never given the program his unequivocal support, complained that the proposal came at a cost to Ecuador's sovereignty, and he threatened to allow transnational energy companies to commence drilling operations in the park.

Organizing protests against extractive policies led to terrorism charges against about two hundred activists. In the most high-profile case, four Indigenous leaders – CONAIE president Marlon Santi and vice-president Pepe Acacho, Ecuarunari president Delfín Tenesaca, and president Marco Guatemal of the Federación Indígena y Campesina de Imbabura (FICI, Indigenous and Campesino Federation of Imbabura) – faced charges for leading protest marches against water and mining acts at a June 2010 ALBA summit in Ecuador. 'This government has declared war on Indigenous peoples,' Tenesaca proclaimed as he denounced the charges as a mechanism of social control.[38] A profound and growing divide emerged between Correa's authoritarian extractivism and Indigenous concepts of the *sumak kawsay*. From an Indigenous perspective, this conflict concerned not only material factors of agrarian economies and environmental issues, but also ideological threats to Indigenous cosmologies.

The president became, as some observed, a manager of state-run capitalism. 'Correa advocates a statist model of development that allows for no real popular participation,' social critic René Báez notes. 'His actions are a violation of the new constitution. Workers, teachers, indigenous organizations, and ecologists have no say in this government.'[39] Correa's policies and style of government led to a growing distance from social movements. The tensions between Correa and social movements were part of a much larger dance between different paths to power in which strategies and ideologies conflicted as much as they coincided, often with bitter accusations being cast across a widening and seemingly insurmountable divide.

Whither Ecuador?

Although at different points all of Latin America's leftist governments have had complicated relationships with social movements, Correa's has been the most difficult. While in international venues such as the WSF, Correa was eager to embrace the social movement process and the broader left, he was also more removed from that political trajectory than his counterparts. Hugo Chávez, for example, had a long history of organizing for revolutionary change within the Venezuelan military. Luiz Inácio Lula da Silva was a union leader in Brazil before becoming president, and in Bolivia Evo Morales kept his leadership position as head of the coca growers' union even after winning the presidency. Uruguayan president José Mujica was an ex-guerrilla. Paraguay's president Fernando Lugo was a Catholic bishop influenced by liberation theology who had long worked with poor and marginalized communities. In Nicaragua Daniel Ortega led the Sandinistas to power in the 1970s. In comparison, as *The Economist* aptly observed, with a doctorate in economics from the University of Illinois and fluent in French and English, Correa was 'an unlikely revolutionary.'[40] He had only a tenuous connection to powerful and well-organized social movements that repeatedly rocked Ecuador's political landscape, and his combative attitudes toward their leaders strained those relations even further.

Was Correa justifiably included as part of a leftward tilt in Latin America, or was his inclusion in this pantheon just a result of rhetoric or hopeful thinking? Analysts now talk of Latin America's 'many lefts.'[41] As Michael Shifter, the vice-president of the Inter-American Dialogue, notes, Latin America 'is swinging in many different directions at the same time.' Despite Correa's attempts to emulate Chávez's strategies, his policies were not nearly as radical as those of his Venezuelan or Bolivian counterparts. Of the many lefts that gained power in Latin America, Correa represented a moderate and ambiguous position closer to that of Lula in Brazil or the Concertación in Chile rather than Chávez's 'twenty-first-century socialism' or Morales's 'communitarian socialism.' As Shifter notes, Correa's policies 'reflected less the embrace of leftism than a desire for a new kind of politics.'[42] Even the business-friendly *Latin American Weekly Report* questioned how radical his reforms really were. 'More investment in health, education and anti-poverty programs, certainly,' they observe. 'But these could simply be defined as social-democratic policies.' His proposed reform of state structures 'appears to be more about style of government than anything else,' they conclude.[43] It was in this context that a mobilized and engaged social movement remained important as a check on a personalistic and populist government. If Correa followed through on any of the hopeful promises of his government, it would be due to this pressure from below and to the left.

Correa remains the most popular politician in Ecuador in decades, owing in no small part to the positive social programs he enacted. Furthermore, the disparate opposition lacked leaders from either the left or the right who could begin to approach the president's level of popularity. For social movements, Correa potentially remained a strong ally because he struck at the entrenched oligarchy's bases of power, and perhaps he was the best that they could hope for at this juncture in history. As Emir Sader contends, the task is to criticize the government for its mistakes but also support its positive moves and to make a common front against the right.[44] The contradictions and tradeoffs that activists face in Ecuador are part of a broader dilemma that much of the rest of the Latin American left, as well as others around the globe, confront. In the face of a seemingly unresolvable situation, it remained the responsibility of environmentalists, rural communities, social movements, and the left in general to push Correa in a positive direction in order to make more inclusive and participatory forms of government.

7 Brazilian president Luiz Inácio Lula da Silva and presidential candidate Dilma Rousseff attend a campaign rally in São Bernardo do Campo, São Paulo, on the eve of the first round of the 2010 presidential elections (credit: Michael Fox).

7 | Brazil: between challenging hegemony and embracing it

'We – the Workers' Party – know that the world is headed toward socialism,' the Brazilian Partido dos Trabalhadores (PT, Workers' Party) president Luiz Inácio Lula da Silva told a packed crowd at the party's first national convention. 'The big question is: Which socialism?'[1]

'The socialism that we want will be defined by all of the people, as a concrete demand of the grassroots struggles,' Lula continued. 'We want a society in which men are valued and where no one has the right to exploit the work of anyone else. A society in which everyone has equal opportunity to realize their potential and aspirations.'

The year was 1981. Despite the strength of the socialist project in Cuba and the revolutionary victory in Nicaragua, Lula and the PT were not willing to quickly define their socialist vision based on what had been implemented elsewhere. That was the job of 'the people,' they said. Clearly impacted by a decade and a half of repressive military rule, the founders of the new party had, in 1979, written into their founding charter a key point that would define the goals of the fledgling organization for years to come: 'There is no socialism without democracy, nor democracy without socialism.'[2]

It was through elections, and not weapons, that the PT planned to democratize Brazil, take power, and carry out the working-class revolution for socialism so dreamed of during the dark years of the dictatorship. They were fairly successful. In Brazil's first open elections, in 1989, Lula lost the presidential election by less than 6 percent. In local elections, thirty-six PT mayors were elected across the country, and began to implement radical programs, such as participatory budgeting, to involve the local community in public decision-making.

At a time when the formal socialist countries were crumbling across the globe, the PT was growing and consolidating.

'The PT is without question the largest explicitly socialist political party in South America, and its growth, particularly in the almost pre-capitalist countryside, is unprecedented in the region,' wrote Brazilian political scientist Emir Sader and journalist Ken Silverstein in 1991. 'Whatever the difficulty in labeling the party, the PT's coalition of

115

forces represents a Brazilian "New Left," and is certainly the most hopeful model for democratic socialism anywhere in South America.'[3]

The PT remained an inspiration for movements and organizers across the region, as the party continued to grow and gain increasing political power. Lula finally won the presidency on 27 October 2002, with over 60 percent of the vote. His successor and former chief of staff Dilma Rousseff was elected and followed in his footsteps on 1 January 2011.

Despite their radical history, Presidents Lula and Rousseff have not joined Chávez, Morales, and Correa in their calls for twenty-first-century socialism. In fact, in order to win the 2002 presidential elections Lula dropped the red star and the word 'socialist' from campaign materials, and promised investors that he would respect the country's financial contracts and obligations. During his second presidential term, Lula went so far as to tell a group of businessmen that he was too old to be leftist.

Internationally, however, Brazil under Lula and Rousseff has played a key role in supporting the more radical left governments and confronting US hegemony both in the region and abroad.

At the 2005 Fourth Summit of the Americas in Mar de Plata, Argentina, Lula helped to unite the region against the US-backed FTAA. While the fiery rhetoric from Venezuelan president Hugo Chávez caught the headlines, the weight of the Brazilian decision was a deal-breaker. No hemispheric-wide trade group could exist without Brazil – by far the largest country and most important economy in Latin America. Brazil's population of almost two hundred million residents equals nearly half of the entire South American population, and its GDP (the sixth-largest in the world) dwarfs all the rest of South America combined.[4]

The other MERCOSUR countries at the time (Argentina, Uruguay, and Paraguay) stood together beside Venezuela and Brazil in opposition to the US-backed pact. It was a defining moment for the region. Latin America's left-leaning countries were capable of blocking US economic interests that had gone relatively unchecked for decades.

For Brazil, it marked a before and after, breaking with a pro-US foreign policy approach that had stood for more than a century. Since then, Lula and Rousseff have promoted regional integration and challenged US hegemony, sheltering the deposed democratically elected Honduran president Manuel Zelaya in its embassy in Tegucigalpa, brokering a nuclear deal between Turkey and Iran that angered the Obama administration, and calling for the United States to lift its blockade on Cuba. Domestically, however, PT policies have been far from groundbreaking. They have decreased inequality by expanding a series of social welfare programs for the poor. But they have also embraced financial capital, multinational corporations, and a booming agro-industry completely at odds with the PT's former companions, Brazil's MST, the largest social movement in the Americas.

Brazil under the PT hasn't tried to significantly alter the status quo, like Venezuela, Bolivia or Ecuador. The Brazilian governments of Lula and Rousseff haven't spoken openly of socialism, nor have they tried to hold a constitutional assembly to revamp the country's laws from the ground up, but as the leaders of the regional economic powerhouse, they have been willing to stand up for the countries that did. This fact has been essential in the region's ability to organize and unite vis-à-vis the United States.

As Richard Nixon remarked in 1971, 'As Brazil goes, so will go the rest of that Latin American Continent.'[5] Brazil, it seems, was willing to challenge hegemony, while also perhaps embracing it.

Dictatorship

In 1964, the Brazilian military dictatorship rolled in like a bad dream. President João Goulart fled to Uruguay, and with him went the hopes of progressive reforms. The first of seventeen military decrees, or Institutional Acts, were issued. Institutional Act 5, decreed by military president Artur da Costa e Silva on 13 December 1968, suspended habeas corpus and disbanded congress. Inspired by the 1959 Cuban revolution, and insurgent guerrilla movements in Argentina, Colombia, Guatemala, Peru, Uruguay, and Venezuela, Communist Party militants went underground and formed armed movements against the dictatorship, including the National Liberation Alliance and the Popular Revolutionary Vanguard, which would later become the Vanguarda Armada Revolucionária Palmares (VAR-Palmares, Revolutionary Armed Vanguard Palmares).

Dissidents were tracked down, arrested, imprisoned, tortured, disappeared, or worse. According to the 2007 report from the Brazilian government's Special Commission on Murders and Political Disappeared entitled 'The right to memory and the truth,' 475 people were disappeared during the twenty-year-long military dictatorship. Thousands were imprisoned and roughly thirty thousand were tortured. More than 280 different types of torture were inflicted on 'subversives' at 242 clandestine torture centers, by hundreds of individual torturers.[6] Current Brazilian president Dilma Rousseff was at the time a student activist who became active in the VAR-Palmares (among other guerrilla groups). She was captured by the Brazilian military on 16 January 1970, tortured, and imprisoned for two and a half years, for participating with the guerrillas. Within a few years the armed resistance to the Brazilian dictatorship had been largely eliminated.

Meanwhile US–Brazilian relations became tighter than ever, as the United States worked to turn Brazil into a 'success story' in the fight against communism. According to a five-and-a-half-year 5,000-page investigation into the human rights violations of the dictatorship, entitled *Brasil Nunca Mais* (Brazil Never Again), CIA agents, such as US officer Dan Mitrione, actively trained hundreds of Brazilian military and police officers in torture techniques, or what they called the 'Scientific Methods to Extract Confessions and Obtain the Truth.' Several documented accounts reveal that Mitrione tested his techniques on street kids and homeless beggars from the streets of Belo Horizonte.[7] Many of these techniques would be replicated across the region through the US-sponsored Plan Condor, as Brazil's neighbors also fell to military dictatorships.

This was the direction in which the United States hoped the region would turn. Internationally, the military dictatorship broke off relations with Cuba and the Soviet bloc, and steered the country back into the US sphere of influence (Cuban–Brazilian relations were not resumed until 1986).[8] 'Never had there been such ideological convergence with the United States,' wrote the former Brazilian ambassador to the United States (1991–93) Ruben Ricupero, 'not just in the perceived continuity and Cold War dangers, but in the acceptance of North American leadership and the feeling among Brazilian leaders that this was an inseparable and defining element in the *internal* struggle against communist subversion.'[9]

Domestically, encouraged by the United States, Brazil liberalized its economy, pushed to increase exports, and opened up for foreign investment, but the economic model didn't stick. Military president Costa e Silva steered the country back toward the import substitution industrialization model that would last through the rest of the dictatorship. Meanwhile, ideologically, Brazilian military leaders continued their fight against the communist threat that would often place them even farther to the right than US officials.

By the end of the 1970s, however, the house of cards was collapsing, and the military junta was already opening space for reform. Exiled activists began to trickle home in 1979 when the junta passed a law granting amnesty to both subversives and the military. While the dictatorship promoted protectionist policies for Brazilian industry, low wages and the lack of freedoms pushed workers to the edge.[10] In May 1978, the workers in the Saab Scania truck assembly plant rejected the wage rise they were offered and stopped work. The strike spread to workers at Volkswagen, Ford, Mercedes-Benz, Chrysler, and the other major foreign-owned car companies. Within a week and a half, 150,000 workers were on strike. The workers won, but the military junta pushed to outlaw strikes in 'essential categories.'

The ABC metalworkers' union and its young leader Luiz Inácio Lula da Silva called for a general strike. Amid a relentless downpour, on 13 May 1979, Lula made a legendary address to 90,000 workers packed into the Primeiro de Maio stadium in the industrial city of São Bernardo do Campo in São Paulo state. Without a sound system, he spoke from on top of a tiny table, his words passed from mouth to mouth among the crowd. The strike continued and the military police responded with repression. While true labor gains would still take time, by the end of 1979 over three million workers had gone on strike around the country.[11] There was no going back.

The birth of the PT and the MST

In 1980, Lula and his fellow workers founded the PT in neighboring São Paulo.

'The PT proposes to be a true political expression of all of those exploited by the capitalist system,' said the PT manifesto, approved on 10 February 1980 at the founding congress. 'The PT is born out of the decision of the exploited to fight against an economic and political system that cannot resolve their problems, because it only exists to benefit a privileged minority.'[12]

The PT was something new, for both Brazil and Latin America. It was Brazil's first truly labor-based party, and it was being built from the bottom up. It was, additionally, rooted in the newly invigorated labor movement, which stood out – in its autonomy, radicalism, and horizontalism – from the more traditional Brazilian unions, which, beginning with the Vargas government, had been subordinated to the Ministry of Labor. The PT was a political entity that could unite all of the grassroots forces in the country, both urban and rural. After years of the repressive dictatorship, the Brazilian left – including the Brazilian Communist Party and its offshoots with their characteristic central party hierarchy – had been largely decimated. The PT, then, was a new force, and without the rigid ideological constraints of past leftist parties or the socialist countries allied with the Soviet Union. The PT believed in a broad definition of socialism and overall had a deep class analysis, understanding that the social democracy of the bourgeois state and capitalist economy would not resolve the problems of the class-based society.

The PT's major allies in the countryside were the landless farmers, who in the late 1970s began to camp along the Encruzilhada Natalino highway intersection in Brazil's southernmost state of Rio Grande do Sul. The occupation would grow to roughly two thousand residents.[13] With the support of Catholic organizations including the Pastoral Land Commission (CPT), the majority of the farmers withstood several years of government repression and intimidation, until the Brazilian government finally agreed to settle them on their own land.

The occupation and the organizing strategy would give birth to the MST in January 1984. It also consolidated the tactic that would become the MST trademark – sustained occupations on fallow land in order to force the Brazilian government to implement land reform as mandated under Brazilian law.

While the MST worked the countryside, the PT struggled for urban reform in the city.

In 1984, the PT participated in the overwhelming *Diretas Já!* (Direct Elections Now!) campaign, demanding an end to military rule and open elections. True elections would not come for another four years, but things were shifting. On 15 January 1985, the Brazilian legislature elected the first civilian president in two decades, Tancredo Neves (prime minister under Goulart). Vice-President José Sarney would assume Neves's position when he became ill and died within two months of the inauguration.

In the first open presidential elections in 1989, Lula faced a powerful media campaign and lost by only 5.7 percent in the runoff vote against the youthful Fernando Collor de Mello. But on the local level, the PT had made important inroads. In 1988, thirty-six PT mayors were elected across the country (up from only one in 1985), including three in state capitals – São Paulo, Porto Alegre, and Vitória – and six in middle-sized industrial cities in the state of São Paulo.[14] In many instances, the party set about redefining local government and open democratic space to the community.

In perhaps the most emblematic case, the Porto Alegre City Hall under PT mayor Olivio Dutra established the now world-renowned process of participatory budgeting (PB), whereby residents could participate directly in the allocation of a chunk of the city budget. For a population that had struggled for two decades beneath a repressive military dictatorship, the experience was revolutionary. The local PT government was rooted in governing with their ethics, and committed to increasing direct and representative democracy in areas that were outside the sphere of traditional community participation in local government. In Porto Alegre, the community responded with increased yearly participation, and by re-electing the PT government throughout the 1990s. The PB experience was replicated across Brazil.

But with a diverse membership, and the relatively vague ideology rooted in socialism and democracy, the PT found it hard to implement a concrete administrative program across the country.

In the 1992 national elections, the PT increased its number of mayoral victories to fifty-four cities, and four capital cities. In 1996, the PT won 115 municipalities. In 2000, it won the mayor's offices in 187 cities, placing roughly 18 percent of Brazil's citizens under PT governments.[15]

But nationally, especially with laws that barred unions from contributing to electoral campaigns, the PT soon realized that it would not be so easy to take power. Lula lost both his second (in 1994) and his third run at the presidency (in 1998) to Fernando Henrique Cardoso of the conservative Partido da Social Democracia Brasileira (PSDB, Brazilian Social Democracy Party). Already, since 1995, internal party power was dominated by a faction known as the Majority Camp, which prioritized winning elections over grassroots activism. Led by Lula, José Dirceu, and their São Paulo allies, the majority coalition won all but one of the party's national internal elections. Meanwhile, Lula consolidated the lessons learned from previous PT elected offices. He spiced up his image with the help of political consultant Duda Mendonça, and entered into a coalition with several parties, including the center-right Partido do Movimento Democrático Brasileiro (PMDB, Brazilian Democratic Movement Party).

On 27 October 2002, in the runoff presidential election, Lula was finally victorious, winning 61.3 percent of the vote and defeating conservative challenger José Serra (PSDB). It was a watershed moment. In São Paulo, supporters poured into Paulista Avenue, crying and waving banners. True change was just around the corner – they could feel it.

Foreign policy – 'South–South relations'

When Lula left office on 1 January 2011 and passed the presidential sash to his successor, Rousseff, he had an impressive approval rating of over 80 percent. While most Brazilians cared more about his domestic policies, for the international community, foreign relations was the defining issue of his administration, and the most progressive. Never had a Brazilian president captured the world's attention and affection like Lula. Friendly and charismatic, Lula offered his hand to anyone who would take it – including US foes Iran and Venezuela – and forged a new Brazilian foreign policy that broke with nearly a century of USA-pandering and lifted Brazil onto the international stage as never before.

At the heart of the innovative foreign policy shift was Celso Amorim, the long-time diplomat who ran the Brazilian Ministry of Foreign Relations for the entirety of Lula's presidency. Amorim prioritized South–South cooperation, regional integration, and multilateral institutions such as the G20 and the BRIC (Brazil, Russia, India, and China), where Brazil played an increasingly important role. In October 2009, *Foreign Policy* magazine blogger David Rothkopf called Amorim 'the world's best foreign minister' for having 'masterminded a transformation of Brazil's role in the world that is almost unprecedented in modern history.'[16] Rothkopf pointed to a plethora of hot-button issues, which Amorim used to 'transform' Brazil 'into one of the most important players on the world stage,' including his use of biofuels to 'forge new dialogues,' or the central Brazilian role in successfully organizing the G20 developing nations against the USA and the EU during the Cancún trade talks in 2003. In August 2011, after defense minister Nelson Jobim was forced to step down over corruption charges, Amorim took over for Jobim, and quickly stated his intention to withdraw Brazilian troops from Minustah, the UN peacekeeping force in Haiti.[17] Despite his comments, Brazilian soldiers show no sign of leaving Haiti any time soon.

The equally competent Marco Aurélio García acted as special foreign policy advisor to both Lula from 2007 on, and now to Rousseff. He has also been credited, alongside Amorim, with building Brazil's autonomous foreign policy, particularly in support of regional integration, MERCOSUR, and Venezuela. García was a professor of political science and philosophy who was exiled in Chile and France, and returned to found the PT alongside Lula.[18]

The year before Lula was elected president, Aurélio García highlighted his own socialist theories in a seminar entitled 'The struggle for 21st century socialism.' Among the eleven themes he discussed, which he believed were important for the agenda of twenty-first-century socialism – including property, social equality, the workplace, and new paradigms of development – the first and most prominent was 'Internationalism.'

'Socialism of the 21st century cannot renounce the construction of a universal community of people, articulated democratically, peacefully, and equally,' said Aurélio García. 'Internationalism cannot be reduced to multilateral accords between nation-states.'[19]

He spoke in favor of regional organizations and alternatives to the IMF and World Bank, and stressed that these organizations had to overcome asymmetries between nations.

Brazilian foreign policy analysts highlight two important features of Lula's foreign policy that represented a break from the past: 1) Since the beginning of the twentieth century, Brazilians have always believed that their country was 'a sleeping giant,' destined for greatness not because of its characteristics and size, but because of consistent financial, social, or political upheavals, never quite taken seriously on the global scene. Under Lula, Brazil actually began to actively participate internationally, finally realizing some of this potential.[20] 2) Brazil had always acted as the sub-imperialist, sub-hegemon, or sidekick to the United States in the region. As mentioned above, the Lula administration broke this pattern and began to carve out a new independent foreign policy, which stood up to the United States (while still continuing cordial relations) and focused on improving South–South relations.

According to Antonio Patriota – an Amorim protégé who now heads the Ministry of Foreign Relations under Rousseff – current Brazilian foreign policy has three pillars: 1) supporting 'traditional' relations, such as Latin American neighbors or important partners from the developed world; 2) diversifying partnerships, especially among South–South relations; and 3) perfecting multilateralism, and improving global governing institutions to make them 'more inclusive, legitimate, and efficient.'[21] An important example of the latter was the Brazilian push under Lula to reform the United Nations and increase the number of countries on the Security Council.

In only the first year of his term, Lula helped to forge the G20 group of developing nations as a counterbalance to US and European interests, a move that the USA criticized as sabotaging trade talks. Within his first four years, Lula had traveled to Africa five times, visiting seventeen countries and opening twelve new embassies, during which time trade between Brazil and the African continent tripled to nearly $15 billion by 2006. Lula was also instrumental in the first Africa–South America Summit, which took place on 29/30 November 2006 in Nigeria.[22]

By October 2009, Lula had visited forty-five countries in only three years and opened thirty-five embassies (mostly in Africa and the Caribbean) since taking office.[23] Brazil now has diplomatic relations with all 192 UN-recognized member nations.[24]

While in office Lula also increased dialogue with the emerging BRIC powers, which have met yearly since 2009. During the BRIC conference in Brasilia on 15 April 2010, Lula called for the 'democratization of the multilateral process of decision making' in international institutions such as the IMF and the UN.

'Developing countries have the right to be heard. Bridging the gap that separates them from the rich countries is not only a matter of justice: The world's economic, social and political stability depends on this. It is our best contribution to peace,' said Lula.[25]

In May 2010, Lula successfully negotiated the Iran–Turkey–Brazil nuclear deal, despite criticism from US Secretary of State Hillary Clinton that the deal was doomed to fail. Just weeks later, Brazil, which held one of the rotating seats on the UN Security Council, voted against further sanctions against Iran. It was the first time that Brazil had ever voted against a UN resolution backed by a majority of the council members.[26]

But it was in western hemispheric relations that Lula truly carved his mark. He signed bilateral agreements with countries across the region, including oil and small business accords with Cuba.[27] He mediated international conflicts between Venezuela and Colombia and oversaw the inauguration of the EU-inspired UNASUR in Brasilia in 2008.

'With Unasur, which is the political-institutional expression of this new regional concept, we can do far more,' said Lula, flanked by Chávez and Morales at a regional summit in 2008, shortly after inaugurating UNASUR; 'the overwhelming majority of our peoples long for development, security, democracy and social justice.'[28] During the meeting they signed an agreement in which Brazil awarded Bolivia a $230 million credit for the construction of a highway linking the landlocked country with Brazil.

The UNASUR South American Defense Council (SADC) was promoted by Lula's defense minister, Nelson Jobim, and approved later that same year. Brazil participated in the creation of the soon-to-be-operating BANCOSUR, offering $4 billion to get it off the ground and holding a preparatory meeting of regional finance ministers in Rio de Janeiro in October 2007.[29] Between 2002 and 2008, Brazilian trade within MERCOSUR increased 310 percent to $36 billion. Brazil was one of the main proponents of Venezuela's incorporation into the trade bloc.[30]

Current president Dilma Rousseff has continued this policy of strongly supporting steps toward regional integration, including UNASUR, MERCOSUR, and CELAC.

Upon taking office, Lula was quick to stand up to the United States. He dined with both Chávez and Fidel Castro within his first twenty-four hours on the job.[31] On several occasions he called on the United

States to lift its blockade of Cuba, including only days after Barack Obama's presidential victory in 2008. 'We await the end of the blockade on Cuba, because there is no explanation for that blockade,' said Lula on 5 November 2008.[32] Under the Lula administration, Brazil also sheltered deposed Honduran president Zelaya for weeks in its embassy in Tegucigalpa, also to the chagrin of US officials, most prominently Hillary Clinton.

'The international community demands that Mr. Zelaya immediately return to the presidency of his country and must be alert to ensure the inviolability of Brazil's diplomatic mission in the capital of Honduras,' Lula told the UN General Assembly in New York to loud applause shortly after Zelaya's arrival at the Brazilian embassy.[33] Two days later Lula said Zelaya could stay 'as long as necessary.'[34]

And yet while Lula stood beside the region's most radical leaders – Castro, Chávez, Correa, Morales, and Zelaya – and was integral in the processes of regional integration, his foreign policy was pragmatic, not radical. In March 2007, Lula met with then US president George W. Bush twice to consolidate a series of ethanol agreements. The second meeting took place at Camp David, when Lula became the first Latin American leader to be received at the US presidential retreat since 1991. Among the accords was a memo of understanding signed between the Brazil and the Unites States – which together account for 75 percent of world ethanol production – in which the two countries agreed to cooperate on research and development, conduct feasibility studies in other countries, and establish global standards for the production and distribution of biofuels. International investors quickly jumped on board and, within a year, they had funding for eight of the proposed thirty projects, in several Latin American countries.[35]

In April 2010, Brazil signed a bilateral military cooperation agreement with the United States. Although very little has surfaced about these accords they ostensibly dealt with Brazilian access to American military technology and arms. While insiders said the deal was at least partly symbolic, it was the first such agreement between the two countries in more than three decades. The then Brazilian defense minister Nelson Jobim said it was an umbrella accord, signed to enable future defense negotiations.[36] There is little doubt that the agreement was at least partially a result of Brazil's interest in the purchase of thirty-six jet airplanes from US manufacturer Boeing, a contract worth $5 billion.[37] Despite increased commercial ties with its closest neighbors, the United States is still Brazil's second-largest trading partner just after China.[38]

'Brazilian foreign policy wasn't against collaboration with anyone.

The United States was a potential partner, as any other,' explains foreign policy analyst Igor Fuser. 'Lula said, "my friend Bush" when George W. Bush came to Brazil. But he also says, "my friend Chávez." He even said, "my friend Ahmadinejad." Everyone is Lula's "friend." This is partially Lula's personal style, but it also reflects the pragmatism of Brazil's position in the world.'

Lula's foreign policy was without doubt the most progressive aspect of his administration, and the area where the PT governments have most stood up to US hegemony in the region. How was Lula able to do it? How did he break Brazil's historic foreign policy rooted in support of the United States? Ironically, by straddling the line in his domestic policy – the area that most concerned Brazilian citizens – where he promoted policies that supported both the poor and the upper class, without alienating the markets, the businessmen, or the bankers.

Domestic policy – 'cautious, calm ... solid'

Just four months before the 2002 presidential elections, financial markets were jittery at the prospect of a Lula victory. Financier George Soros cautioned that a Lula win would plunge Brazil into economic 'chaos,' and the corporate media warned of rising inflation. Lula responded by publishing a 'Letter to the Brazilian people' in which he promised to respect 'the country's contracts and obligations,' or in other words, continue the neoliberal policies of his conservative predecessor Fernando Henrique Cardoso (1995–2002). It was a huge statement for the leader of the PT, which had once had socialism as the central pillar of its campaign platform.

By then, however, the socialist aspirations of the PT had been largely scrapped, replaced by the realities of winning office and holding it. This was Lula's fourth run at the presidency. It was do or die.

He won, and kept his promise to the markets. To the Finance Ministry, he appointed fiscally conservative Antonio Palocci, who had privatized public services while mayor of Ribeirão Preto. He then tagged Henrique Meirelles, the former president of the International Bank of Boston, to head the Central Bank. The idea was to reassure investors that Lula would push for economic stability, following the model of the anti-inflationary Real Plan, laid out in 1994.[39] Government orthodox policy kept official interest rates high, and inflation was kept relatively under check.

Rather than refuse to pay the Brazilian debt to the IMF, as Lula and the PT had promised for years, Meirelles agreed to pay it off even more quickly. Long-time supporters were dumbstruck.

When Lula spoke to a jubilant crowd of thousands at the 2003 WSF in Porto Alegre, less than a month after taking office, the energy was electric. Just two years later, at the same forum, instead of bathing in euphoria, Lula was heckled. Some center-left supporters were satisfied with the minor gains they had achieved in his first two years as president. But jeers droned through the entirety of Lula's speech, reminding everyone in attendance that he had failed to live up to expectations. In 2004, the fledgling Partido Socialismo e Liberdade (PSOL, Socialism and Freedom Party) was founded after a group of progressive PT congressional representatives were expelled for voting against Lula's social security reform. In mid-2005, the *mensalão*, or 'big monthly payment,' scandal broke. Representatives in the Brazilian Congress had been paid off for several years to support key projects introduced by the Lula administration. Crisis rocked the party just months before Lula's bid for re-election. The PT grouping Socialist Popular Action split from the party, carrying five additional congressional representatives to the PSOL.

These realities, perhaps, weren't wholly unexpected. In order to win the 2002 presidency, Lula had watered down his radical platform, dropping the word 'socialist,' and embraced rival parties, including the center-right Partido Liberal (PL, Liberal Party). He placed PL millionaire businessman José Alencar on the ticket as his vice-president.

While progressives were looking for radical answers, Lula had been clear about his first steps as president: 'Cautious, calm ... solid.' Many supporters were willing to give him time. It made sense. After all, he had to start off cautiously in order to avoid scaring away investment. He had to build a solid economy first, and then he could focus on the issues he had been championing for decades.

Poverty alleviation

Once in power, Lula turned to reformist poverty alleviation programs that wouldn't upset the markets. In 2003, he declared that he would eradicate hunger in Brazil, an issue that personally resonated with the president, who had been born into a poor family, the seventh of eight children, in the impoverished northeast of Brazil. In 2003/04, Lula launched a subsidized residential electricity program, a literacy campaign, and *Fome Zero* (Zero Hunger), a package of social programs including soup kitchens and water cisterns for rural communities, and *Bolsa Família* (Family Stipend), a monthly cash support for low-income families with children in school. By the end of 2006, more than eleven million families (roughly 25 percent of the population) received *Bolsa*

Família benefits.[40] Lula's *Fome Zero* and *Bolsa Família* programs were widely popular among a lower-class electorate that was traditionally used by politicians for their votes and then ignored once in office.

Lula's programs had concrete results. According to government statistics, extreme poverty in Brazil decreased from 12 percent in 2003 to 4.8 percent in 2008. During the Lula presidency over twenty-eight million Brazilians were lifted out of poverty.[41] But systems such as the *Bolsa Família*-style conditional cash transfers (CCTs) are not the radical programs of a revolutionary socialist government.

There are currently CCT programs in thirty countries, including Colombia, Costa Rica, Nigeria, India, Pakistan, Peru, the Philippines, and Panama.[42] These are not revolutionary nations. Nearly half of the programs are at least partially financed by the World Bank, including Brazil's, which received World Bank loans of $572 million (2004) and $200 million (2010).[43] Brazil's *Bolsa Família* program is by far the largest of the world's CCT programs. By 2009, poor families enrolled in the program could receive up to $116 a month.[44] By September 2010, the number of recipients had risen to 12.7 million families, or nearly fifty million people.[45] This has helped lift millions out of poverty, and ensured that millions of lower-class Brazilian children remain in school, an important step for their education and future. However, like welfare programs anywhere, *Bolsa Família* offers little space for participation, empowerment, or community organizing. This is a crucial difference between Lula's poverty alleviation programs and the social programs of the more radical Venezuela, where participation and organization are promoted and encouraged.

In Venezuela, in most cases (as already covered in Chapter 4), in order to receive support from the national government, communities must organize. Communities must form communal councils and communes to provide the space through which to receive funds from the federal government and to decide collectively how to allocate those resources, be it in socio-economic projects or in the repair of local roads or community infrastructure.

In Brazil, the Workers' Party has been at the forefront of the fight to 'democratize democracy' and open the space for community participation through experiences such as PB and popular councils. But although PB was founded by the PT in Porto Alegre in 1989, and has been implemented in well over one hundred municipalities across Brazil, Lula decided not to pursue it on a national level.

Big business – big winners

Nevertheless, with Lula's social programs, inequality in Brazil has declined. The Brazilian Gini coefficient – the international standard for measuring inequality (the lower the number the greater the equality) – reached an all-time low of 0.53 in 2010, down from 0.6 in 2003.[46] The number, however, is still high compared with most of Brazil's neighbors. Venezuela's Gini coefficient in 2009 was down to 0.39, and the United States' in 2008 had risen to 0.46.[47]

In Brazil in the decade from 2000 to 2010, the income of the poorest 20 percent grew more than that of the top 20 percent (6.3 and 1.7 percent respectively).[48] The big winners under Lula, however, were the richest 1 percent of the population, whose income grew more, proportionately, than the improvement of the lower classes. As Brazilian economist Paulo Kliass explained in a 2011 *NACLA Report on the Americas* article, 'This is because during Lula's eight years in office, the transfer of resources from the federal budget to the financial system and the Brazilian elite occurred in the form of interest payments on the debt – about $600 billion worth. That is 10 times the amount of resources allocated to programs aimed at the low-income population.'[49] Windfall profits to the financial sector increased the growing hold of banks and other financial institutions over the economy, while capital became further concentrated in large economic conglomerates.[50]

Nevertheless, Brazil's economic resilience to the 2008 financial crisis was unprecedented. The Lula government responded to the meltdown by breaking the orthodox economic mold. It adopted Keynesian counter-cyclical policies, invested locally, offered tax breaks and fiscal stimulus to key sectors, and raised the minimum wage yet again. After a short economic slump in 2009, the Brazilian economy was booming again by the following year with 7.5 percent economic growth. Brazil quickly became increasingly enticing for international financial players looking to invest. Just a month and a half after General Motors (GM) filed for bankruptcy on 2 June 2009, and was bailed out by the US government, subsidiary GM Brasil announced its largest investment in Brazil in the company's eighty-four-year history in the country – totaling over $1 billion.[51] Despite investments like this, Brazil's manufacturing sector dropped from over 19 percent of Brazilian GDP in 2004 to 15.8 percent in 2010. Manufacturing (including airplanes; automobiles; machines and equipment; electronics; and paper, plastic, rubber, and textile) products fell to 39 percent of total exports in 2010 from 55 percent in 2005.[52]

Paradoxically, Brazil's agribusiness explosion – both a pillar of the country's financial program and the issue that has caused the greatest backlash from agrarian movements – also played an essential role in the recovery. Much of Brazilian growth comes from the production and export of primary products, including agricultural commodities and extractive goods. These products represent over half of all exports, including iron ore (14.3 percent), oil (8 percent), soybeans (5.5 percent), sugar (4.6 percent), chicken (2.9 percent), and coffee (2.6 percent).[53] Despite the lack of growth over the last three years, the Brazilian agro-industry was responsible for 22.4 percent of Brazilian GDP in 2010, and the Ministry of Agriculture says this could increase to 25 percent in 2011. According to the National Agricultural Confederation, a third of all jobs are in the Brazilian agro-industry.[54]

Brazil is the world's third-largest agricultural exporter behind the United States and the European Union. It ranks number one in world production and exports of coffee and sugar, and number two in soybeans, tobacco, beef, and poultry.[55] Like the overall economy, Brazil's agro-industry did experience a slump in 2009, but it quickly rebounded and is once again registering record figures. During the twelve months from May 2010 through April 2011, Brazilian agro-industry exports grew by over 20 percent and topped $80 billion with soy, beef, ethanol, sugar, and forest products among the largest exported products.[56]

Over the last decade, the Brazilian agro-industry – led by US companies Bunge and Cargill (and with Unilever, Nestlé, and ADM also in the top ten) – has grown exponentially.[57] Even during the difficult year of 2009, the Brazilian agro-industry made over $56 billion. As of 2010, Bunge had 150 factories in sixteen Brazilian states and employed over 17,000 people. The Minnesota-based Cargill, the largest agribusiness corporation in the world, had over $8 billion in sales in Brazil in 2009, nearly 70 percent of which were in exports.

According to the Food and Agricultural Policy Research Institute, by the end of this decade Brazil is expected to produce half of the world's coarse grains, one third of the world's soybeans, and a quarter of the world's sugar. Half of the world's fowl and beef will come from Brazil, and the country is expected to double its production of ethanol.[58]

For obvious reasons, both the Lula and Rousseff governments have banked on the agro-industry, and have been vocal supporters of the ever-growing agribusiness sector. In 2007, Lula praised the sugar mill owners as the 'true heroes' of the country, despite running an industry known for its poor working conditions, low wages, and a record of workplace accidents. Ironically, Rousseff has praised both agribusiness and family agriculture as essential components of her new government.[59] Only a few months later, however, she supported changes to the Brazilian Forest Code that could open up the Amazon to greater deforestation and the concentration of land into fewer and bigger hands. Rousseff's support for Big Ag and her refusal to open the door to greater environmental protection in the Amazon while serving as Lula's chief-of-staff appear to be a major impetus for Marina Silva's decision to step down as environmental minister in May 2008.[60]

For Brazil's MST, the increasing Brazilian government support for the powerful agribusiness is disturbing. They are now fighting 'not just against the landowner, but a multinational corporation, which means that there is no space for land distribution and agrarian reform,' explained MST leader Marina dos Santos at the movement's twenty-fifth anniversary in January 2009. During the meeting, movement leaders ratified that they were now primarily fighting against the multinational agro-industry.[61]

'We spent many years struggling against the large landowners alone, because we believed – and we believe – that the *latifundio* is the principal cause of the poverty and inequality in the countryside,' said MST leader João Pedro Stédile during the meeting. 'But over the last few years, capitalism has transformed itself and dramatically altered the model of agricultural production in the world, and in our country. Now, because of this new dominance of financial capital, large multinational corporations indirectly control the land, the production, the seeds, and the agricultural riches.'

According to the MST, the Lula government gave ten times more subsidies to multinational agribusiness than to family farming. According to the latest Brazilian census, land was concentrated in fewer hands in 2006 than in 1920.[62] Meanwhile, the MST says that agrarian reform actually decreased under Lula.

The actual numbers are complicated. According to Dataluta, a scientific pro-agrarian reform project at the State University of São Paulo, the Lula government created 2,517 new agrarian reform settlements and settled 416,015 families between 2003 and 2009, while Cardoso created 3,924 settlements and settled 393,842 families. This would mean that Cardoso created more settlements and Lula settled more families. However, the Lula administration claims to have settled 164,000 families more than these figures.[63] Lula's overblown figure is largely due to the fact that his administration included families officially 'regularized' – in which an already settled family acquired the title to their land – as newly settled families.

Even the fact that Lula had to compete with Cardoso over who

131

settled more families is disturbing considering the PT and MST's long collaboration, and the fact that land reform was a historic and central component of the PT platform.

Few MST members expect a spike in agrarian reform under the Rousseff administration, but they continue to struggle, not just for their own piece of land but for the 'other world' they believe is possible.

Social movements – socialism and decline

According to MST figures, by 2009 the movement had forced the expropriation of 35 million acres of land; 370,000 families had acquired their own land in MST settlements, and 100,000 families were in encampments waiting for land. The movement had built hundreds of public schools, taught tens of thousands of its members to read and write, and formed 400 associations and cooperatives to collectively produce their food. But as local MST member in Brazil's southernmost state, Rio Grande do Sul, João Amaral said in July 2008, it is the democracy of the movement which has held the movement together.

'Everything is discussed. There is no voting. Discussions tend to be by consensus. Perhaps that is one of the secrets of the unity of the MST. That's why we have not been divided over every issue where you have to make a decision,' said Amaral.

Since its foundation, the MST has organized around three fundamental objectives: struggling for land, land reform, and for a more just and fraternal society.[64] While MST members aren't necessarily vocal over their socialist aspirations, many are conscious that this is the goal of their daily actions.

'Our struggle for agrarian reform now needs to project socialist values, including our way of organizing – practicing how socialism is going to be,' said Ana Hanauer, an MST leader who grew up on an MST settlement in southern Brazil, in 2009.

Democracy and participation are central to the organization, and the MST ideal of socialism. When families first join the MST, they often must live for several years on encampments in makeshift homes of scrap wood and black plastic tarps before they acquire land from the Brazilian state. Families in these encampments are organized into base nuclei of twenty to thirty families each. Everyone participates in their nuclei, where the decisions of the occupation are made. The coordinators of the encampment are made up of the spokespeople of each base nucleus. Individuals participate in different collective chores, be they planting, food preparation, cooking, water collection, childcare, or the security of the encampment.

'This way of doing things influences people's relationships, and it helps you to get over some of the values of individualism, and the collective values become more important. Solidarity, sharing ... there's no way that you don't change,' says Hanauer.

The MST isn't the only Brazilian group still talking about socialism. In April 2011, members of the PSOL held the first national meeting of PSOL Ecosocialists in Curitiba, where they discussed how to transform the PSOL into an eco-socialist party.[65]

'What is at stake for humanity is the challenge of building a new society that can be, at one and the same time, politically democratic, socially just and egalitarian, culturally and ethnically diverse and environmentally sustainable,' read the closing paragraph of their charter, which outlined the principles and campaigns they planned to promote within the PSOL and throughout Brazil.[66]

According to Joel Kovel, a social scientist who co-authored, with anthropologist Michael Löwy, the 'Ecosocialist Manifesto,' Brazil has been a hotbed for eco-socialism organizing for many years, even if organizers didn't call it that.

In his essay 'What is eco-socialism?' Löwy pointed to the struggle of Brazilian environmental union leader Chico Mendes and his Coalition of the People of the Forest as a 'particularly exemplary movement, for both its social and ecological reach.'[67] In the 1980s, Mendes was able to organize small farmers, agricultural workers, union members, rubber tappers, and indigenous tribes against the large landowners who were cutting down the Amazon forest to make way for pasture. Mendes was killed by hired hit-men in December 1988, but for Löwy, because of 'the articulation between Socialism and Ecology, campesino and indigenous struggles, survival of the local populations and life preserver of a global challenge (the protection of the last great tropical forest), this movement could become a paradigm of future popular mobilizations in the "South."'

Interestingly, while the PT governments may have shied away from using the word 'socialism' and attempting to implement it on a national level, the third PT Congress in September 2007 placed 'PT Socialism' as one of its central themes. The congress approved a resolution reaffirming this and other important concepts from the party's long history. In late 2010, the PT launched a nationwide political education campaign to reach 100,000 PT members. Among the materials were a series of popular education books about the PT, the first of which dealt extensively with the PT struggle for socialism, in which it reprinted (among other things) the opening text of the PT's first party platform:

'The Brazil that we want is a free, just, and sovereign country. A nation founded on solidarity and social equality, and where individual and collective rights are the center of the political agenda.'[68]

For many, this is exactly what the PT governments have been able to provide.

'It's a different context now with the PT in government. We went from a period of resistance to a period of achievement,' said Anderson Campos, youth advisor to the Executive Council of the Central Única dos Trabalhadores (CUT, Unified Workers' Central), a close PT ally. 'We no longer had to fight against the privatization of the public sector. Instead, we fought for a minimum wage increase. Now that employment has risen, our demand for 2011 is work with dignity. So the agenda is much more favorable today than ten years ago.'

According to Campos, Brazil's labor movement was 'far more victorious' under the Lula government than in the 1990s, winning increased salaries and workers' rights.[69]

But after a decade of national PT governments, many social movements are experiencing an unprecedented decline. In southern Brazil, for instance, fewer people are joining these MST occupations, which the movement has traditionally relied on for new recruits and to push the Brazilian government for land reform. The drop in participation is at least partially a result of Lula's poverty alleviation programs, which appear to have satisfied some of Brazil's lower class enough that they don't feel the urge to struggle for their own piece of land.

The PT government has also been a drain on the movement as many leaders have been tagged to fill some of the nearly 23,000 positions for appointees in the Lula and now Dilma governments.[70] The same has occurred across Brazil's social movements and even in the traditional grassroots groups, *núcleos de base*, of the PT.

'In the sense of grassroots organization, [the PT presidential victory] was a defeat,' said Brasilia-based MST leader José Batista de Oliveira in an interview in late 2010. 'It weakened the social struggle, and it didn't truly alter the institutionalism of inequalities, agrarian and urban reform.'

The MST has continued to launch countless occupations of *latifundios*, government buildings, and agro-business property, but large-scale mobilizations involving thousands had, until late 2011, been largely absent against the PT governments.[71] Meanwhile, despite its original platform that committed it to promoting 'economic and social development in a democratic way while respecting the environment,' the PT governments have continued to base their development on extractive and exploitative industries.

Neo-extractivism and renewable energy

In October 2011, at a Brazil–EU summit in Brussels, Rousseff re-affirmed that Brazil's natural resources were 'essential' for the develop-ment of the country's industry and modern agriculture.[72] As with even its more radical neighbors, resource extraction has continued as the root of Brazil's development model under the PT, and it is growing.

In October 2006, Brazil discovered the massive Tupi oilfield, other-wise known as *Pre-Sal*, deep-water oil reserves off the coast of Rio de Janeiro, which could contain more oil than Mexico, Canada, and the United States combined. Production on the oilfield began in April 2009 and the Brazilian semi-state oil company Petrobras plans to be extracting 500,000 barrels of oil daily from Tupi by 2020. Petrobras is already the largest company in Latin America, with a daily oil produc-tion of roughly two million barrels. Brazil is now dreaming of one day joining OPEC.

The Brazilian company Fibria, formed in September 2009 with the merger between Aracruz and Votorantim Celulose e Papel, is now the largest paper pulp company in the world.[73] The former state mining company Vale is the second-largest mining company in the world, and the largest producer of iron ore and pellets, and the second largest of nickel. The company also operates nine hydroelectric plants.

Hydroelectricity has been an important source of energy for Brazil, which likes to promote its sustainable image. The country obtains 45.9 percent of its energy from renewable resources, largely from hydro-electric dams and biofuels.[74] This percentage is impressive considering the global average of 12.9 percent.[75] However, even these renewable energies have had negative effects on the environment and society.

Brazil plans to build over thirty hydroelectric dams in the Amazon by 2020, potentially flooding conservation zones and removing in-digenous peoples.[76] In 2011, the Brazilian government's push to build the massive Belo Monte dam captured international headlines. When completed in 2015, Belo Monte – located in the Amazon on the Xingu river – would be the world's third-largest hydroelectric dam. In June 2011, the Brazilian government gave the green light to go ahead with the licensing.[77] The approval sparked an enormous uproar from Brazil-ian citizens, who denounced the potential environmental and human rights violations for the 22,000 or so indigenous peoples that will have to be removed for the dam's construction. Petitions from the Brazilian chapter of the global rights organization Avaaz.org and the Gota d'Auga Movement, started by celebrities who oppose the dam, each received over a million signatures.[78]

Brazil is also the world's second-largest producer of ethanol, after the United States, and the largest exporter of ethanol. In 2008, Brazilian sugar cane plantations (from which Brazilian ethanol is made) grew by 14 percent, to more than seventeen million acres in production. The 2010/11 sugar cane harvest produced 27.6 billion liters of ethanol, up 7 percent from the previous year.[79] Nearly half of all Brazilian cars run off ethanol, leading Brazil to be considered as having the world's first 'sustainable' biofuels economy. Nevertheless, while ethanol may be cheaper at the pump, and less polluting than petroleum, critics say the use of farmland for fuel rather than food is dangerous given the potential for a global food crisis. The mono-crop sugar plantations are also pesticide and labor intensive, and characterized by low wages and human rights violations. In 2008, Brazil surpassed the United States to become the largest consumer of pesticides (agro-toxins) on the planet. In 2010, over a billion liters of pesticides were used on Brazilian crops.[80]

Trade policy – neo-developmentalism and contradictions

When Lula came to power in 2003, both the economy and trade had been slowly liberalized under the neoliberal push of the 1990s. The Brazilian government had sold off $110 billion worth of assets, including over half of its most important state businesses, and trade had been disassociated from foreign policy, with a push for free trade agreements, eliminating tariffs and opening access.[81]

Lula, however, steered Brazil back in the direction of a 'national-developmentalist' agenda. He regrouped trade policy as a strategic branch of Brazilian foreign policy, which he wielded in his leadership role in the creation of the G20 in World Trade Organization agricultural negotiations, as the 'underdeveloped' countries largely united to protect their domestic industries against 'dumping' from highly subsidized Northern markets.[82]

He promoted regional and bilateral trade agreements with a developmentalist approach, acknowledging the asymmetries between neighboring countries. Brazil supported the creation of MERCOSUR's Structural Convergence Fund, which has distributed over $1 billion, largely to the bloc's junior members, Paraguay and Uruguay, in a push to gradually eliminate asymmetries between them and Argentina and Brazil.[83]

'The only country in the region that has the technological and financial ability to take on such resource extraction and industrialization projects is Brazil,' wrote Uruguayan journalist Raúl Zibechi in May

2012, 'through Vale (second-largest mining company in the world), Petrobras (fourth-largest oil company), Braskem (fifth-largest petrochemical), and its large construction firms such as Odebrecht, OAS, Andrade Gutierrez, Camargo Correa and Queiroz Galvão. And count on the Banco Nacional de Desenvolvimento Econômico e Social (BNDES, Brazilian Development Bank) – the world's largest development bank – to finance any project.'[84]

With development policies, there is frequently conflict between the national or international agenda and the interests of the local community. And there have been inevitable contradictions in regional integration even among the 'leftist' governments. Since 2007, both Ecuador and Bolivia have expelled major Brazilian construction firms over faulty work or their failures to fulfill a scheduled timeline.[85]

The Initiative for the Integration of the Regional Infrastructure of South America (IIRSA) was launched in 2000 in Brasilia among the South American countries, with the goal of building a network of regional infrastructure in transportation, energy, and communications.[86] According to the non-governmental organization International Rivers, which monitors development plans, '335 projects have been identified as part of IIRSA, with an overall budget of $37.4 billion.'[87] Among the projects are roads, waterways, ports, and energy and communications interconnections, and the initiative has come under frequent attack for developing projects, such as the great southern gas pipelines, without the input of local communities.

With the economic brute force of Latin America's largest economy behind them, Brazilian businesses have long looked to operate in the new markets of the region's weaker economic neighbors. This reality is probably the largest point of contention for true mutually beneficial regional integration. Brazilian agribusiness behemoths have gobbled up land in eastern Paraguay, on which they have transformed once native jungles into mono-crop deserts of soy. Local communities have been bought out, chased off, or forced off their land by the company thugs or toxic plumes of pesticides that cover their homes and their subsistence farms. By 2005, more than 40 percent of the largest businesses in Latin America were Brazilian. In comparison, fewer than 35 percent were Mexican, 10 percent Colombian, and roughly 6 percent were Argentine.[88]

These types of asymmetries have caused animosity among Brazil's less powerful neighbors. Like multinational corporations anywhere, Brazilian businesses have sought manifest-destiny-style expansion in South America. Brazil's strength is a double-edged sword: it is both a powerful economic force for potential change – a voice of support for the region's leftward government – and also weighted down by its own financial power and regional aspirations; its corporations replicating the same colonialist dreams of profit the PT administrations professed to want to do away with.

Beyond Lula

Before taking office, Rousseff and her team had been clear that they would follow the foreign policy path of her predecessor. She picked Amorim protégé and career diplomat Antônio Patriota to head the Foreign Affairs Ministry, and asked Marco Aurélio García to continue as foreign policy advisor under her.

In an interview in November 2010, García said that there would be no change in foreign policy under the new government, that the president-elect wouldn't shy away from intervening on the international scene as Lula had, and that 'MERCOSUR and South America will continue to be among the top priorities.'

With Patriota, a foreign ambassador to the United States, US–Brazilian relations are expected to continue on a par. In March 2011, Rousseff met with President Barack Obama in Rio de Janeiro during his brief Latin American tour. The visit, however, was overshadowed by Obama's authorization of the Libya bombing. Other than an expression of US interest in purchasing Brazilian oil, no concrete agreements were made.

However, some shifts in Rousseff's foreign policy have been clear. She has distanced herself from some of Lula's more controversial positions, such as his close ties to both former Libyan president Muammar Gaddafi and Iranian president Mahmoud Ahmadinejad. She has been more vocal over human rights, and in March 2010 she supported the UN vote to monitor human rights in Iran, a reversal of Lula's policy of frequently abstaining or voting against sanctions enforced by the UN Security Council.[89]

Brazil has been pushing for a permanent seat on the Security Council, and analysts read Rousseff's reversal as political maneuvering to acquire support for the request.

Rousseff is also coming into her own. In September 2011, she became the first woman to open the debate at the UN General Assembly. She discussed the European debt crisis, conflict in the Arab world, combating global warming, and building gender equality. She also broke from the US line and vocally supported Palestine's request for statehood.

'Recognizing the legitimate right of the Palestinian people to sovereignty and self-determination increases the possibilities of [reaching] a lasting peace in the Middle East. Israel's legitimate concerns for peace with its neighbors, security on its borders, and regional political stability can only be achieved by creating a free and sovereign Palestine,' said Rousseff.[90]

But her government, like Lula's in 2005, has been rocked by a corruption scandal under which several of her top cabinet members have resigned, including chief-of-staff Antonio Palocci and defense minister Nelson Jobim. Thousands of Brazilians have protested in support of Dilma's campaign to clean up her administration.

Challenging hegemony and embracing it

While the Lula and Rousseff administrations have not championed the cause of twenty-first-century socialism like Venezuela or Bolivia, their role in regional affairs has been crucial. Considering the size and economic strength of the country, a conservative Brazilian government would have been a disaster for Latin America's left turn over the last decade and the development of twenty-first-century socialism. With the support of Brazil, several regional initiatives were launched and expanded, including the BANCOSUR, the SADC, UNASUR, and countless bilateral agreements.

Brazil, under both Lula and Rousseff, has stood up to US doctrine and policies both regionally and internationally.

The Lula government, with Celso Amorim at the helm of the Ministry of Foreign Affairs, broke a Brazilian foreign policy paradigm that with few exceptions had guided Brazil for the last century. At the same time, it led Brazil onto the international stage as almost never before, causing many to wonder whether perhaps finally the 'sleeping giant' of Brazilian potential had truly awoken. Rousseff has carried this torch, breaking new ground, and defining her own powerfully gendered foreign policy. In August 2011, Forbes ranked her third among the world's 100 most powerful women.[91]

How was the PT able to so dramatically shift Brazilian foreign policy? Charisma, domestic policy, powerful support? The answer is a combination of everything. After years of struggle as a union leader, Lula had the political clout for popular support in Brazil, and his welfare poverty alleviation programs helped to raise millions out of poverty. At the same time he was careful not to rock the financial boat once in office. He paid off the Brazilian debt to the IMF, and proved that he would support large capital and agro-industry. The richest Brazilians made more than ever before. Lula was able to be more flexible with his foreign relations, because he proved that he was willing to toe the line.

Dilma is now following in his footsteps: outspoken, and also playing it safe.[92]

For progressive Brazilians, the governments have been disappointing domestically – the revolutionary changes long defined in the party's original platform ignored or forgotten. But for the Latin America left, Brazil under the PT has played a pivotal role in standing up to US hegemony, integrating the region, and supporting the more radical governments in their push for 'twenty-first-century socialism.'

8 Santiago de Cuba, 2010 (credit: Lewis Watts).

8 | Cuba: 'updating' twentieth-century socialism?

Cuba is undergoing a major transformation. The Sixth Communist Party Congress of April 2011 proclaimed that Cuba is 'updating the economic model.' This simple phrase does not begin to capture what is going on. The Congress issued 313 *lineamientos* – guidelines or recommendations – to move the country forward. Among these guidelines are a potpourri of measures, calling for an array of changes and adaptations. There are also statements that appear to sustain the old order. A committee of ninety-eight people has been set up to go over the *lineamientos* and issue policy recommendations.

'The call to update the economic model opens up a new scenario for ... the Cuban economy,' writes Julio Díaz Vázquez, a professor at the Center for Investigations of the International Economy at the University of Havana, and a strident critic of the old state-dominated economic order. 'Its concrete implementation will dramatically alter the national economic reality, fomenting strategic changes in the social order ... and in the sociopolitical renewal of the country.'[1]

This opening in Cuba began with the ascent of Raúl Castro, well before the 2011 party congress. Raúl became acting president in mid-2006 when his brother Fidel Castro fell ill. In February 2008 he was elected president by the National Assembly, Cuba's legislative body. While Fidel is charismatic and perhaps the greatest revolutionary strategist of the late twentieth century, Raúl has paid closer attention to organization, administration, and the rejuvenation of an economy that is largely moribund. Already in mid-2007, as acting president, Raúl announced 'the need to make structural and conceptual transformations' in Cuban socialism. Stymied by three devastating hurricanes that struck Cuba in the latter half of 2008, he assured the National Assembly at the end of that year that 'none of the issues I have referred to recently have been shelved ... Partial measures have been implemented as permitted by the circumstances, and progress will be made, without any hurry or excessive idealism.'[2] Raúl made a series of important changes from 2007 to 2009 to streamline and decentralize the activities of the government, reducing the number of ministries, and introducing the Comptroller

General's office with powers to audit and oversee all governmental and economic activities, an autonomous body often found in capitalist states like those of Chile and Spain.

Perhaps the most important early initiative of Raúl Castro was the call for a *consulta* (consultation) with the Cuban people. Barrio committees, factory workers, local party organizations, and others were encouraged to meet and register their thoughts and complaints. By August 2009, 5.1 million people out of a total Cuban population of 11.2 million had participated in the consultation. There were 3.3 million registered comments of which almost half were critical.[3] The most recurring criticism was of limited food production and the daily problems people faced in securing three meals a day for their families. Comments on corruption in government enterprises were also prevalent.

Patricia Grogg, a long-time resident of Havana of Chilean descent who works for the Inter Press Service, a news agency based in Havana, noted that in her barrio 'the spontaneity and wide ranging comments were striking.' Some criticized deteriorating medical and educational facilities. One woman asserted that Cubans abroad should be able to invest in community projects. 'People felt free to speak their minds without any fear of retribution,' said Grogg. Raúl Castro himself embraced the results of the *consulta*, saying it was an important 'rehearsal' for shaping the proceedings of the Sixth Party Congress.[4]

A number of important changes have already been introduced. People are being given title to the homes they reside in, which can be exchanged and sold on the market. Apartheid tourism has been ended, meaning that Cubans can go to hotels, restaurants, clubs, and beaches that were once designated only for foreign tourists. One hundred and eighty-one occupations, such as those of food vendors, hair stylists, taxi drivers, tour guides, and shoe repairmen, can now be licensed as *trabajo por cuenta propia* – self-employment or independent work. Anyone can solicit the government for 10 hectares of idle land that can be held and farmed in usufruct for ten years with the opportunity for renewal. Agricultural produce of just about every kind is now sold in open markets in urban and rural areas alike.

The big question is: what do these changes mean for socialism? What type of socialism is being constructed in Cuba and how does it compare with other countries? Cubans draw a distinction between socialism *in* the twenty-first century and socialism *of* the twenty-first century (*socialismo* en *el siglo 21* and *socialismo* del *siglo 21*). This difference in wording reflects the fact that the socialism being constructed in the rest of Latin America is unique to the new millennium, whereas in Cuba it has a much longer trajectory. Aurelio Alonso, sub-director of the magazine *Casa de las Américas*, points out that the *'punta de partida'* (point of departure) is different for Cuba and the rest of Latin America, both in terms of time and politics.

'The Cuban process today is an attempt to advance the socialism that triumphed in the twentieth century while in Latin America at large the left is in a protracted struggle with the oligarchy to construct a new socialism of the twenty-first century,' says Alonso.[5] Socialism has very different protagonists and antagonists in each region. For Cuba the opposition is not the oligarchy but the bureaucracy and elements within the Communist Party that want to hold on to the old twentieth-century order with a centralized economy and an authoritarian state.

Cuba is also different from the Latin American continent in that its historic trajectory is related to the other surviving socialisms of the twentieth century, particularly those of China and Vietnam. All three countries in their earlier stages adopted the Soviet model in one form or another with the centralization of their economies and state ownership of the means of production. The market played only a marginal role as the state set prices and issued five-year plans to determine production goals.

The two Asian countries moved much earlier than Cuba to market economies; China beginning in 1978 under Deng Xiaoping with its 'modernization' policies, and Vietnam in 1986 with its 'renovation' program that it adopted in the face of widespread food shortages and famine. Both were largely rural societies at the time, and many of the early reforms were directed at the countryside and quickly succeeded in increasing agricultural production. The Cubans believe that the Chinese encouragement of rural manufacturing via township and village enterprises is a particularly relevant innovation, especially in the processing of foodstuffs and materials needed for housing construction. In Cuba under the new economic policy, municipal enterprises and cooperatives are being encouraged to set up food processing centers and to produce inputs, implements and supplies needed for farming.

China, Vietnam, and now Cuba share the belief that the market should not be identified exclusively with capitalism. The market functioned in feudal societies and it can help distribute resources in an efficient manner in a socialist economy. But free rein cannot be given to individuals to dominate and manipulate the market. The marketplace itself needs to be regulated.

The Cuban leadership does not express an official viewpoint on the large-scale accumulation of private capital and the emergence of a new bourgeoisie in China that have been a result of the market economy. But informally Cuban academics and even some party leaders acknowledge that extremes of wealth and poverty are growing in China and that the new bourgeoisie has a presence within the Chinese Communist Party. It is at this point that Cubans assert that their reform process will be different from both the Chinese and Vietnamese experiences, because they are 'Asiatic societies,' whereas Cuba is firmly rooted in the 'Western tradition.' There are critical differences in culture and history, perspectives on leadership, and the role of the peasantry and the workers. Differences in geography and the size of the populations also weigh heavily in determining what types of economic and political institutions evolve under market socialism in each country.[6]

In Cuba there is a determination to prevent the rise of a new bourgeoisie. The uncontrolled accumulation of capital would enable the Cuban exile community in Miami to move back into the country to invest and even take over key sectors of the economy, particularly tourism and finance. More importantly, the leadership is committed to 'updating the model' as opposed to 'changing the model,' meaning that the fundamental socialist goals of equality and economic justice as well as free education and access to healthcare will be maintained. The slogan 'socialismo o muerte' is seen on billboards around the country.

'This is a revolution of the humble and for the humble,' said Raúl on 1 January 2009, in his speech on the fiftieth anniversary of the revolution. The leadership 'will never rob or betray this trust.'

At the same time, the Cuban leadership is determined that the updating of the model will not be allowed to spin out of control. Cubans draw on the Soviet experience as an example of how not to proceed. Fidel and Raúl believe that glasnost under Mikhail Gorbachev in the 1980s led to the demise of the Communist Party as the glue holding the country together. At the same time perestroika and economic reform failed to advance. Gorbachev soon lost control of the entire process, leading to the collapse of the Soviet Union in 1991.[7]

Almost from the start of his government, Raúl Castro has recognized that a transformation of the agricultural economy is the key to the survival and future of the Cuban revolution. In recent years, Cuba, a country rich in agricultural resources, has imported up to 70 percent of its food needs. In 2005 it even imported sugar, the export commodity that the island is identified with historically.[8] Accordingly, Castro has issued an urgent call for increased agricultural production and announced the distribution in usufruct of idle fields and forests so that 'the lands and resources are in the hands of those who are capable of efficient production.' He added that those who till the land 'should receive the material remuneration they deserve,' which will come from setting fair prices and allowing a portion of their production to be sold in the open market.[9]

Under a law passed in July 2008, over 1.2 million hectares were distributed to more than 132,000 beneficiaries by mid-2011. There has even been a notable movement of people leaving the cities to take up farming. But the gains in production have been limited. Agricultural produce for the domestic market remained largely the same in 2010 and 2011. Armando Nova, an agricultural economist at the Center for the Study of the Cuban Economy, said in April in Havana, 'the agricultural system remains in crisis.'

'We need an agrarian revolution to drive the country forward and it is still blocked. The middle-level bureaucracy and even sectors of the party, particularly at the provincial level, are determined to prevent market innovations for fear of losing their status and privileges,' declared Nova.[10]

The lack of adequate inputs ranging from fertilizers and seeds to well pumps and farm implements is a critical bottleneck. State enterprises provide most of these inputs only sluggishly, and it has been difficult to set up private or cooperative enterprises to take over as intermediate suppliers. There are also complaints about pricing and marketing. Seventy percent of the produce is sold to the government at prices it sets and the rest is sold in the open market.

The sugar industry, which does not lend itself to small-scale production, is 'obsolete,' according to Nova. Sugar is a potential source of major export revenue (especially with the growing use of sugar cane to produce biofuels), but there have been no major investments in the sugar industry since the Soviet era. As it lacks capital for renovation, Nova believes joint ventures with foreign capital are necessary. The Brazilians have recently undertaken such a project to modernize one of Cuba's major sugar mills. To remove the industry from the realm of politics, the Ministry of Sugar was recently abolished and turned into an autonomous state enterprise. Another issue is how the sugar mills and plantations should be run and managed. In the 1990s most of the the industry was shifted from state enterprises to cooperatives with very limited operational autonomy. Control and management by the workers in these cooperatives has never been very effective.

To deal with the redundant labor force, and the low productivity of the economy, Raúl announced in 2011 that half a million workers would be laid off. Trade unions and local party organizations immediately reacted, protesting that the independent or self-employed occupations could not begin to absorb the 500,000 laid-off workers. The government retreated. It did not want to 'shock' the economy and cause widespread unemployment and discontent as had happened in other Latin American countries with the application of the neoliberal policies advocated by the IMF.

However, the existence of an inefficient workforce presents a conundrum for the country. The social, health, and educational programs, the core achievements of the revolution, are being undermined by the fact that they account for 65 percent of the country's economic activities. Basic services (utilities, transportation, etc.) take up another 15 percent, leaving the productive economy with only about 20 percent.[11] In addition, Vázquez estimates that Cuba has a million professionals owing to its free universal educational system. But many of them cannot find appropriate employment and good salaries. The social programs enjoyed by Cubans are not sustainable unless this skilled workforce is utilized to increase productivity and export competitiveness. The imbalance between social progress and low productivity has to be corrected if Cuba is to flourish as a socialist society in the twenty-first century.

There are a host of other difficulties involved in the process of updating the economic model. At present, cooperatives exist exclusively in the area of agriculture. There are incipient plans to extend them into the urban areas to factories and a host of other enterprises. But there is a question over the balance that should be struck between cooperatives and *trabajo por cuenta propia*. This is an intense debate within the party. Some argue that the productive forces can be unleashed only by allowing individual initiative to predominate. Cooperatives and worker-managed enterprises are difficult to run and, owing to its contemporary history of state dominance, Cuba lacks a 'culture of cooperatives.' But as Camila Piñeiro Harnecker, who works at the Center for the Study of the Cuban Economy, points out in her influential article published in the Cuban magazine *Temas*: 'Only by democratizing or socializing the economy ... can we advance toward a society that has as its horizon human development and not simply the redistribution of income.' She adds that if this direction is not taken, 'we run the risk ... that the logic of profit will be converted ... into the "rational" abandonment of the socialist horizon.'[12]

There are endless concrete examples of the difficulties of initiating even small- and medium-sized enterprises that avoid exploitation. For example, a barber shop usually employs one or two people and should be *trabajo por cuenta propia*, but it could be different with a hair stylist or beauty salon which could have a dozen employees doing various tasks. Should they be organized cooperatively, or should there be a single boss who would hire and fire workers at will and set salaries at a level so that she or he would earn a profit? Each approach has very different implications for how the new society evolves. The dilemma is that while it is so much easier to set up private enterprises, the socialization of society is advanced with cooperatives in which profits are shared and decisions are made collectively. In twenty-four hours someone can get a license to work independently, whereas the process of forming a cooperative is more complicated and could take a month or longer.

The transformations in the Cuban economy come at a precipitous moment in world affairs. Just over a decade ago Cuba found itself largely isolated in the international arena, still in difficult straits from the economic after-effects of the collapse of the Soviet bloc and the continuing US economic blockade. The rise of the new left governments in Latin America starting with the election of Chávez in Venezuela in 1998 and Lula in Brazil in 2002 altered this situation dramatically. By the Sixth Summit of the Americas held in April 2012 in Cartagena, Colombia, the tables had turned against the United States. The entire panoply of Latin American and Caribbean nations demanded that Cuba be included in any future summit. Barack Obama said at the event: 'I'm not somebody who brings to the table here a lot of baggage from the past.' But in fact the United States, and not the Latin American nations, remains in a Cold War time warp, by refusing to end the embargo against Cuba.

Just as importantly, trade relations have now shifted and the United States also finds itself isolated. Over 50 percent of Cuba's trade is with five emerging markets: Venezuela, China, Brazil, Mexico, and Russia. The relationship with Venezuela is unique, as is Cuba's partnership with ALBA.

China has become Cuba's major merchandise trading partner. It ships durable and consumer goods to Cuba while Cuba exports nickel, sugar, and iron. The trade surplus rests with China, and the Chinese complain that the Cubans frequently fail to meet export commitments. Chinese investments are also critical in the Cienfuegos petroleum refinery and in offshore exploration of deep-sea oil reserves. Brazil under Lula significantly expanded economic relations with Cuba. Of particular importance is Brazilian involvement in the $957 million project to expand and modernize the port of Mariel. It will be a major transit point for Latin American and European trade, serving also as a terminal for deep-water petroleum and as a trade zone for light manufacturing.[13]

While the debate within the government and the Cuban Communist Party over the direction of the economy is comprehensive, the leadership has made it clear that Cuba will remain a one-party state. However, important changes are taking place within the political and state apparatus. With the demise of Fidel and the limits of Raúl, who is now in his eighties, the 'historic leadership' of the revolution is drawing to a close. A new generation is coming to the fore and it will need to act more collectively than Fidel and Raúl, who both synthesized the debates and controversies, acting as the final arbitrators. There will never again be such an entrenched leadership. Legislation is being advanced in the National Assembly that will limit all upper-level government positions to two five-year terms. The National Assembly itself will also become more important as a center of debate and discussion over policies, while the election of delegates to the Assembly will be more competitive than in the past.[14]

The leadership justifies the adherence to the one-party state as a defensive strategy against US intervention. Throughout Latin America, the United States has repeatedly intervened in electoral politics to back parties and movements that it is aligned with. Since its founding in 1983, NED has been a prominent force throughout the continent, funding opposition movements against left governments in the region. In 1988–90 in Chile it was instrumental in bringing to power the Concertación, a coalition of political parties that excluded the Communist Party of Chile and the Movimiento de Izquierda Revolucionaria (MIR, Left Revolutionary Movement). In 1990 in Nicaragua, NED played a decisive role in funding the opposition that defeated incumbent Sandinista president Daniel Ortega.

Cuba has drawn the appropriate lesson from these blatant political interventions, realizing that if opposition political parties were permitted, the US government and the Cuban exile community would rush in to back the opposition. But the one-party state is shifting, reflecting the changes that have occurred in Cuban society as it becomes more diversified. As Harlan Abrahams and Arturo Lopez-Levy note in their book *Raúl Castro and the New Cuba*, 'there is an emerging convergence of people who live within the system – workers, artists, intellectuals, and students – advocating for reform.'[15] A widespread debate is taking place within the party over the direction of the economy and the society.

'Although there are no formal currents or camps in the party, there are a lot of opinions; some can be characterized as liberalizing, others as Marxists, some as social democratic, and still others as pro-Chinese,' says Juan Valdes Paz.[16]

'There are more polemics and discussions than ever before,' explains Alonso. 'No one is oppressed. There is an openness to hear criticisms. The discussion is broader than even during the period of revolutionary fervor in the 1960s, when the slogan was everything within the revolution, nothing outside of it.'[17]

Cuba at present is a society in motion. Although the economic model has not been consolidated and growth is limited, it is difficult not to notice a certain vibrancy in the society at large. The opening of opportunities for individual work and the end of apartheid tourism have meant that more income is circulating at the grassroots. The United States and the exile community are dead wrong if they think that regime change will take place at any time in the near future. Socialism in Cuba is very much alive and well. It will be its own unique model, different from the socialist countries of the twentieth century, Vietnam and China, and from the countries in South America that have taken up the banner of twentieth-first-century socialism.

9 Seven hundred women from Vía Campesina and Brazil's Landless Workers' Movement (MST) march against a 44,000-acre eucalyptus plantation in Rio Grande do Sul, Brazil, in early 2009. Through hundreds of land occupations over the last twenty-seven years, 370,000 MST families have acquired their own land by forcing the Brazilian government to carry out land reform (credit: Jefferson Pinheiro/ COLETIVO CATARSE).

Conclusion: socialism and the long Latin American spring

This is a period of turbulence and transitions. It is not an age of armed revolution as was the century past. Twenty-first-century socialism in Latin America is part of a complex process of change sweeping the region. As our profiles of Bolivia, Ecuador, and Venezuela reveal, the banner of socialism is unfurling at a very distinct pace in each country. The quest for socialism is most advanced in Venezuela, both politically and economically, while in Ecuador the concept of socialism is only infrequently raised in public discourse, owing in part to the wide breach between the social movements and Rafael Correa's self-proclaimed citizens' revolution. Bolivia occupies a middle ground in which innovative discussions are taking place within and between the government and social movements that relate socialism to the indigenous concept of *buen vivir*.

At the moment, no singular project, socialist or otherwise, is capturing the imagination of the peoples of Latin America as occurred in the 1960s and 1970s with the Cuban revolution and the Chilean democratic experiment with socialism under Salvador Allende. Nevertheless, today different explorations, or counter-hegemonic processes, are at work throughout the hemisphere. As Arturo Escobar – a Colombian-American anthropologist known for his contribution to post-development theory – writes in 'Latin America at a crossroads':

Some argue that these processes might lead to a re-invention of socialism; for others, what is at stake is the dismantling of the neo-liberal policies of the past three decades – the end of the 'the long neo-liberal night,' as the period is known in progressive circles in the region – or the formation of a South American (and anti-American) bloc. Others point at the potential for un nuevo comienzo (a new beginning) which might bring about a reinvention of democracy and development or, more radically still, the end of the predominance of liberal society of the past 200 years founded on private property and representative democracy. Socialismo del siglo XXI, pluri-nationality, interculturality, direct and substantive democracy, revolución ciudadana, endogenous development centered on the buen vivir of the people, territorial and cultural autonomy, and decolonial projects towards post-liberal societies are some of the concepts that seek to name the ongoing transformations.[1]

This is an exciting and innovative period that has been ongoing for more than a decade, a 'Latin American spring,' rich in social advances and political openings. The unrest and turbulence in Latin America are decentralized, a multiplicity of struggles on many different fronts. No singular ideology is driving this change in Latin America.

The central characteristic of the three countries that have raised the banner of socialism is that they are committed to democratic procedures. As the Appendix reveals, during the fourteen years of Chávez, starting with his first presidential election, there were sixteen elections or referendums, while during the seven years of Morales there were seven, and during Correa's six years there were seven.

Some journalists on the right, such as Juan Forero of *The Washington Post*, are arguing that this use of democracy is merely a façade for moving to authoritarianism. In an article entitled 'Latin America's new authoritarians,' Forero asserts 'charismatic populists are posing the most serious challenge to democratic institutions in Latin America since the 1980s, when rebel wars and dictators were the norm.'[2] These popular democracies are eroding 'the checks and balances' and 'closing media outlets,' he adds. In reality what is upsetting Forero and others is that the old systems of privileged rule are being overturned, in particular by democratically elected constituent assemblies, while the right-wing press, which has called for coups and has spread lies, is prevented from engaging in such egregious behavior. Moreover, Forero says not a word about the coups in Honduras and Paraguay that have overthrown two popularly elected presidents. These are the true authoritarians who hark back to the dictatorships of the past.

The commitment to democratic procedures means that twenty-first-century socialism in Latin America is tied to the electoral cycle. A likelihood exists that in Venezuela, Bolivia or Ecuador, the incumbent presidents or their designated successors will eventually be voted out of office. This will mark a new unpredictable phase in the struggle for socialism. Will the new non-socialist leaders seek to overturn the deep reforms of their more radical predecessors? Or will they have to accept many of the changes, particularly the economic reforms that have benefited the popular classes? Will new openly socialist candidates win back the presidential office in future elections? Here the words of Bolivian vice-president Álvaro García Linera ring true: the transition to socialism 'will not be easy, it could take decades, even centuries.'[3]

A key question facing the popular forces is what type of democracy should be constructed. At present the economic and political systems where the new left has come to power can be described as liberal in the classical sense. Broadly speaking, this liberal paradigm emerged with the philosophies of John Locke and Thomas Hobbes. It consolidated in the eighteenth century with the American, French, and industrial revolutions, based on the concepts of private property, representative democracy, individual rights, and the market as the organizing principle of the economy and social life.[4] With the rise of capital, dominant economic interests have manipulated the state, resulting in controlled democracies where citizens are allowed to vote every few years for candidates that generally do not question the capitalist order or respond to the interests of the people. Today in Latin America there is growing disillusionment with this liberal form of government and representative democracy.

In the region, individuals, movements, and governments are now visualizing a democracy that is participatory, starting at the local level. Communal self-rule is assuming ever greater importance in Latin America, beginning with the Zapatistas in Mexico and extending through Venezuela with its communal councils, to Bolivia with the indigenous communities, and elsewhere across the region. In Venezuela, Bolivia, and Ecuador, constituent assemblies have drafted new constitutions that allow for greater popular participation and full citizenship for all the ethnic groups that have been excluded and exploited since colonial times.

The constitutions of Bolivia and Ecuador call for people to live in harmony with 'Pachamama,' Mother Earth, and for *buen vivir*, or good living – a holistic cosmovision of the world where people strive for harmony. It is more than a hollow dream; it influences contemporary policies in opposition to capitalist development. For example, food sovereignty as it is conceived of in the Andean countries is adapted to *buen vivir*. It breaks with the traditional concept of development, asserting that food production should not be driven simply by the marketplace, especially the international market. Food sovereignty means that people have access to nutritious and sanitary foods that are produced at the community level by local producers in accordance with local needs and cultures, be they Andean or non-Andean. As Francisco Hidalgo Flor, an Ecuadorean sociologist, asserts in his October 2011 article 'Land: food sovereignty and *Buen Vivir*,' 'the state has the responsibility to stimulate production ... to provide support to small and medium scale producers,' ensuring that they have adequate technical assistance and credit.[5] Land should be controlled or owned by those who work it. The promotion of cooperatives and a solidarity economy are part of the effort to construct a participatory society, be it in Brazil with the MST or in Bolivia with the indigenous communities.

The Achilles heel of these counter-hegemonic processes is the difficulty of conceiving and implementing a new economic model. As we saw earlier, all of the countries with new left governments are grappling with the dilemma of what to do with their extractivist exports: petroleum in Venezuela, natural gas and minerals in Bolivia, petroleum in Ecuador. The list even includes South America's largest economy, Brazil, which earns over half of its export revenue from minerals and commodities such as coffee and soybeans.

The Uruguayan sociologist Raúl Zibechi argues that the region's dependence on extractive exports means that countries like Bolivia and Ecuador are mired in a second phase of neoliberalism and have not escaped from dependent capitalist development.[6] But this is an ahistoric argument. The economies of Latin America have always been driven by extractive exports. To expect this to change in a decade or so is entirely unrealistic. What we are witnessing in the short term is the determination of these countries to capture a much larger portion of the rents that come from exports and to use this revenue to expand social programs and to encourage endogenous development.

In the arena of international trade and financing, some of the new left countries of Latin America are also trying to break with the existent terms of trade and the old patterns of dependency. The most notable example in trade is ALBA, which encourages barter and reciprocal trade agreements among its member states as well as the creation of petroleum and processing agreements on concessionary terms.

Although these state-level economic initiatives are limited in scope, a transformative and radical dialogue is taking place at the grassroots. There, civil society and local movements are questioning the process of development itself because it harms the environment and is intricately linked to capitalism. Social movements and many of the new left governments have increasingly clashed over development projects. In Bolivia the dispute over a road that would link previously fragmented parts of the country, but which would run through TIPNIS, raised fundamental questions about issues of development, indigenous autonomy, and the rights of Mother Earth.

In Ecuador the social movements are denouncing President Rafael

Correa for moving to exploit the country's petroleum and mineral resources at the expense of local communities. CONAIE, the major indigenous organization in Ecuador, is openly challenging Correa's developmentalist policies in mining, water rights, and the exploitation of oil reserves in one of the most biodiverse areas in the world.

Bolivian vice-president García Linera puts a positive spin on these developments, asserting that these conflicts are inherent in a transformative process. The popular forces will have different factions that try to push their particular interests and visions of where they want the society to go. The vice-president calls these 'creative tensions' and even argues that they are essential for social and political progress to take place.[7]

There are a different set of challenges for the advance of socialism in Cuba. Because its roots are in twentieth-century socialism, Cuba is a one-party state with a command economy. At present the country is trying to transition to market socialism and is more open to discussion and criticism than at any other moment in the revolution's history. The outcome of this process, however, is unpredictable. Will Cuba end up like China with an emergent bourgeoisie and an authoritarian state, or will it go in the opposite direction, uplifting the economic well-being of the majority of the population while allowing for greater popular participation in the governing structures? The world will be watching. The eventual outcome of the Cuban process will affect the evolution of socialism in the rest of Latin America.

The struggle in Latin America is Gramscian, 'a prolonged battle for hegemony, or war of position,' argues Brazilian political scientist Emir Sader in his 2011 book *The New Mole*. He does not believe that by aligning with the center-left governments the left is subordinated to the bourgeoisie, as was the case with the earlier reformist governments of the twentieth century. Instead, Sader notes that the left today is consciously 'seeking to create an anti-liberal and anti-capitalist alternative.' He believes that Venezuela, Bolivia, and Ecuador have converged on this strategy.[8]

'Their aim is to overcome neoliberalism and develop processes of regional integration that strengthen the resistance to imperial hegemony, so as to develop post-neoliberal models,' writes Sader. Neoliberalism is still a very potent force, and the left needs to unite with the new left governments, whether reformist or radical, to decisively defeat their reactionary and right-wing adversaries. If the left and the social movements engage in internecine battles with the new left governments, the right will take advantage of the situation.

This is indeed a turbulent process of transition. The challenge for the left and the social movements is to find the proper balance between prodding the new left governments to advance toward post-neoliberal and socialist societies without creating divisions that allow the right to strengthen.

'Latin America is living through a crisis of hegemony of enormous proportions,' writes Sader. 'The old is struggling to survive, while the new has difficulty in replacing it.'[9]

Latin America is a cauldron of political and social ferment. Socialism is a central component of the brew that is being stirred up by the social movements and the popular forces. Rather than a lineal historic clash between capitalism and socialism, we are now witnessing a plethora of struggles and confrontations that zigzag across the pages of history: between classic liberalism and post-liberal politics, *extractivismo* and post-development, transnational agribusiness and food sovereignty, patriarchy and feminism, exclusionary educational systems and free democratic centers of learning, nation-states dominated by the descendants of the colonizers and the new pluri-national states.

Instead of a singular socialist horizon, a multiplicity of groups and movements are now imagining new utopias. 'One world with room for many worlds,' proclaim the Zapatistas. In the short term, twenty-first-century socialism could flounder or experience setbacks in any one of the countries in the hemisphere where the socialist banner has been planted – Venezuela, Bolivia, Ecuador, or Cuba. But it will not disappear. The history of socialism in the hemisphere runs too deep, and the need for alternatives to a turbulent global capitalist order is ever increasing.

Appendix: nationwide elections in Venezuela, Bolivia and Ecuador

Venezuela

1 6 December 1998: presidential election in which Chávez wins first term
2 25 April 1999: referendum on whether to convoke a constituent assembly
3 25 July 1999: election of constituent assembly members
4 15 December 1999: referendum on the new constitution
5 30 July 2000: 'mega-elections' of all elected officials, from mayors to president, based on new constitution
6 3 December 2000: election of local representatives (*consejos municipales*)
7 15 August 2004: presidential recall referendum
8 31 October 2004: regional elections (mayors and governors)
9 17 July 2005: municipal elections (city councils)
10 4 December 2005: National Assembly election
11 3 December 2006: presidential election
12 2 December 2007: constitutional reform referendum
13 23 November 2008: regional elections
14 15 February 2009: constitutional amendment referendum (on term limits)
15 26 September 2010: National Assembly election
16 7 October 2012: presidential election
   Total: 16 nationwide votes in 14 years

Bolivia

1 18 December 2005: national elections for president, National Assembly and departmental prefects
2 2 July 2006: elections for constituent assembly and referendum on departmental autonomy
3 10 August 2008: presidential and prefectural recall referendum
4 25 January 2009: referendum on new constitution
5 6 December 2009: elections for president and new Plurinational Legislative Assembly

6   4 April 2010: departmental and municipal elections

7   16 October 2011: judicial elections

Total: 7 nationwide votes in 7 years

Ecuador

1   15 October 2006: first round of presidential elections

2   26 November 2006: runoff elections for president

3   15 April 2007: referendum to convoke constituent assembly

4   30 September 2007: elections for delegates to the constituent assembly

5   28 September 2008: referendum to approve new constitution

6   26 April 2009: presidential elections

7   7 May 2011: referendum on ten key issues covering the judicial system, the media, and gambling

Total: 7 nationwide votes in 6 years

Notes

Introduction

1 'US Watches for LatAm "Geopolitical Turbulence,"' Agence France-Presse, 6 March 2012, www.google.com/hostednews/afp/article/ALeqM 5jdoFrn59zBhrIoipz CpEUAxx I5kQ?docId=CNG.f6e2b cf973ed6c 8290bbd6d1bc39f23a.a91.

2 See Roger Burbach, 'The global revolt of 2011: a turning point in history,' *Global Alternatives*, 21 November 2011, globalalternatives.org/node/118. See also Burbach, 'The global revolt and Latin America,' *NACLA Report on the Americas*, 6 January 2012, nacla.org/news/2012/1/6/global-revolt-and-latin-america.

3 Jordi Zamora, 'China's trade with Latin America raises eyebrows,' Agence France-Presse, 4 September 2011, www.hurriyet dailynews.com/default.aspx?pageid =438&n=china8217s-trade-with-latin-america-raises-eyebrows-2011-09-04.

4 See the Appendix for a list of the elections and referendums in these three countries.

5 Marta Harnecker, 'Cinco reflexiones sobre el socialismo del siglo XXI,' *Rebelión*, 26 March 2012, www.rebelion.org/docs/147047.pdf.

6 Jorge Castañada, *Utopia Unarmed: The Latin American Left after the Cold War* (Alfred A. Knopf, 1993).

7 Emir Sader, *The New Mole: Paths of the Latin American Left* (Verso, 2011).

8 Katu Arkonada and Alejandra Santillana, 'Ecuador y Bolivia: estado, gobierno y campo popular en la transición,' *Rebelión*, 13 September 2009, www.rebelion.org/noticia.php?id=135502.

9 See Jean-Guy Allard and Eva Golinger, *USAID, NED y CIA: la agresión permanente* (MINCI, 2009).

10 Federico Fuentes, 'Paraguay: US makes gains from coup against Lugo,' *Green Left Weekly*, 15 July 2012, www.greenleft.org.au/node/51636.

1 Globalization

1 David Harvey, *The New Imperialism* (Oxford University Press, 2003), p. 56.

2 William I. Robinson, *Latin America and Global Capitalism, A Critical Globalization Perspective* (Johns Hopkins University Press, 2008), p. 15.

3 Ibid., p. 55.

4 Economic Commission for Latin America and the Caribbean, *Foreign Investment in Latin America and the Caribbean 2007* (ECLAC, 2007), p. 27.

5 Ian F. Fergusson, 'The World Trade Organization: background and issues,' Congressional Research Service, 9 May 2007, www.national aglawcenter.org/assets/crs/98-928.pdf.

6 'Encuesta Latinobarómetro 1999–2000,' Latinobarómetro, www.latinobarometro.org/latino/LAT Contenidos.jsp.

7 Economic Commission for Latin America and the Caribbean, *Social Panorama of Latin America, 2000–2001* (ECLAC, 2002), p. 71.

8 Mark Weisbrot and David Rosnick, *Another Lost Decade? Latin America's Growth Failure Continues into the 21st Century* (Center for Economic and Policy Research [CEPR], 2003), p. 5.

9 Max Spoor, 'Policy regimes and performance of the agricultural sector in Latin America and the Caribbean during the last three decades,' *Journal of Agrarian Change*, 2(3) (2002): 398.

10 George Ciccariello-Maher, 'The Fourth World War started in Venezuela,' *Counterpunch*, 3–5 March 2007, www.counterpunch.org/2007/03/03/the-fourth-world-war-started-in-venezuela/.

11 Roger Burbach, Orlando Nunez and Boris Kagarlitsky, *Globalization and Its Discontents: The Rise of Postmodern Socialisms* (Pluto Press, 1997), pp. 30–32.

12 Marta Harnecker, with the collaboration of Federico Fuentes, *Ecuador: Una nueva izquierda en busca de la vida en plenitud* (Abya Yala, 2011), p. 44.

13 Roger Burbach, 'Ecuador: the popular rebellion against the "Partidocracia" and the neoliberal state,' *Global Alternatives*, n.d., globalalternatives.org/rebellion_against_the_partidocracia.

14 Victor Breton and Francisco García (eds), *Estado, Etnicidad y Movimientos Sociales en América Latina: Ecuador en Crisis* (Icaria Editorial, 2003), pp. 194–6.

15 Allen Gerlach, *Indians, Oil and Politics: A Recent History of Ecuador* (Scholarly Resources, 2003), p. 71.

16 Roger Burbach, *Globalization and Postmodern Politics: From Zapatistas to Hightech Robber Barons* (Pluto Press, 1997), pp. 115–28.

17 For a broader discussion of this view, see ibid.

18 James Petras and Henry Veltmeyer, *The New Development Politics: The Age of Empire Building and New Social Movements* (Ashgate Publishing, 2003), pp. 101–4.

19 Francisco Garcia, 'Político, estado y diversidad cultural: a proposito del Movimiento Indígena ecuatoriano,' in Breton and García, *Estado, Etnicidad y Movimientos Sociales en América Latina*, p. 196.

20 Daniel Hellinger, 'Venezuela: movements for rent?', in Gary Prevost, Carlos Oliva Campos and Harry E. Vanden (eds), *Social Movements and Leftist Governments in Latin America: Confrontation or Co-optation?* (Zed Books, 2012), pp. 140–41; Marta Harnecker, *Haciendo camino al andar: experiencias de ocho gobiernos locales de América Latina* (Monte Avila, 2005).

21 Marta Harnecker and Federico Fuentes, *MAS-IPSP de Bolivia: Instrumento político que surge de los movimientos sociales* (Centro Internacional Miranda, 2008), p. 92.

22 Angus Wright, *To Inherit the Earth: The Landless Movement and the Struggle for a New Brazil* (Food First Books, 2003), pp. 75–6.

23 Ibid., p. 75.

24 Peter Rosset, Raj Patel and Michael Courville, with a Foreword by Carmen Diana Deere, *Promised Land, Competing Visions of Agrarian Reform* (Food First Books, 2006), p. 223.

25 See Roger Burbach, *The Pinochet Affair: State Terrorism and Global Justice* (Zed Books, 2003).

26 Michael Hardt and Antonio Negri, *The Multitude: War and Democracy in the Age of Empire* (Penguin Books, 2005), pp. 68–9.

2 The pink tide

1 Rachael Boothroyd, 'CELAC, counter-OAS organization inaugu-

rated in Caracas,' *Venezuela Analysis*, 5 December 2011, venezuelanalysis. com/news/6668.

2 'Era of U.S. hegemony in Latin America is over, says CFR task force,' Council of Foreign Relations website, 14 May 2008, www.cfr.org/ americas/era-us-hegemony-latin-america-over-says-cfr-task-force/ p16245.

3 '¿Que es el ALBA-TCP?', *Portal ALBA-TCP*, 3 December 2009, www. alianzabolivariana.org/modules. php?name=Content&pa=showpage& pid=2080.

4 Fabiana Frayssinet, 'Nueva etapa geopolítica de Mercosur,' Inter Press Service, 31 July 2012, www.ipsnoticias.net/nota. asp?idnews=101305.

5 This is a sentiment Hugo Chávez and Evo Morales have expressed with regard to MERCOSUR. See Jason Tockman, 'Chávez, Morales seek transformation of MERCOSUR trade bloc,' *Venezuela Analysis*, 22 January 2007, venezuelanalysis.com/analysis/2187.

6 See Martin Hart-Landsberg, 'Learning from ALBA and the Bank of the South: challenges and possibilities,' *Monthly Review*, 61(4) (2009): 1–17.

7 Roger Burbach, 'The United States: orchestrating a civic coup in Bolivia,' *Global Alternatives*, 17 November 2008, globalalternatives. org/node/95.

8 William I. Robinson, *Latin America and Global Capitalism, A Critical Globalization Perspective* (Johns Hopkins University Press, 2008), p. 36.

9 For a discussion of the US global decline, see Giovanni Arrighi, 'Hegemony unravelling – 1,' *New Left Review*, 32 (March/April 2005), and Giovanni Arrighi, 'Hegemony

unravelling – 2,' *New Left Review*, 33 (May/June 2005). See also David Harvey, *The New Imperialism* (Oxford University Press, 2003).

10 Arrighi, 'Hegemony unravelling – 1.'

11 Rafael Valdez Mingramm, Ke-Li Wang, Antonio Jiménez and Jesús J. Reyes, 'China–Latin America commodity trade and investment,' *SinoLatin Capital*, November 2010, www.sinolatincapital.com.

12 Sara Miller Lana and Andrew Downie, 'In Brazil Hu Jintao aims for bigger piece of Latin American trade,' *Christian Science Monitor*, 15 April 2010, www.csmonitor.com/ Business/2010/0415/In-Brazil-Hu-Jintao-aims-for-bigger-piece-of-Latin-America-trade.

13 Greg Grandin, 'Muscling Latin America,' *The Nation*, 21 January 2010, www.thenation.com/article/ muscling-latin-america.

14 Examples of this dualism include Jorge Castañeda, 'Latin America's left turn,' *Foreign Affairs*, 85(3) (May/June 2006).

15 See Greg Grandin, 'Why stop at two?', *London Review of Books*, 31(20, 22).

16 André Gorz, *Strategy for Labor* (Beacon Press, 1967), pp. 7–8.

3 Neo-extractivism and socialism

1 Cleto A. Sojo, 'Venezuela's Chávez closes World Social Forum with call to transcend capitalism,' *Venezuela Analysis*, 31 January 2005, venezuelanalysis.com/print/907.

2 'Latin American presidents address the World Social Forum,' *Canadian Centre for Policy Alternatives Monitor*, April 2009, www. asadismi.ws/latinamericanrevolution 1.html.

3 Mario Osava, 'World Social Forum: presidents for feminist

socialism,' Inter Press Service, 30 January 2009, www.globalissues.org/news/2009/01/30/483.

4 'Latin American presidents address the World Social Forum.'

5 Paul Walder, 'Álvaro García Linera, Vicepresidente de Bolivia: "El movimiento social empuja el cambio político,"' *Punto Final*, 14 October 2011, www.puntofinal.cl/744/movimiento_social.php.

6 Eduardo Gudynas, 'The new extractivism of the 21st century: ten urgent theses about extractivism in relation to current South American progressivism,' Americas Program, Center for International Policy (CIP), 21 April 2010, news.infoshop.org/article.php?story=20100421011214362.

7 Walder, 'Álvaro García Linera.'

8 Eduardo Gudynas, 'Las nuevas intersecciones entre pobreza y desarrollo: tensiones y contradicciones de la sociedad civil y los gobiernos progresistas,' *Surmania*, 4 (September 2010), p. 98.

9 See John Holloway, *Change the World Without Taking Power: The Meaning of Revolution Today* (Pluto Press, 2002); *Crack Capitalism* (Pluto Press, 2010), and also John Holloway, 'How far away is Latin America from Nottingham,' *Upside Down World*, 8 November 2010, upsidedownworld.org/main/international-archives-60/2773-how-far-away-is-latin-america-from-vancouver.

10 Ramor Ryan, 'John Holloway, crack capitalism and Latin America,' *Upside Down World*, 8 November 2010, upsidedownworld.org/main/mexico-archives-79/2772-john-holloway-crack-capitalism-and-latin-america.

11 Benjamin Dangl, *Dancing with Dynamite: Social movements and states in Latin America* (AK Press, 2010), p. 5.

12 Roberto Regalado, *Latin America at the Crossroads: Domination, crisis, popular movements and political alternatives* (Ocean Press, 2007), p. 225.

13 Marta Harnecker, 'Latin America & twenty-first century socialism: inventing to avoid mistakes,' *Monthly Review*, 62(3) (2010): 63.

14 Claudio Katz, *Las disyuntivas de la izquierda en América Latina* (Ediciones Luxemburg, 2008), pp. 39–40.

15 Raúl Zibechi, *Dispersing Power: Social Movements as Anti-State Forces* (AK Press, 2010).

4 Venezuela's socialism

1 Michael Lebowitz, *Build It Now: Socialism for the 21st Century* (Monthly Review Press, 2006), p. 109.

2 Ibid.

3 For an overall view of this vision of twenty-first-century socialism, see Michael Lebowitz, *The Socialist Alternative: Real Human Development* (Monthly Review Press, 2010).

4 Fernando Coronil, *The Magical State: Nature, Money and Modernity in Venezuela* (University of Chicago Press, 1997), p. 8; Lebowitz, *Build It Now*, p. 87.

5 Fernando Coronil, 'It's the oil, stupid!!!', *ReVista: Harvard Review of Latin America*, VIII(1) (2008): 20.

6 Jorge Pérez Mancebo, 'Una historia económica de Venezuela: balance de realizaciones y desafíos,' in *I Encontro de Historiadores 200 Anos de Independência: Olhar o Futuro numa Perspectiva Sul-Americana* (Fundação Alexandre de Gusmão, 2008), p. 33.

7 Bernard Mommer, 'Petróleo subversivo,' in Luis E. Lander (ed.), *Poder y Petróleo en Venezuela* (Publicaciones PDVSA, 2003), p. 28.

8 Pérez Mancebo, 'Una historia económica de Venezuela,' p. 41.

9 Ibid., p. 42.

10 Margarita López Maya, *Protesta y cultura en Venezuela: los marcos de acción colectiva en 1999* (CLACSO, 2000), pp. 9–10, 19.

11 Iain Bruce, *The Real Venezuela: Making Socialism in the 21st Century* (Pluto Press, 2008), pp. 25–30.

12 Daniel Hellinger, 'Venezuela: movements for rent?', in Gary Prevost, Carlos Oliva Campos and Harry E. Vanden (eds), *Social Movements and Leftist Governments in Latin America: Confrontation or Co-optation?* (Zed Books, 2012), pp. 144, 165.

13 Article 62, Constitución de la República Bolivariana de Venezuela, www.tsj.gov.ve/legislacion/constitucion1999.htm.

14 Lebowitz, *Build It Now*, pp. 94–5.

15 Federico Fuentes, 'VENEZUELA: Uprising defeats US-backed coup,' *Green Left Weekly*, 24 April 2002, www.greenleft.org.au/node/25488.

16 José Honorio Martínez, 'La política petrolera del gobierno Chávez o la redefinición del estado ante la globalización neoliberal,' *Historia Actual Online*, 24 (Winter 2011), p. 12.

17 'Profile: Hugo Chavez,' *BBC News*, 29 February 2012, www.bbc.co.uk/news/mobile/world-latin-america-10086210.

18 Juan Forero, 'Documents show C.I.A. knew of a coup plot in Venezuela,' *New York Times*, 3 December 2004, www.nytimes.com/2004/12/03/international/americas/03venezuela.html?_r=1.

19 Vonk Netherlands and Hands off Venezuela, 'Venezuela and the Netherlands,' *Hands Off Venezuela*, 13 January 2010, www.handsoffvenezuela.org/venezuela_and_netherlands.htm.

20 Dow Jones, 'Venezuela's Chávez: won't accept rulings by ICSID court,' *Wall Street Journal*, 8 January 2012, online.wsj.com/article/BT-CO-20120108-703460.html.

21 Victor Álvarez, *Venezuela: Hacia donde va el modelo productivo? Crítica al modelo rentístico venezolano generador de desempleo, pobreza y exclusión social; razones para transformarlo en un nuevo modelo productivo socialista; políticas y planes del Gobierno bolivariano para impulsar la economía social; y evaluación de los resultados obtenidos entre 1999–2008* (Centro Internacional Miranda, 2010), p. 38.

22 Bruce, *The Real Venezuela*, p. 43.

23 Luis Bilbao, *Venezuela en Revolución: Renacimiento del socialismo* (Capital Intelectual, 2008), p. 111.

24 Ibid., pp. 108–11.

25 Federico Fuentes and Tamara Pearson, 'Venezuela: combating food shortages,' *Green Left Weekly*, 1 February 2008, www.greenleft.org.au/node/38973.

26 Mark Weisbrot, Rebecca Ray and Luis Sandoval, *The Chávez Administration at 10 Years: The Economy and Social Indicators* (Center for Economic and Policy Research, 2009), p. 12.

27 Humberto Márquez, 'Venezuela declares itself illiteracy-free,' Inter Press Service, 28 October 2005, www.ipsnews.net/africa/interna.asp?idnews=30823; Bilbao, *Venezuela en Revolución*, p. 122.

28 MINCI, *Misiones Bolivarianas* (MINCI, 2007), p. 10. The term *adhocracia* (adhocracy) is used in Alberto Muller Rojas, 'Adhocracia vs. burocracia,' *Aporrea*, 29 December

2007, www.aporrea.org/ideologia/a48176.html.

29 Nadeska Silva Querales, 'Organizaciones y redes sociales en las políticas de inclusión social,' in Jorge Giordani, Asdrúbal Baptista, Elías Eljuri, Nadeska Silva, Lourdes Urdaneta de Ferrán, Pedro Sainz and José Félix Rivas Alvarado (eds), *Inclusión Social y Distribución del Ingreso* (BCV, 2006), pp. 293–8; 298.

30 José Luis Hernández, 'Sistematización y análisis de la Misión Zamora,' *INNOVAVEN*, www.innovaven.org/quepasa/agropol1.pdf; Lebowitz, *Build It Now*, p. 98; Dick Parker, 'Chávez y la búsqueda de una seguridad y soberanía alimentarías,' *Revista Venezolana de Economía y Ciencias Sociales*, 14(3) (2008): 133.

31 Bruce, *The Real Venezuela*, p. 90.

32 Camila Piñeiro Harnecker, 'The new cooperative movement in Venezuela's Bolivarian process,' *MRZine*, 12 May 2005, mrzine. monthly review.org/2005/harneckero51205.html.

33 Camila Piñeiro Harnecker, 'Principales desafíos de las cooperativas en Venezuela,' *Capaya: Revista Venezolana de Economía Social*, 8(15) (2008): 38.

34 Ibid., p. 38.

35 Álvarez, *Venezuela: Hacia donde va el modelo productivo?*, p. 258.

36 Dario Azzellini, 'Economía solidaria, formas de propiedad colectiva, nacionalizaciones, empresas socialistas, co- y autogestión en Venezuela,' *ORG y DEMO*, 10(1/2) (2009): 11.

37 Steve Ellner, 'The Venezuelan labor movement under Chávez: autonomous branch of civil society or instrument of political control?', *A Contracorriente*, 2(3) (2005): 120.

38 Haiman El Troudi, *La Política Económica Bolivariana (PEB) y los dilemas de la transición socialista en Venezuela* (Monte Avila, 2010), p. 51.

39 Mark Weisbrot and Rebecca Ray, *Update on the Venezuelan Economy* (Center for Economic and Policy Research, 2010), p. 3.

40 Álvarez, *Venezuela: Hacia donde va el modelo productivo?*, p. 241.

41 Weisbrot and Ray, *Update on the Venezuelan Economy*, p. 3.

42 Antonio J. González Plessmann, 'La desigualdad en la Revolución Bolivariana. Una década de apuesta por la democratización del poder, la riqueza y la valoración del estatus,' *Revista Venezolana de Economía y Ciencias Sociales*, 14(3) (2008): 195.

43 Álvarez, *Venezuela: Hacia donde va el modelo productivo?*, p. 208.

44 Eva Golinger has written extensively on US intervention in Venezuela. Her writings can be found at www.chavezcode.com.

45 Federico Fuentes, 'Venezuela: Reform battle continues as Chavez ally split,' *Green Left Weekly*, 12 November 2007, www.greenleft.org.au/node/38621.

46 Weisbrot and Ray, *Update on the Venezuelan Economy*, p. 4.

47 AFP, Reuters and DPA, 'Chávez anuncia nuevo plan de ayuda a familias venezolanas en pobreza extrema,' *La Jornada*, 13 December 2011, www.jornada.unam.mx/2011/12/13/mundo/027n1mun.

48 'Factbox: Venezuela's state takeovers under Chavez,' Reuters, 26 April 2011, www.reuters.com/article/2011/04/26/us-venezuela-nationalizations-idUSTRE73P7N620110426.

49 Federico Fuentes, 'Venezuela: The struggle for industry to serve people,' *Green Left Weekly*, 29 August

2008, www.greenleft.org.au/node/40184.

50 'Factbox: Venezuela's state takeovers under Chavez.'

51 Dan Molinski, 'Chávez nationalizes auto lubricants company,' *Wall Street Journal*, 11 October 2010, online. wsj.com/article/SB10001424052748703 3585045755448640890103340.html.

52 'Factbox: Venezuela's state takeovers under Chavez.'

53 Federico Fuentes, 'Venezuela's revolution faces crucial battles,' *Green Left Weekly*, 20 February 2010, www.greenleft.org.au/node/43252.

54 Ramon Sahmkow, 'El peso del Estado se hace cada vez mayor en la economía venezolana,' Agence France-Presse, 15 March 2010, economia.noticias24.com/noticia/18349/el-peso-del-estado-se-hace-cada-vez-mayor-en-la-economia-venezolana/.

55 Federico Fuentes, 'VENEZUELA: "When the working class roars, capitalists tremble,"' *Green Left Weekly*, 30 May 2009, www.greenleft.org.au/node/41751.

56 The *Plan Guayana Socialista* can be downloaded at www.revistacritica.com.ar/39_40/03_venezuela_plan.html.

57 Federico Fuentes, 'Venezuela: Workers' control to solve power problems,' *Green Left Weekly*, 17 April 2010, www.greenleft.org.au/node/43647.

58 'Giordani: Boligarquía se ha encargado de amasar fortuna en nombre de la revolución,' *El Nacional*, 13 October 2010, el-nacional.com/www/site/p_contenido.php?q=nodo/159920/Econom%C3%ADa/Giordani:-Boligarqu%C3%ADa-se-ha-encargado-de-amasar-fortuna-en-nombre-de-la-revoluci%C3%B3n.

59 Jesús E. Machado M., 'Partici-pación social y consejos comunales en Venezuela,' *Revista Venezolano de Economía y Ciencias Sociales*, 15(1) (2009): 177.

60 Ley de Consejos Comunales, Art. 2, infocentro.gob.ve/archivos/locc.pdf.

61 Cited in Hellinger, 'Venezuela: movements for rent?', p. 158.

62 Ibid., p. 157.

63 Machado M., 'Participación social y consejos comunales,' pp. 179–84.

64 Juan Reardon, 'Chavez supporters march in Caracas for "radicalization" of the revolution and against "imperialism and bureaucratism,"' *Venezuela Analysis*, 29 November 2010, venezuelanalysis.com/news/5820; Venezuelanalysis.com, 'Venezuelan workers march again to demand socialism at the workplace,' *Venezuela Analysis*, 31 March 2011, venezuelanalysis.com/news/6106.

65 Aporrea.org., 'MARCHA NACIONAL contra el sicariato, la impunidad y la criminalización este MARTES 7 DE JUNIO,' *Aporrea*, 6 June 2011, www.aporrea.org/ddhh/n182352.html.

66 Scarlet Soto, 'Encuentro nacional por el control obrero,' Plan Guayana website, 22 May 2011, www.planguayana.com/pgs_documentos/encuentro_nacional_co.htm.

67 Federico Fuentes, 'Venezuela: Socialist party seeks shake up,' *Green Left Weekly*, 1 May 2011, www.greenleft.org.au/node/47465.

68 Referring to the idea that Venezuela is polarized between the anti-patriotic capitalist opposition 'pole' and those that support the revolutionary 'pole.'

69 VTV, 'Pdte. Chávez con-voca a organizaciones sociales a conformar Gran Polo Patriótico,'

Venezolana de Televisión, 6 October 2011, www.vtv.gov.ve/index.php/nacionales/68813-pdte-chavez-convoca-a-organizaciones-sociales-a-la-conformacion-del-gran-polo-patriotico-.

70 See Ewan Robertson, 'Revolutionary democracy in the economy? Venezuela's worker control movement and the Plan Socialist Guayana,' *Venezuela Analysis*, 3 August 2012, venezuelanalysis.com/analysis/7151.

71 Pepe Mejía, 'Entrevista a Gonzalo Gomez, co-fundador de Aporrea: "Un general golpista venezolano involucrado en un atentado con explosivos contra la embajada de España en Caracas,"' *Kaos en la Red*, 9 January 2012, kaosenlared.net/america-latina/item/3298-un-general-golpista-venezolano-involucrado-en-un-atentado-con-explosivos-contra-la-embajada-de-espa%C3%B1a-en-caracas/3298-un-general-golpista-venezolano-involucrado-en-un-atentado-con-explosivos-contra-la-embajada-de-espa%C3%B1a-en-caracas.html.

5 Bolivia's socialism

1 Hugo Blanco, 'Bolivia-Perú,' *Rebelión*, 4 January 2006, www.rebelion.org/noticia.php?id=25053'f.

2 With regard to the idea of the long and short memory of struggle, see Silvia Rivera, *Oprimidos pero no vencidos: Luchas del campesinado aymara y qhechwa de Bolivia, 1900–1980* (Yachaywasi, 2003) and Pablo Stefanoni and Hervé do Alto, *Evo Morales, de la coca al palacio: una oportunidad para la izquierda indígena* (Imprenta Cervantes, 2007). For background material on these struggles, see Marta Harnecker and Federico Fuentes, *MAS-IPSP de Bolivia: Instrumento político que surge de los movimientos sociales* (Centro Internacional Miranda, 2008), in particular the introduction by Federico Fuentes.

3 Pablo Stefanoni, '¿Pueblo enfermo o raza de bronce? Etnicidad e imaginación nacional en Bolivia (1900–2010),' in Maristella Svampa, Pablo Stefanoni and Bruno Fornillo, *Debatir Bolivia: Perspectivas de un proyecto de descolonialización* (Taurus, 2010), p. 97.

4 Álvaro García Linera, 'El socialismo comunitario, una aporte de Bolivia al mundo,' *Revista de Análisis, Reflexiones sobre la Coyuntura* (February 2010), p. 15.

5 Ibid., p. 17.

6 Luís Alberto Arce Catacora, 'El nuevo modelo económico, social, comunitario y productivo,' *Economía Plural*, Publicación Mensual del Ministerio de Economía y Finanzas Publicas, Year 1, no. 1 (September 2011), p. 3.

7 David M. Robinson, 'Economic roots of Bolivia's social revolution,' *WikiLeaks*, 17 May 2006, wikileaks.vicepresidencia.gob.bo/ECONOMIC-ROOTS-OF-BOLIVIA-S-SOCIAL.

8 Benjamin Kohl and Linda Farthing, *Impasse in Bolivia: Neoliberal Hegemony and Popular Resistance* (Zed Books, 2005), pp. 109, 112.

9 Ibid., pp. 61, 63, 68, 71–2.

10 Ibid., p. 69.

11 Evo Morales, *La revolución democrática y cultural: Diez discursos de Evo Morales* (Editorial Malatesta, 2006), p. 25.

12 Ibid., p. 34.

13 Arce Catacora, 'Introducción,' *Economía Plural*, p. 1.

14 Arce Catacora, 'El nuevo modelo económico, social, comunitario y productivo,' *Economía Plural*, p. 7.

15 Ibid., p. 4.

16 Luis Hernández Navarro, 'El pueblo boliviano vive la mayor revolución social,' *La Jornada*, 7 February 2012, pp. 2–3, translation from johnriddell.wordpress. com/2012/02/19/bolivias-garcia-linera-moving-beyond-capitalism-is-a-universal-task/.

17 Álvaro García Linera, *Las Empresas del Estado: Patrimonio colectivo del pueblo boliviano* (Vicepresidencia del Estado, 2011), pp. 54, 61.

18 Walter Vásquez, 'Un tercio de la subvención se desvió al contrabando,' *La Razón*, 12 January 2012, www.la-razon.com/nacional/tercio-subvencion-desvio-contrabando_0_1539446142.html; Lourdes Chang, 'Bolivia to build third largest gas megaplant in LatAm,' *Prensa Latina*, 26 October 2011, www.plenglish.com/index.php?option=com_content&task=view&id=428825&Itemid=1.

19 Ap-Agencias, 'Sindicatos mineros rechazan nacionalización de Morales,' *Los Tiempos*, 19 April 2011, www.hidrocarburosbolivia.com/bolivia-mainmenu-117/42-nacionalizaci/41856-sindicatos-mineros-rechazan-nacionalizacion-de-morales.html.

20 García Linera, *Las Empresas del Estado*, pp. 17–33, 40–41, 73.

21 Telesur, 'Tras nacionalización de hidrocarburos Bolivia incremento en mas de un 300% su recaudación,' HidrocarburosBolivia.com, 22 January 2012, www.hidrocarburosbolivia.com/bolivia-mainmenu-117/gobierno-relacionamiento-mainmenu-121/49164-tras-nacionalizacion-de-hidrocarburos-bolivia-incremento-en-mas-de-un-300-su-recaudacion.html; Álvaro García Linera, *El 'Oenegismo', Enfermedad Infantil del Derechismo (o como la 'reconducción' del Proceso de Cambio es la restauración neoliberal)* (Vicepresidencia del Estado, 2011), p. 20; García Linera, *Las Empresas del Estado*, p. 38.

22 'Estado generó 485.574 empleos en cinco años,' *Cambio*, 4 July 2011, www.cambio.bo/noticia.php?fecha=2011-07-04&idn=49025.

23 'Pequeñas empresas estatales crecen, se espera que sindicatos las manejan,' *Cambio*, 28 November 2011, www.cambio.bo/noticia.php?fecha=2011-11-28&idn=59332.

24 Juan Carlos Rojas Calizaya, 'Tierra, propiedad y poder,' constituyentesoberana.org/3/docsanal/122011/201211_1.pdf.

25 'La empresa estatal amplió su apoyo productivo de 6 mil a 90 mil hectáreas desde 2007,' *Cambio*, 22 February 2011, www.cambio.bo/noticia.php?fecha=2011-02-22&idn=39409.

26 For figures, see EMAPA, *Informe de Gestion 2010*, www.emapa.gob.bo/files/informe20EMAPA20GESTION2020101.pdf.

27 García Linera, *Las Empresas del Estado*, p. 109.

28 García Linera, *El 'Oenegismo'*, pp. 15, 19.

29 Ibid., pp. 120–21.

30 John Riddell, 'Progress in Bolivia: a reply to Jeff Webber,' *Socialist Project*, www.socialistproject.ca/bullet/499.php.

31 Federico Fuentes, 'Bolivia fights for sovereignty over military,' *Green Left Weekly*, 7 August 2011, www.greenleft.org.au/node/48426.

32 Martin Sivak, 'The Bolivianisation of Washington–La Paz relations: Evo Morales' foreign policy agenda in historical context,' in Adrian J. Pearce (ed.), *Evo Morales and the Movimiento al Socialismo in Bolivia: The First Term in Context, 2006–2010* (Institute for the Studies of the Americas, 2010), p. 162.

33 Ibid., p. 164.

34 These are: Confederación Sindical Única de Trabajadores Campesinos de Bolivia (CSUTCB, Unique Confederation of Rural Laborers of Bolivia), Federación Nacional de Mujeres Campesinas de Bolivia – Bartolina Sisa (FNMCB-BS, National Federation of Peasant Women of Bolivia – Bartolina Sisa), Confederación Sindical de Colonizadores de Bolivia (CSCB, Confederation of Colonizers' Unions of Bolivia), Confederación de Pueblos Indígenas de Bolivia (CIDOB, Confederation of Indigenous Peoples of Bolivia) and Consejo Nacional de Ayllus y Markas del Qullasuyu (CONAMAQ, National Council of Ayllus and Markas of Qullasuyu).

35 Sivak, 'The Bolivianisation of Washington–La Paz relations,' p. 172.

36 'Fundamental principles of the Peoples' Trade Treaty – TCP,' ALBA-TCP website, alba-tcp.org/en/contenido/fundamental-principles-tcp.

37 Redacción Bolpress, 'Sudamérica siglo XXI: trascender UNASUR y crear un "Estado región,"' Bolpress, 27 May 2011, www.bolpress.com/art.php?Cod=2011052702.

38 'President Evo Morales of Bolivia to arrive at Copenhagen Conference,' Climate Justice Now, www.climate-justice-now.org/president-evo-morales-of-bolivia-to-arrive-at-copenhagen-conference/.

39 The Cochabamba Declaration can be viewed at pwccc.wordpress.com/2010/04/24/peoples-agreement/.

40 Sven Harten, The Rise of Evo Morales and the MAS (Zed Books, 2011), pp. 70–77.

41 The declassified US file can be found at www.bigwood.biz/Bolivia_docs/20020730-BO-DoS-USAID-Evo_Morales-MAS.pdf.

42 Eva Golinger, 'Newly declassified documents reveal more than $97 million from USAID to separatist projects in Bolivia,' Bolivia Rising, 22 May 2009, boliviarising.blogspot.com.au/2009/05/newly-declassified-documents-reveal.html.

43 Federico Fuentes, 'Bolivia's struggle for justice, against right-wing offensive,' Green Left Weekly, 10 August 2008, www.greenleft.org.au/node/40074.

44 For a detailed description of the US-backed civic coup and the central role of the DEA, see Roger Burbach, 'The United States: orchestrating a civic coup in Bolivia,' Global Alternatives, 17 November 2008, globalalternatives.org/node/95.

45 'Ex diputado denuncia que golpe de estado contra Evo no fue desmontado,' ABI, 23 September 2008, www.grupoapoyo.org/basn/node/1393.

46 Stefanoni, '¿Pueblo enfermo o raza de bronce?', p. 122.

47 Gonzalo Lema, La Bolivia que se va, la Bolivia que viene: entrevista a líderes políticos nacionales (Los Tiempos, 2011), pp. 93–4.

48 See Federico Fuentes, 'Bolivia: When fantasy trumps reality,' Green Left Weekly, 22 May 2010, www.greenleft.org.au/node/44208; Federico Fuentes, 'Bolivia: Social tensions erupt,' Green Left Weekly, 15 August 2010, www.greenleft.org.au/node/45140; and Federico Fuentes, 'Fuel backdown shows pressures,' Green Left Weekly, 24 January 2011, www.greenleft.org.au/node/46490 for more detail on these struggles.

49 'Fundación Milenio: la conflictividad tiene un cifra record en el gobierno del MAS,' Erbol, 24 February 2012, www.erbol.com.bo/noticia.php?identificador=2147483955061.

50 Alejandro Almaraz, Gustavo

Guzmán, Raúl Prada et al., 'Manifiesto 22 de junio,' *Herramienta*, www.herramienta.com.ar/herramienta-web-9/bolivia-manifiesto-22-de-junio.

51 See Federico Fuentes, 'Bolivia: Amazon protest – development before environment,' *Green Left Weekly*, 8 September 2011, www.greenleft.org.au/node/48774; Federico Fuentes, 'Bolivia: Conflict deepens over disputed highway,' *Green Left Weekly*, 27 September 2011, www.greenleft.org.au/node/48959; and 'Bolivia: Jumble over jungle far from over,' *Green Left Weekly*, 20 November 2011, www.greenleft.org.au/node/49515.

52 Álvaro Garcia Linera, *Las Tensiones Creativas de la Revolución: la quinta fase del Proceso de Cambio* (Vicepresidencia del Estado, 2010).

53 Ibid., p. 24

54 Ibid., p. 38.

55 Ibid., p. 47.

56 Ibid., pp. 47–8.

57 Ibid., p. 63.

58 See, for example, CIDOB-USAID, 'Proyecto de desarrollo de capacidades de liderazgo y fortalecimiento de la capacidad de gestión territorial,' *CIDOB*, 2010, www.cidob-bo.org/index.php?&view=article&id=394.

59 Emir Olivares Alonso, 'La revolución en Bolivia, a caballo de las contradicciones, dice García Linera,' *La Jornada*, 8 February 2012, www.jornada.unam.mx/2012/02/08/politica/020n1pol.

60 Helen Argirakis Jordan, 'La conflictividad como epistemología y pedagogía del poder en Bolivia,' *La Época*, 21 May 2012, www.la-epoca.com.bo/index.php?opt=front&mod=detalle&id=1740.

6 Ecuador's socialism

1 Marc Becker is Professor of Latin American History at Truman State University. His research focuses on constructions of race, class, and gender within popular movements in the South American Andes. His most recent book is *Pachakutik: Indigenous movements and electoral politics in Ecuador.*

2 Carlos de la Torre, 'Corporatism, charisma, and chaos: Ecuador's police rebellion in context,' *NACLA Report on the Americas*, 44(1) (2011): 25–32.

3 Virgilio Hernández E. and Fernando Buendía G., 'Ecuador: avances y desafíos de Alianza PAÍS,' *Nueva Sociedad*, 234 (July/August 2011), p. 136.

4 Carlos de la Torre, *Populist Seduction in Latin America*, 2nd edn, Ohio University research in international studies, Latin America series: Research in international studies, no. 50 (Ohio University Press, 2010).

5 José Zepada, 'Entrevista al presidente de Ecuador, Rafael Correa,' Radio Netherlands Wereldomroep, n.d., sites.rnw.nl/documento/Entrevista%20al%20presidente%20de%20Ecuador.pdf.

6 Rafael Correa, 'Por fin América Latina se atreve a generar pensamiento propio: el socialismo del siglo XXI,' in Rafael Correa (ed.), *Ecuador y América Latina: El Socialismo del Siglo XXI* (APDH, 2007).

7 'Correa reigns over institutional chaos,' *Latin American Weekly Report*, WR-07-16 (26 April 2007), p. 4.

8 Francisca Cabieses Martínez, 'Rafael Correa, de "indignado" a presidente de la República: Revolución Ciudadana, el camino del Ecuador,' *Punto Final*, 758 (25 May 2012), pp. 16–18.

9 Greg Wilpert, *Changing Venezuela by Taking Power: The History and Policies of the Chavez Government* (Verso, 2007).

10 Boaventura de Sousa Santos, 'Las paradojas de nuestro tiempo y la Plurinacionalidad,' in Alberto Acosta and Esperanza Martínez (eds), *Plurinacionalidad: Democracia en la diversidad* (Abya Yala, 2009), p. 26.

11 Correa, 'Por fin América Latina se atreve a generar pensamiento propio.'

12 'Correa attempts to define modern socialism,' *Latin American Weekly Report*, WR-09-02 (15 January 2009), p. 3.

13 Alfredo Vera Arrata, *Política* (Editorial El Conejo, 2005), p. 11.

14 Juan Antonio Montecino, *Decreasing Inequality under Latin America's 'Social Democratic' and 'Populist' Governments: Is the Difference Real?* (Center for Economic and Policy Research, 2011).

15 Juan Ponce and Alberto Acosta, 'La pobreza en la "revolución ciudadana" o ¿pobreza de revolución?', *Ecuador Debate*, 81 (December 2010), pp. 7–20; Instituto Nacional de Estadística y Censos (INEC), 2012,'Pobreza por ingresos,' www.inec. gob.ec/estadisticas/?option=com_ content &view=article&id=65&Item id=35. 'Indigenous' is used as a proper noun in this chapter, and henceforth is capitalized.

16 'Las ONG dejan su huella en Ciudad Alfaro,' *El Comercio*, 6 July 2008, p. 7.

17 Instituto Científico de Culturas Indígenas (ICCI), 'Uno es el discurso ... otra la realidad,' *Boletín ICCI-Rimay*, 9(105) (2007): 6.

18 'Correa appears to backtrack on debt,' *Latin American Weekly Report*, WR-08-47 (27 November 2008), p. 4.

19 Catherine M. Conaghan, 'Ecuador: Correa's plebiscitary presidency,' *Journal of Democracy*, 19(2) (2008): 55.

20 Luis Ángel Saavedra, '"We've balanced out the power,"' *Latinamerica Press*, 39(19) (2007): 1.

21 República del Ecuador, Constitución de 2008, pdba.georgetown.edu/Constitutions/Ecuador/ecuador08.html.

22 'Last US forces abandon Manta military base in Ecuador,' *MercoPress*, 19 September 2009, en.mercopress.com/2009/09/19/last-us-forces-abandon-manta-military-base-in-ecuador; 'Anti-drug accord sealed with US,' *Latin American Weekly Report*, WR-09-37 (17 September 2009), pp. 4–5.

23 'Ecuador set to leave OPEC,' *New York Times*, 18 September 1992, www.nytimes.com/1992/09/18/business/ecuador-set-to-leave-opec.html.

24 'Correa pide eficiencia a Petroecuador para no privatizarla,' *El Comercio*, 6 August 2011, www.elcomercio.com/politica/Correa-pide-eficiencia-Petroecuador-privatizarla_0_530946942.html.

25 'La CONAIE toma distancia con el Gobierno,' *Ayni Solidaridad*, 2(16) (2008): 8.

26 Carlos Zorrilla, 'Large-scale mining to test rights of nature in Ecuador,' *Upside Down World*, 1 July 2011, upsidedownworld.org/main/ecuador-archives-49/3105-large-scale-mining-to-test-rights-of-nature-in-ecuador.

27 Paul Dosh and Nicole Kligerman, 'Correa vs. social movements: showdown in Ecuador,' *NACLA Report on the Americas*, 42(5) (2009): 24.

28 Jennifer Moore, 'Swinging from the right: Correa and social movements in Ecuador,' *Upside Down World*, 13 May 2009, upsidedownworld.org/main/ecuador-archives-49/1856-swinging-

from-the-right-correa-and-social-movements-in-ecuador-.

29 Alberto Acosta, 'Siempre más democracia, nunca menos. A manera de prólogo,' in Alberto Acosta and Esperanza Martínez (eds), *El Buen Vivir: Una vía para el desarrollo* (Abya Yala, 2009), pp. 27–8; Alberto Acosta, 'El buen vivir, una oportunidad por construir,' *Ecuador Debate*, 75 (December 2008), pp. 45–6.

30 Raúl Zibechi, 'Ecuador: The logic of development clashes with movements,' *IRC Americas Program*, 17 March 2009, americas.irc-online. org/am/5965.

31 Comisión Comunicación CONAIE-ECUARUNARI, 'Pueblos indígenas del Ecuador rechazan declaraciones del presidente Correa,' 18 January 2009, movimientos.org/ show_text.php3?key=13604.

32 Instituto Científico de Culturas Indígenas (ICCI), 'Plurinacionalidad, territorios y democracia: los límites del debate,' *Yachaykuna*, 8 (April 2008), p. 8.

33 Luis Ángel Saavedra, 'The good with the bad,' *Latinamerica Press*, 40(1) (2008): 4.

34 Zibechi, 'Ecuador: The logic of development clashes with movements.'

35 Correa, 'Por fin América Latina se atreve a generar pensamiento propio.'

36 'Correa's get-tough stance founders on one fatality,' *Latin American Weekly Report*, WR-09-39 (1 October 2009), p. 6.

37 Amazon Watch, 'Indigenous blockades escalate after police violently attack protest in the Ecuadorian Amazon,' *Amazon Watch*, 1 October 2009, amazonwatch. org/news/2009/1001-indigenous-blockades-escalate- after-police-violently-attack-protest-in-the-

ecuadorian-amazon. On Peru, see Gerardo Rénique, 'Law of the jungle in Peru: Indigenous Amazonian uprising against neoliberalism,' *Socialism and Democracy*, 23(3) (2009): 117–35.

38 'ONG: 189 indígenas están acusados de terrorismo y sabotaje,' *Hoy*, 19 July 2011, www.hoy.com.ec/ noticias-ecuador/ong-189-indigenas-estan-acusados-de-terrorismo-y-sabotaje-488777.html.

39 Roger Burbach, 'Movements face off with Ecuador's President Correa,' *Z Magazine*, 23(3) (2010): 16.

40 'Spearheading dissent,' *The Economist* (17 July 2010), p. 44, www. economist.com/node/16595284.

41 Greg Grandin, 'Why stop at two?', *London Review of Books*, 31(20) (October 2009).

42 Alexei Barrionvuevo, 'Chilean vote is another sign of Latin America's fading political polarization,' *New York Times*, 20 January 2010, p. A6.

43 'Correa attempts to define modern socialism,' *Latin American Weekly Report*, WR-09-02 (15 January 2009), p. 3.

44 Emir Sader, 'Cuervos y buitres,' 4 November 2011, lalineadefuego.info/2011/11/04/ cuervos-y-buitres-por-emir-sader/.

7 Brazil

1 'Discurso de Luiz Inácio Lula da Silva na 1ª Convenção Nacional do Partido dos Trabalhadores,' Fundação Perseu Abramo, 1981, fpabramo.org.br.

2 PT, 'Carta de Principios do PT,' 1 May 1979, pt.org.br/arquivos/ cartadeprincipios.pdf.

3 Emir Sader and Ken Silverstein, *Without Fear of Being Happy: Lula, the Workers' Party and Brazil* (Verso, 1991), pp. 3–4.

4 World Development Indicators, 'Gross domestic product 2009,' Database, World Bank, 14 April 2011, siteresources.worldbank.org/DATA STATISTICS/Resources/GDP.pdf.

5 Richard Nixon, 'Toasts of the President and President Medici of Brazil,' *American President Project*, transcript, 7 December 1971, presidency.ucsb.edu/ws/index. php?pid=3247#axzz1R6EC1AqK.

6 E. Bradford Burns, *A History of Brazil* (Columbia University Press, 1993), p. 457.

7 Cardinal Paulo Evaristo Arns, *Brasil Nunca Mais*, 1985, dhnet.org. br/dados/projetos/dh/br/tnmais/ index.html; Esteban Cuya, 'Las Comisiones de la Verdad en América Latina,' derechos.org/koaga/iii/1/ cuya.html; Dan Mitrione was transferred to Uruguay in 1969, which was battling the Tupamaros, perhaps the most successful urban guerrilla movement in Latin America at the time. In July 1970 Mitrione was kidnapped by the Tupamaros, and shot and killed eleven days later, after the Brazilian government refused their demand that it release 150 political prisoners.

8 Beto Almeida, 'Cuba–Brasil, 25 anos do reatamento,' *Carta Maior*, 29 June 2011, vermelho.org.br/noticia. php?id_noticia=157481&id_secao=7.

9 Ruben Ricupero, *Visões do Brasil: Ensaios sobre a história e a inserção internacional do Brasil* (Record, 1995), p. 339.

10 Labor statistics show that the average 1978 pay for workers in the Brazilian automobile industry was the equivalent of 60 cents an hour. Meanwhile, inflation was constantly on the rise. According to a secret World Bank report leaked to the press, the Brazilian government was manipulating its inflation figures.

Between 1973 and 1974, the salary of Brazilian workers lost 34.1 percent of its real value. Sader and Silverstein, *Without Fear of Being Happy*, pp. 42, 53.

11 Peter Robb, *A Death in Brazil: A Book of Omissions* (Henry Holt & Co., 2004), pp. 133–5.

12 PT, 'Manifesto de Fundação,' 10 February 1980, pt.org.br/arquivos/ manifesto.pdf.

13 Gabriel Ondetti, *Land, Protest, and Politics: The Landless Movement and the Struggle for Agrarian Reform in Brazil* (Pennsylvania State University Press, 2008), p. 68.

14 Wendy Hunter, *The Transformation of the Workers' Party in Brazil, 1989–2009* (Cambridge University Press, 2010), p. 81.

15 Ibid.; Gianpaolo Baiocchi, *Radicals in Power: The Workers' Party and Experiments in Urban Democracy in Brazil* (Zed Books, 2003), p. 13.

16 David Rothkopf, 'The world's best foreign minister,' *Foreign Policy*, 7 October 2009, rothkopf. foreignpolicy.com/posts/2009/10/07/ the_world_s_best_foreign_minister.

17 Center for Economic and Policy Research, 'MINUSTAH: Mission (almost) accomplished?', blog, 11 August 2011, cepr.net/index. php/blogs/relief-and-reconstruction-watch/minustah-mission-almost-accomplished.

18 'New Brazilian government ratifies Lula da Silva's regional foreign policy,' *MercoPress*, 30 November 2010, en.mercopress. com/2010/11/30/new-brazilian-government-ratifies-lula-da-silva-s-regional-foreign-policy.

19 Marco Aurélio García, *Socialismo do Seculo XXI* (Fundação Perseu Abramo, 2005), pp. 18–26.

20 This is not to say that Brazil had never participated internationally. It had, and extensively.

President Fernando Henrique Cardoso even held an unprecedented summit of Latin American countries in September 2000, but beyond that on the international scene, it was never truly taken seriously. Stephen Buckley, 'Colombia eclipses summit / South American leaders fear Vietnam-like fallout from U.S. aid,' *Washington Post*, 1 September 2000, articles.sfgate.com/2000-09-01/news/17659839_1_plan-colombia-colombian-government-drug-traffickers.

21 Antonio de Aguiar Patriota, 'O Brasil no início do século XXI: uma potência emergente voltada para a paz,' *Politica Externa*, 19(1) (2010): 21.

22 Ministry of External Relations, 'Africa–South America summit takes place this week in Nigeria,' Press release, Embassy of Brazil in London website, 27 November 2006, brazil.org.uk/press/press releases_files/20061127.html.

23 *Newsweek*, 'Brazil's Lula befriends Iran's Ahmadinejad,' blog, 12 October 2009, newsweek.com/blogs/wealth-of-nations/2009/10/12/brazil-s-lula-befriends-iran-s-ahmadinejad.html.

24 De Aguiar Patriota, 'O Brasil no início do século XXI,' pp. 22–3.

25 Luiz Inácio Lula da Silva, 'Brazilian President Lula: BRIC countries must forge a transparent system of global governance,' *Christian Science Monitor*, 16 April 2010, csmonitor.com/Commentary/Global-Viewpoint/2010/0416/Brazilian-President-Lula-BRIC-countries-must-forge-a-transparent-system-of-global-governance.

26 'An Iranian banana skin,' *The Economist*, 17 June 2010, economist.com/node/16377307.

27 Carmen Gentile, 'Analysis: Brazil, Cuba sign oil pact,' UPI, 16 January 2008, upi.com/Business_News/Energy-Resources/2008/01/16/Analysis-Brazil-Cuba-sign-oil-pact/UPI-53491200507730/; 'Brazil offers Cuba help to develop small businesses,' BBC, 21 September 2010, bbc.co.uk/news/world-latin-america-11381472.

28 'Lula da Silva praises strength and speed of regional integration,' *MercoPress*, 18 July 2008, en.mercopress.com/2008/07/18/lula-da-silva-praises-strength-and-speed-of-regional-integration.

29 Correo del Orinoco International, 'Bank of the South to initiate operations this year,' *Venezuela Analysis*, 20 May 2011, venezuelanalysis.com/news/6204; 'Bank of the South sets launch date on Nov. 3 in Venezuela,' Associated Press, 8 October 2007, antiracismdsa.blogspot.com/2007/10/bank-of-south-created.html.

30 De Aguiar Patriota, 'O Brasil no início do século XXI,' p. 22.

31 Alan Clendenning, '"Axis of good" for Brazil, Cuba and Venezuela?', AP, 3 January 2003, commondreams.org/headlines03/0103-01.htm.

32 'Lula salutes Obama, asks him to lift Cuba embargo,' *Earth Times*, 5 November 2008, earthtimes.org/articles/news/240283,lula-salutes-obama-asks-him-to-lift-cuba-embargo.html.

33 'At U.N., Brazil's Lula demands Zelaya reinstatement,' Reuters, 23 September 2009, reuters.com/article/2009/09/23/us-honduras-un-chavez-sb-idUSTRE58M2YW20090923.

34 Zelaya had been overthrown on 28 June 2009 in a *coup d'état* that installed the coup regime of Roberto Micheletti, and paved the way for the presidency of Porfirio 'Pepe' Lobo, a conservative elected in November 2009. In September 2009 he had

returned to Honduras to push to regain power, but retreated to the Brazilian embassy. He said he chose to seek support from the Brazilian embassy 'because of the democratic inclination of Brazil, president Lula, and Marco Aurélio García. And also for the international weight that they have'; Bruno Garcez, 'Zelaya permanecerá em embaixada enquanto for necessário, diz Lula,' BBC Brasil, 25 September 2009, bbc.co.uk/portuguese/noticias/2009/09/090925_lula_honduras_bg_cq.shtml; "Brasil não sabia dos meus planos," diz Zelaya,' *Folha Online*, 23 September 2009, www1.folha.uol.com.br/folha/mundo/ult94u627883.shtml.

35 Within a few months, however, the financial crisis in 2008 caused oil prices to fall, forcing many US ethanol producers into bankruptcy. Brazilian producers were not as affected because they produce most of their ethanol from sugar cane, which is cheaper than producing it from corn, as in the United States. 'The future of U.S.–Brazil energy relations: an opportunity for change, or more of the same?', Council on Hemispheric Affairs, 11 February 2009, coha.org/the-future-of-us-brazil-energy-relations-an-opportunity-for-change-or-more-of-the-same.

36 Phil Stewart and Raymond Colitt, 'Brazil to sign defense cooperation accord,' Reuters, 7 April 2010, reuters.com/article/2010/04/07/brazil-usa-military-idUSN0714692520100407.

37 The US airline manufacturer Boeing is a major contender for the contract against France's Dassault and Sweden's Saab AB. Interestingly, in late September 2011 the former US ambassador to Brazil, Donna Hrinak, was named president of Boeing Brazil. 'U.S. and Brazil sign defense pact, no decision on jets,' Reuters, 14 April 2010, menwithfoilhats.com/2010/04/u-s-and-brazil-sign-defense-pact-no-decision-on-jets/; 'Former US ambassador named president of Boeing Brazil,' Associated Press, 28 September 2011, washingtonpost.com/business/former-us-ambassador-named-president-of-boeing-brazil/2011/09/28/gIQA1DU74K_story.html.

38 Michael Fox, 'Brazil eager to be a force of change and moderation,' *Deutsche Welle*, 30 December 2010, dw-world.de/dw/article/0,,14744104,00.html.

39 Paulo Kliass, 'Lula's political economy: crises and continuity,' *NACLA Report on the Americas*, 44(2) (March/April 2011).

40 Wendy Hunter and Timothy J. Power, 'Rewarding Lula: executive power, social policy, and the Brazilian elections of 2006,' *Latin American Politics and Society*, 49(1) (2009): 19.

41 'Almost 40 million Brazilians climbed to middle class in the last eight years,' *MercoPress*, 28 June 2011, en.mercopress.com/2011/06/28/almost-40-million-brazilians-climbed-to-middle-class-in-the-last-eight-years; Marcelo Neri (ed.), 'Os emergentes dos emergentes: reflexões globais e ações locais para a nova classe média brasileira,' Fundación Getulio Vargas, July 2011, cps.fgv.br/pt-br/brics.

42 World Bank, 'Conditional cash transfers,' go.worldbank.org/BWUC1CMXM0.

43 World Bank, 'Lifting families out of poverty in Brazil – Bolsa Familia program,' go.worldbank.org/QCZI04L470.

44 Berta Rivera Castiñera, Luis Currais Nunes and Paolo Rungo, 'Impacto de los programas de transferencia condicionada de

renta sobre el estado de salud: el programa Bolsa Família de Brasil,' *Revista Española de Salud Pública*, 83(1) (2009): 87; CIA *World Factbook*, online.

45 World Bank, 'Lifting families out of poverty in Brazil.'

46 Neri, 'Os emergentes dos emergentes.'

47 'Background note: Venezuela,' US State Department, 8 February 2011, state.gov/r/pa/ei/bgn/35766. htm; Richard Warnick, 'The Gini index,' *OneUtah*, 13 September 2010, oneutah.org/2010/09/13/the-gini-index/.

48 Neri, 'Os emergentes dos emergentes.'

49 Kliass, 'Lula's political economy: crisis and continuity'; Câmara dos Deputados, 'Lei Orçamentária Anual para 2011,' 9 February 2011.

50 Paulo Kliass, 'Mais uma vez, os incomensuráveis lucros dos bancos,' *Carta Maior*, 5 February 2011, www.cartamaior.com.br/templates/colunaMostrar.cfm?coluna_id=4974.

51 'Investimento é o maior da história da GM,' *Jornal do Comércio*, 16 July 2009, jcrs.uol.com.br/site/noticia.php?codn=3321.

52 'Fatia da manufatura no PIB caiu para 15,8% em 2010,' *Agência Estado*, 12 September 2011, dgabc. com.br/News/5913029/fatia-da-manufatura-no-pib-caiu-para-15-8-em-2010.aspx; 'Economia brasileira,' webpage, Sua Pesquisa, suapesquisa. com/geografia/economia_brasileira. htm.

53 Paulo Kliass, 'Nossas exportações: opção política ou vocação natural?,' *Carta Maior*, 27 January 2011, www.cartamaior. com.br/templates/colunaMostrar. cfm?coluna_id=4941.

54 Bruna Saniele, 'Agronegócio pode chegar a 25% do PIB em 2011, diz ministério,' *Terra*, 6 October 2011, alfonsin.com.br/agronegcio-pode-chegar-a-25-do-pib-em-2011-diz-ministrio/.

55 USDA Foreign Agricultural Service, 'Brazil,' webpage, updated 22 November 2010, fas.usda.gov/country/Brazil/Brazil.asp.

56 'Exportações do agronegócio ultrapassam US$ 80 bilhões,' *Porkworld*, 12 May 2011, porkworld. com.br/noticias/post/exportacoes-do-agronegocio-ultrapassam-us-80-bilhoes; figures from the Brazilian Ministry of Agriculture.

57 Márcio Juliboni, 'As 10 maiores empresas de agronegócio do Brasil,' *Exame.com*, 15 September 2010, memes.com.br/jportal/portal. jsf?post=27820.

58 Food and Agricultural Policy Research Institute, 'FAPRI 2008 World Agricultural Outlook,' Ames: Center for Agriculture and Rural Development (Iowa State University, 2008).

59 'Portal do Agronegócio', portaldoagronegocio.com.br/conteudo.php?id=51229.

60 Claudia Andrade, 'Marina Silva pede demissão do Meio Ambiente e alega falta de sustentação à política ambiental,' *Uol Notícias*, 13 May 2008, noticias.uol.com.br/ultnot/2008/05/13/ult23u2288.jhtm.

61 Michael Fox, 'Brazil's Landless Movement turns 25, opens "new phase" of struggle,' *Upside Down World*, 28 January 2009, upsidedown world.org/main/content/view/1688/1/.

62 'A luta pela reforma agrária continua,' *Brasil de Fato*, 4 April 2011, brasildefato.com.br/node/6127.

63 Cliff Welch, 'Lula and the meaning of agrarian reform,' *NACLA Report on the Americas*, 44(2) (2011): 28–9.

64 'Nossos objetivos,' MST, 7 July 2009, mst.org.br/node/7703.

65 PSOL, 'First national meeting of PSOL Ecosocialists approves Curitiba Charter,' *International Viewpoint*, April 2011, international viewpoint.org/spip.php?article2119.

66 Ibid.

67 Michael Löwy, 'O que é o Ecosocialismo?', combate.info/index2.php?option=com_content&do_pdf=1&id=94.

68 Secretaria de Formação Politica do Diretório Nacional do PT, *Caderno de Formação, Modulo 1, Conhecer o que foi feito para elhor prosseguir* (Fundação Perseu Abramo, 2009), p. 35.

69 Sílvia Leindecker and Michael Fox, 'After Lula: the Brazilian Workers' Party in transition,' *NACLA Report on the Americas*, 44(2) (2011): 14.

70 O Globo, 'Gasto de Lula com cargos de confiaça cresceu 119%,' *O Globo* (Rio de Janeiro), 22 February 2010, www.pbagora.com.br/conteudo.php?id=20100222150839.

71 Dan La Botz, 'Strike wave sweeps Brazil: no sector unaffected; a new union movement on the march,' *International Viewpoint*, October 2011, internationalviewpoint.org/spip.php?article2317.

72 EFE, 'Dilma: equilíbrio fiscal é compatível com desenvolvimento humano,' 4 October 2011, economia.terra.com.br/noticias/noticia.aspx?idNoticia=201110041513_EFE_80294181.

73 'VCP e Aracruz formam maior empresa do mundo em cellulose,' Reuters, 1 September 2009, economia.terra.com.br/noticias/noticia.aspx?idNoticia= 200909011405_RTR_12518139 14nN01483779&idtel=.

74 Nearly 20 percent of the country's energy is produced at the world's largest hydroelectric plant, Itaipu, on the Paraná river between Paraguay, Argentina, and Brazil.

75 Instituto de Pesquisa Econômica Aplicada (Ipea), 'Comunicado do Ipea nº 77: Energia e meio ambiente no Brasil. Parte da série Eixos do Desenvolvimento Brasileiro,' 15 February 2011, ipea. gov.br/portal/index.php?option =com_conte nt&view=article&id=726 3&Itemid=7.

76 Zachary Hurwitz, 'Dirty business in Brazil: Rousseff backslides on the environment,' *NACLA Report on the Americas*, 45(1) (2012): 17.

77 Amazon Watch, 'Belo Monte dam may lead Brazil to OAS High Court,' Press release, 16 June 2011, amazonwatch.org/news/2011/0616-belo-monte-dam-may-lead-to-oas-high-court.

78 Hurwitz, 'Dirty business in Brazil,' pp. 17–19.

79 Ministério do Desenvolvimento, Indústria e Comércio Exterior, 'Álcool combustível,' mdic.gov.br/sitio/interna/interna.php?area=2&menu=999.

80 It is estimated that the majority of the pesticides were used for the production of soy, sugar cane, and corn. 'Mais venenos nos alimentos, mais doenças,' *Jornal dos Trabalhadores Rurais Sem Terra*, February/March 2011, p. 5; the US agricultural biotech multinational Monsanto is one of the top suppliers to Brazil of both pesticides and genetically modified (GMO) seeds. Although GMO seeds were approved in Brazil only in 1998, today Brazil is the second-largest producer of GMOs, with thirty varieties of seeds already approved. Over 75 percent of the 2010/11 soy harvest was GMO, and that number is expected to increase to over 80 percent by next year.

'Supersoja à brasileira,' *Carta Capital*, 14 September 2011, cib.org.br/midia.php?ID=68650&data=20110914.

81 In Brazil, trade policy had traditionally been subordinated to foreign policy objectives. Since Brazilian elites traditionally most feared foreign threats to their economic interests, both Brazilian foreign and trade policy were shaped to support and protect national development. This was consolidated in 1957 when the country rooted itself in a model of import substitution industrialization that was then continued, largely under the Brazilian military dictatorship, for nearly three decades. Local industry, automobile manufacturing, and agro-industry were diversified and protected. This protectionist paradigm, or 'Brasília consensus,' led Brazil through periods of extensive economic growth, such as the country's so-called 'economic miracle' (1968–73), during which time the country's GDP grew by more than 11 percent a year. After the slow return to democracy, however, President José Sarney began to liberalize the economy and trade, with a series of quick unilateral tariff reductions in 1988 and the removal of non-tariff barriers beginning in 1991. These new neoliberal policies and privatizations continued under Presidents Fernando Collor de Mello and Fernando Henrique Cardoso. Between 1991 and 2001, the Brazilian government sold $110 billion worth of assets, including the country's telecommunications giant, Telebrás, and the mining behemoth Vale. Before Cardoso, thirty-eight out of one hundred Brazilian firms were government owned. Today, only thirteen are state owned. Cardoso, ironically a former Marxist academic, also pushed to

separate trade negotiations from larger foreign policy goals; Pedro da Motta Veiga, 'Brazil's trade policy: moving away from old paradigms?', in Lael Brainard and Leonardo Martinez-Diaz (eds), *Brazil as an Economic Superpower?: Understanding Brazil's Changing Role in the Global Economy* (Brookings Institution, 2009), pp. 114–17; 'Brazil – economy,' *Encyclopedia of the Nations*, nationsencyclopedia.com/Americas/Brazil-ECONOMY.html; Lael Brainard and Leonardo Martinez-Diaz, 'Brazil: The "B" belongs in the BRICS,' in Brainard and Martinez-Diaz, *Brazil as an Economic Superpower?*, pp. 165–6.

82 Da Motta Veiga, 'Brazil's trade policy,' p. 123.

83 'Mercosur "structural convergence fund" has distributed 1.1bn USD in 37 projects,' *MercoPress*, 29 June 2011, en.mercopress.com/2011/06/29/mercosur-structural-convergence-fund-has-distributed-1.1bn-usd-in-37-projects.

84 Raúl Zibechi, 'Will Latin America become the new Middle East?', *La Jornada*, translated and published through *Upside Down World/ALC*, 10 May 2012, alcnoticias.net/interior.php?codigo=21891&format =columna&lang=688.

85 'Cutting things down to size,' *Newsweek*, 14 November 2008, thedailybeast.com/newsweek/2008/11/14/cutting-things-down-to-size.html; Terra Brasil, 'Bolivia rompe contrato con la brasileña Queiroz Galvao "por incumplimiento,"' 14 September 2007, terranoticias.terra.es/articulo/html/av21848931.htm.

86 'Institutional,' IIRSA official webpage, iirsa.org//Institucional_ENG.asp?CodIdioma=ENG.

87 'IIRSA,' International Rivers, internationalrivers.org/latin-america/iirsa.

88 Ben Ross Schneider, 'Big business in Brazil,' in Brainard and Martinez-Diaz, *Brazil as an Economic Superpower?*, pp. 173–5.

89 Felicia Bryson, 'Dilma steps out from Lula's shadow,' *Rio Times*, riotimesonline.com/brazil-news/front-page/dilma-steps-out-from-lulas-shadow/#.

90 Mac Margolis, 'Dilma thumps for women,' *Daily Beast*, 21 September 2011, thedailybeast.com/articles/2011/09/21/dilma-rousseff-s-u-n-address-championing-women-s-rights.html.

91 Forbes staff, 'The world's 100 most powerful women,' *Forbes*, 24 August 2011, forbes.com/wealth/power-women.

92 Raymond Colitt and Maria Luiza Rabello, 'Rousseff more popular than Lula as crisis skirts by Brazil,' Bloomberg, 16 December 2011, businessweek.com/news/2011-12-19/rousseff-more-popular-than-lula-as-crisis-skirts-by-brazil.html.

8 Cuba

1 Julio Díaz Vázquez, 'Un balance crítico sobre la economía cubana: notas sobre dirección y gestión,' *Temas* (April–June 2011), p. 128.

2 Inter Press Service, *2009 Annual Political Report*, n.d.

3 Ibid.

4 Patricia Grogg, interview, April 2012.

5 Aurelio Alonso, interview, April 2012.

6 Díaz Vázquez, 'Un balance crítico sobre la economía cubana,' p. 128. Also interview with Juan Valdes Paz, April 2012.

7 Juan Valdes Paz, interview, April 2012. See also Perry Anderson, 'The two revolutions: rough notes,' *New Left Review*, 61 (January/February 2010). Anderson describes how the Soviet economy unraveled with the collapse of the Communist Party's central coordinating role, while the Chinese Communist Party provided direction for the emergence and rapid growth of the market economy.

8 'More sugar mills may be shut down,' *The Free Library*, Cuba News, 2005, www.thefreelibrary.com/More+sugar+mills+may+be+closed+down.-a0133904328.

9 Inter Press Service, *Resumen Político Anual 2010, La Cuba Real*, p. 5.

10 Armando Nova, interview, April 2012.

11 Richard E. Feinberg, *Reaching Out, Cuba's New Economy and the International Response* (Latin America Initiative at Brookings, 2011), pp. 11–12.

12 Camila Piñeiro Harnecker, 'Empresas no estatales en la economía cubana: ¿construyendo el socialismo?', *Temas*, 67 (July–September 2011), p. 77.

13 Feinberg, *Reaching Out*, p. 34.

14 Juan Valdes Paz, interview, April 2012.

15 Harlan Abrahams and Arturo Lopez-Levy, *Raúl Castro and the New Cuba, a Close-Up View of Change* (McFarland and Co., Inc., 2011), p. 113.

16 Juan Valdes Paz, interview, April 2012.

17 Aurelio Alonso, interview, April 2012.

Conclusion

1 Arturo Escobar, 'Latin America at a crossroads,' *Cultural Studies*, 24(1) (2010): 2.

2 Juan Forero, 'Latin America's new authoritarians,' *Washington Post*, 23 July 2012, www.washingtonpost.com/world/the_americas/2012/07/22/gJQAMdtD3W_story.html.

3 Álvaro García Linera, 'Bolivia deja el Estado aparente e impulsa

el Estado Socialista,' Arzobispado de La Paz, 22 January 2010, www.arzobispadolapaz.org/noticias/Nacional.

4 Escobar, 'Latin America at a crossroads,' p. 9.

5 Francisco Hidalgo Flor, 'Tierra: soberanía alimentaría y buen vivir,' *La Línea de Fuego*, 14 October 2011, lalineadefuego.info/2011/10/14/tierra-soberania-alimentaria-y-buen-vivir-por-francisco-hidalgo/.

6 Raúl Zibechi, 'Ecuador: A new model of domination,' Latin America Bureau, trans. Alex Cachinero-Gorman, 5 August 2011.

7 Álvaro García Linera, *Las Tensiones Creativas de la Revolución: la quinta fase del Proceso de Cambio* (Vicepresidencia del Estado, 2010).

8 Emir Sader, *The New Mole: Paths of the Latin American Left* (Verso, 2011), p. 104.

9 Ibid., p. 158.

Bibliography

Interviews

Alonso, Aurelio, April 2012
Groog, Patricia, April 2012
Nova, Armando, April 2012
Valdés Paz, Juan, April 2012

Publications/broadcasts

ABI (2008) 'Ex diputado denuncia que golpe de estado contra Evo no fue desmontado,' *ABI*, 23 September, www.grupoapoyo.org/basn/node/1393.

Abrahams, H. and A. Lopez-Levy (2011) *Raúl Castro and the New Cuba, a Close-Up View of Change*, McFarland and Co., Inc.

Acosta, A. (2008) 'El buen vivir, una oportunidad por construir,' *Ecuador Debate*, 75, December.

— (2009) 'Siempre más democracia, nunca menos. A manera de prólogo,' in A. Acosta and E. Martínez (eds), *El Buen Vivir: Una vía para el desarrollo*, Abya Yala.

Acosta, A. and E. Martínez (eds) (2009) *Plurinacionalidad: Democracia en la diversidad*, Abya Yala.

— (2009) *El Buen Vivir: Una vía para el desarrollo*, Abya Yala.

AFP (2012) 'US watches for LatAm "geopolitical turbulence,"' Agence France-Presse, 6 March, www.google.com/hostednews/afp/article/ALeqM5jdoFrn59zBhrIoipzCpEUAxxI5kQ?docId=CNG.f6e2bcf973ed6c8290bbd6d1bc39f23a.a91.

AFP, Reuters and DPA (2011) 'Chávez anuncia nuevo plan de ayuda a familias venezolanas en pobreza extrema,' *La Jornada*, 13 December, www.jornada.unam.mx/2011/12/13/mundo/027n1mun.

Agência Estado (2011) 'Fatia da manufatura no PIB caiu para 15,8% em 2010,' *Agência Estado*, 12 September, dgabc.com.br/News/5913029/fatia-da-manufatura-no-pib-caiu-para-15-8-em-2010.aspx.

ALBA-TCP (n.d.) 'Fundamental principles of the Peoples' Trade Treaty – TCP,' ALBA-TCP website, alba-tcp.org/en/contenido/fundamental-principles-tcp.

Allard, J.-G. and E. Golinger (2009) *USAID, NED y CIA: la agresión permanente*, MINCI.

Almaraz, A., G. Guzmán, R. Prada et al. (n.d.) 'Manifiesto 22 de junio,' *Herramienta*, www.herramienta.com.ar/herramienta-web-9/bolivia-manifiesto-22-de-junio.

Almeida, B. (2011) 'Cuba–Brasil, 25 anos do reatamento,' *Carta Maior*, 29 June, vermelho.org.br/noticia.php?id_noticia=157481&id_secao=7.

Álvarez, V. (2010) *Venezuela: Hacia donde va el modelo productivo? Crítica al modelo rentístico venezolano generador de desempleo, pobreza y exclusión social; razones para transformarlo en un nuevo modelo productivo socialista; políticas y planes del Gobierno bolivariano para impulsar la economía social; y evaluación de los resultados obtenidos entre 1999–2008*, Centro Internacional Miranda.

Amazon Watch (2009) 'Indigenous blockades escalate after police violently attack protest in the Ecuadorian Amazon,' *Amazon Watch*, 1 October, amazonwatch.org/news/2009/1001-indigenous-blockades-escalate-after-police-violently-attack-protest-in-the-ecuadorian-amazon.

— (2011) 'Belo Monte Dam may lead Brazil to OAS High Court,' Press release, 16 June, amazonwatch.org/news/2011/0616-belo-monte-dam-may-lead-to-oas-high-court.

Anderson, P. (2010) 'The two revolutions: rough notes,' *New Left Review*, 61, January/February.

Andrade, C. (2008) 'Marina Silva pede demissão do Meio Ambiente e alega falta de sustentação à política ambiental,' *Uol Notícias*, 13 May, noticias.uol.com.br/ultnot/2008/05/13/ult23u2288.jhtm.

Ap-Agencias (2011) 'Sindicatos mineros rechazan nacionalización de Morales,' *Los Tiempos*, 19 April, www.hidrocarburosbolivia.com/bolivia-mainmenu-117/42-nacionalizaci/41856-sindicatos-mineros-rechazan-nacionalizacion-de-morales.html.

Aporrea.org. (2011) 'MARCHA NACIONAL contra el sicariato, la impunidad y la criminalización este MARTES 7 DE JUNIO,' *Aporrea*, 6 June, www.aporrea.org/ddhh/n182352.html.

Arce Catacora, L. A. (2011) 'El nuevo modelo económico, social, comunitario y productivo,' *Economía Plural*, Publicación mensual del Ministerio de Economía y Finanzas Publicas, Year 1, no. 1, September.

Argirakis Jordan, H. (2012) 'La conflictividad como epistemología y pedagogía del poder en Bolivia,' *La Época*, 21 May, www.la-epoca.com.bo/index.php?opt=front&mod=detalle&id=1740.

Arkonada, K. and A. Santillana (2009) 'Ecuador y Bolivia: Estado, gobierno y campo popular en la transición,' *Rebelión*, 13 September, www.rebelion.org/noticia.php?id=135502.

Arrighi, G. (2005) 'Hegemony unravelling – 1,' *New Left Review*, 32, March/April.

— (2005) 'Hegemony unravelling – 2,' *New Left Review*, 33, May/June.

Associated Press (2007) 'Bank of the South sets launch date on Nov. 3 in Venezuela,' Associated Press, 8 October, antiracismdsa.blogspot.com/2007/10/bank-of-south-created.html.

— (2011) 'Former US ambassador named president of Boeing Brazil,' Associated Press, 28 September, washingtonpost.com/business/former-us-ambassador-named-president-of-boeing-brazil/2011/09/28/gIQA1DU74K_story.html.

Aurélio García, M. (2005) *Socialismo do Seculo XXI*, Fundação Perseu Abramo.

Ayni Solidaridad (2008) 'La CONAIE toma distancia con el Gobierno,' *Ayni Solidaridad*, 2(16), June.

Azzellini, D. (2009) 'Economía solidaria, formas de propiedad colectiva, nacionalizaciones, empresas socialistas, co- y autogestión en Venezuela,' *ORG y DEMO*, 10(1/2).

Baiocchi, G. (2003) *Radicals in Power: The Workers' Party and Experiments in Urban Democracy in Brazil*, Zed Books.

Barrionvuevo, A. (2010) 'Chilean vote is another sign of Latin America's fading political polarization,' *New York Times*, 20 January, p. A6.

BBC (2010) 'Brazil offers Cuba help to develop small businesses,'

BBC, 21 September, bbc.co.uk/news/world-latin-america-113 81472.

— (2012) 'Profile: Hugo Chavez,' *BBC News*, 29 February, www.bbc.co.uk/news/mobile/world-latin-america-10086210.

Bilbao, L. (2008) *Venezuela en Revolución: Renacimiento del socialismo*, Capital Intelectual.

Blanco, H. (2006) 'Bolivia–Perú,' *Rebelión*, 4 January, www.rebelion.org/noticia.php?id=25053'f.

Boothroyd, R. (2011) 'CELAC, counter-OAS organization inaugurated in Caracas,' *Venezuela Analysis*, 5 December, venezuelanalysis.com/news/6668.

Brainard, L. and L. Martinez-Diaz (2009) *Brazil as an Economic Superpower?: Understanding Brazil's Changing Role in the Global Economy*, Brookings Institution.

— (2009) 'Brazil: The "B" belongs in the BRICS,' in L. Brainard and L. Martinez-Diaz (eds), *Brazil as an Economic Superpower?: Understanding Brazil's Changing Role in the Global Economy*, Brookings Institution.

Brasil de Fato (2011) 'A luta pela reforma agrária continua,' *Brasil de Fato*, 4 April, brasildefato.com.br/node/6127.

Breton, V. and F. García (eds) (2003) *Estado, Etnicidad y Movimientos Sociales en América Latina: Ecuador en Crisis* (Icaria Editorial, 2003).

Bruce, I. (2008) *The Real Venezuela: Making Socialism in the 21st Century*, Pluto Press.

Bryson, F. (n.d.) 'Dilma steps out from Lula's shadow,' *Rio Times*, riotimesonline.com/brazil-news/front-page/dilma-steps-out-from-lulas-shadow/#.

Buckley, S. (2000) 'Colombia eclipses summit / South American leaders fear Vietnam-like fallout from U.S. aid,' *Washington Post*, 1 September, articles.sfgate.com/2000-09-01/news/17659839_1_plan-colombia-colombian-government-drug-traffickers.

Burbach, R. (1997) *Globalization and Postmodern Politics: From Zapatistas to Hightech Robber Barons*, Pluto Press.

— (2003) *The Pinochet Affair: State Terrorism and Global Justice*, Zed Books.

— (2008) 'The United States: orchestrating a civic coup in Bolivia,' *Global Alternatives*, 17 November, globalalternatives.org/node/95.

— (2010) 'Movements face off with Ecuador's President Correa,' *Z Magazine*, 23(3), March.

— (2011) 'The global revolt of 2011: a turning point in history,' *Global Alternatives*, 21 November, globalalternatives.org/node/118.

— (2012) 'The global revolt and Latin America,' *NACLA Report on the Americas*, 6 January, nacla.org/news/2012/1/6/global-revolt-and-latin-america.

— (n.d.) 'Ecuador: the popular rebellion against the "Partidocracia" and the neoliberal state,' *Global Alternatives*, globalalternatives.org/rebellion_against_the_partidocracia.

Burbach, R., O. Nunez and B. Kagarlitsky (1997) *Globalization and Its Discontents: The Rise of Postmodern Socialisms*, Pluto Press.

Burns, E. B. (1993) *A History of Brazil*, Columbia University Press.

Cabieses Martínez, F. (2012) 'Rafael Correa, de "indignado" a presidente de la República: Revolución Ciudadana, el camino del Ecuador,' *Punto Final*, 758, 25 May.

Câmara dos Deputados (Brasil), 'Lei Orçamentária Anual para 2011,' 9 February 2011.

Cambio (2011) 'La empresa estatal amplió su apoyo productivo de 6 mil a 90 mil hectáreas desde 2007,' Cambio, 22 February, www.cambio.bo/noticia. php?fecha=2011-02-22&idn=39409.

— (2011) 'Estado generó 485.574 empleos en cinco años,' Cambio, 4 July, www.cambio.bo/noticia. php?fecha=2011-07-04&idn=49025.

— (2011) 'Pequeñas empresas estatales crecen, se espera que sindicatos las manejan,' Cambio, 28 November, www.cambio. bo/noticia.php?fecha=2011-11-28&idn=59332.

Canadian Centre for Policy Alternatives Monitor (2009) 'Latin American presidents address the World Social Forum,' Canadian Centre for Policy Alternatives Monitor, April, www.asadismi.ws/ latinamericanrevolution1.html.

Carta Capital (2011) 'Supersoja à brasileira,' Carta Capital, 14 September, cib.org.br/midia. php?ID=68650&data=20110914.

Castañada, J. (1993) Utopia Unarmed: The Latin American Left after the Cold War, Alfred A. Knopf.

— (2006) 'Latin America's left turn,' Foreign Affairs, 85(3), May/June.

Center for Economic and Policy Research (2011) 'MINUSTAH: Mission (almost) accomplished?', blog, 11 August, cepr.net/ index.php/ blogs/relief-and-reconstruction-watch/minustah-mission-almost-accomplished.

Chang, L. (2011) 'Bolivia to build third largest gas megaplant in LatAm,' Prensa Latina, 26 October, www.plenglish.com/index. php?option=com_content&task= view&id=428825&Itemid=1.

CIA World Factbook (n.d.), online.

Ciccariello-Maher, G. (2007) 'The Fourth World War started in Venezuela,' Counterpunch, 3–5 March, www.counterpunch. org/2007/03/03/the-fourth-world-war-started-in-venezuela/.

CIDOB-USAID (2010) 'Proyecto de desarrollo de capacidades de liderazgo y fortalecimiento de la capacidad de gestión territorial,' CIDOB, www.cidob-bo.org/index. php?&view=article&id=394.

Clendenning, A. (2003) '"Axis of good" for Brazil, Cuba and Venezuela?', AP, 3 January, commondreams.org/ headlines03/0103-01.htm.

Climate Justice Now (n.d.) 'President Evo Morales of Bolivia to arrive at Copenhagen conference,' Climate Justice Now, www. climate-justice-now.org/president-evo-morales-of-bolivia-to-arrive-at-copenhagen-conference/.

Colitt, R. and M. L. Rabello (2011) 'Rousseff more popular than Lula as crisis skirts by Brazil,' Bloomberg, 16 December, businessweek. com/news/2011-12-19/rousseff-more-popular-than-lula-as-crisis-skirts-by-brazil.html.

Comisión Comunicación CONAIE-ECUARUNART (2009) 'Pueblos indígenas del Ecuador rechazan declaraciones del presidente Correa,', 18 January, movimientos.org/show_text. php3?kpy=13604.

Conaghan, C. M. (2008) 'Ecuador: Correa's plebiscitary presidency,' Journal of Democracy, 19(2), April.

Constitución de la República Bolivariana de Venezuela (n.d.), www.tsj.gov.ve/legislacion/ constitucion1999.htm.

Coronil, F. (1997) The Magical State: Nature, Money and Modernity in

Venezuela, University of Chicago Press.

— (2008) 'It's the oil, stupid!!!', *ReVista: Harvard Review of Latin America*, VIII(1), Fall.

Correa, R. (2007) 'Por fin América Latina se atreve a generar pensamiento propio: el socialismo del siglo XXI,' in R. Correa (ed.), *Ecuador y América Latina: El Socialismo del Siglo XXI*, APDH.

— (ed.) (2007) *Ecuador y América Latina: El Socialismo del Siglo XXI*, APDH.

Correo del Orinoco International (2011) 'Bank of the South to initiate operations this year,' *Venezuela Analysis*, 20 May, venezuelanalysis.com/news/6204.

Council of Foreign Relations (2008) 'Era of U.S. hegemony in Latin America is over, says CFR task force,' Council of Foreign Relations website, 14 May, www.cfr.org/americas/era-us-hegemony-latin-america-over-says-cfr-task-force/p16245.

Council on Hemispheric Affairs (COHA) (2009) 'The future of U.S.–Brazil energy relations: an opportunity for change, or more of the same?', COHA, 11 February, coha.org/the-future-of-us-brazil-energy-relations-an-opportunity-for-change-or-more-of-the-same.

Cuya, E. (n.d.) 'Las Comisiones de la Verdad en América Latina,' derechos.org/koaga/iii/1/cuya.html.

Da Motta Veiga, P. (2009) 'Brazil's trade policy: moving away from old paradigms?', in L. Brainard and L. Martinez-Diaz (eds), *Brazil as an Economic Superpower?: Understanding Brazil's Changing Role in the Global Economy*, Brookings Institution.

Dangl, B. (2010) *Dancing with Dynamite: Social movements and states in Latin America*, AK Press.

De Aguiar Patriota, A. (2010) 'O Brasil no início do século XXI: uma potência emergente voltada para a paz,' *Politica Externa*, 19(1), June/July/August.

De la Torre, C. (2010) *Populist Seduction in Latin America*, 2nd edn, Ohio University research in international studies, Latin America series: Research in international studies, no. 50, Ohio University Press.

— (2011) 'Corporatism, charisma, and chaos: Ecuador's police rebellion in context,' *NACLA Report on the Americas*, 44(1), January/February.

De Sousa Santos, B. (2009) 'Las paradojas de nuestro tiempo y la Plurinacionalidad,' in A. Acosta and E. Martínez (eds), *Plurinacionalidad: Democracia en la diversidad*, Abya Yala.

Díaz Vázquez, J. (2011) 'Un balance crítico sobre la economía cubana: notas sobre dirección y gestión,' *Temas*, April–June.

Dosh, P. and N. Kligerman (2009) 'Correa vs. social movements: showdown in Ecuador,' *NACLA Report on the Americas*, 42(5), September/October.

Dow Jones (2012) 'Venezuela's Chávez: won't accept rulings by ICSID court,' *Wall Street Journal*, 8 January, online.wsj.com/article/BT-CO-20120108-703460.html.

Earth Times (2008) 'Lula salutes Obama, asks him to lift Cuba embargo,' *Earth Times*, 5 November, earthtimes.org/articles/news/ 240283,lula-salutes-obama-asks-him-to-lift-cuba-embargo.html.

Economic Commission for Latin America and the Caribbean

(2002) *Social Panorama of Latin America, 2000–2001*, ECLAC.

— (2007) *Foreign Investment in Latin America and the Caribbean 2007*, ECLAC.

Economist (2010) 'An Iranian banana skin,' *The Economist*, 17 June, economist.com/node/16377307.

— (2010) 'Spearheading dissent,' *The Economist*, 17 July, www.economist.com/node/16595284.

EFE (2011) 'Dilma: equilíbrio fiscal é compatível com desenvolvimento humano,' 4 October, economia.terra.com.br/noticias/noticia.aspx?idNoticia=201110041513_EFE_80294181.

El Comercio (2008) 'Las ONG dejan su huella en Ciudad Alfaro,' *El Comercio*, 6 July.

— (2011) 'Correa pide eficiencia a Petroecuador para no privatizarla,' *El Comercio*, 6 August, www.elcomercio.com/politica/Correa-pide-eficiencia-Petroecuador-privatizarla_0_530946942.html.

El Nacional (2010) 'Giordani: Boligarquía se ha encargado de amasar fortuna en nombre de la revolución,' *El Nacional*, 13 October, el-nacional.com/www/site/p_contenido.php?q=nodo/159920/Econom%C3%ADa/Giordani:-Boligarqu%C3%ADa-se-ha-encargado-de-amasar-fortuna-en-nombre-de-la-revoluci%C3%B3n.

El Troudi, H. (2010) *La Política Económica Bolivariana (PEB) y los dilemas de la transición socialista en Venezuela*, Monte Avila.

Ellner, S. (2005) 'The Venezuelan labor movement under Chávez: autonomous branch of civil society or instrument of political control?', *A Contracorriente*, 2(3), Spring.

EMAPA (2010) *Informe de Gestion 2010*, www.emapa.gob.bo/files/informe20EMAPA20GESTION2020101.pdf.

Encyclopedia of the Nations (n.d.) 'Brazil – economy,' *Encyclopedia of the Nations*, nationsencyclopedia.com/Americas/Brazil-ECONOMY.html.

Erbol (2012) 'Fundación Milenio: la conflictividad tiene un cifra record en el gobierno del MAS,' *Erbol*, 24 February, www.erbol.com.bo/noticia.php?identificador=2147483955061.

Escobar, A. (2010) 'Latin America at a crossroads,' *Cultural Studies*, 24(1), January.

Evaristo Arns, Cardinal P. (1985) *Brasil Nunca Mais*, dhnet.org.br/dados/projetos/dh/br/tnmais/index.html.

Feinberg, R. E. (2011) *Reaching Out, Cuba's New Economy and the International Response*, Latin America Initiative at Brookings.

Fergusson, I. F. (2007) 'The World Trade Organization: background and issues,' Congressional Research Service, 9 May, www.nationalaglawcenter.org/assets/crs/98-928.pdf.

Folha Online (2009) '"Brasil não sabia dos meus planos," diz Zelaya,' *Folha Online*, 23 September, www1.folha.uol.com.br/folha/mundo/ult94u627883.shtml.

Food and Agricultural Policy Research Institute (2008) 'FAPRI 2008 World Agricultural Outlook,' Ames: Center for Agriculture and Rural Development, Iowa State University.

Forbes staff (2011) 'The world's 100 most powerful women,' *Forbes*, 24 August, forbes.com/wealth/power-women.

Forero, J. (2004) 'Documents show C.I.A. knew of a coup plot in Venezuela,' *New York Times*,

3 December, www.nytimes.
com/2004/12/03/international/
americas/03venezuela.html?_r=1.

— (2012) 'Latin America's new authoritarians,' Washington Post, 23 July, www.washingtonpost.com/world/the_americas/2012/07/22/gJQAMdtD3W_story.html.

Fox, M. (2009) 'Brazil's Landless Movement turns 25, opens "new phase" of struggle,' Upside Down World, 28 January, upsidedownworld.org/main/content/view/1688/1/.

— (2010) 'Brazil eager to be a force of change and moderation,' Deutsche Welle, 30 December, dw-world.de/dw/article/0,,14744104,00.html.

Frayssinet, F. (2012) 'Nueva etapa geopolítica de Mercosur,' Inter Press Service, 31 July, www.ipsnoticias.net/nota.asp?idnews=101305.

Free Library (2005) 'More sugar mills may be shut down,' The Free Library, Cuba News, www.thefreelibrary.com/More+sugar+mills+may+be+closed+down.-a0133904328.

Fuentes, F. (2002) 'VENEZUELA: Uprising defeats US-backed coup,' Green Left Weekly, 24 April, www.greenleft.org.au/node/25488.

— (2007) 'Venezuela: Reform battle continues as Chavez ally split,' Green Left Weekly, 12 November, www.greenleft.org.au/node/38621.

— (2008) 'Bolivia's struggle for justice, against right-wing offensive,' Green Left Weekly, 10 August, www.greenleft.org.au/node/40074.

— (2008) 'Venezuela: The struggle for industry to serve people,' Green Left Weekly, 29 August, www.greenleft.org.au/node/40184.

— (2009) 'VENEZUELA: "When the working class roars, capitalists tremble,"' Green Left Weekly, 30 May, www.greenleft.org.au/node/41751.

— (2010) 'Venezuela's revolution faces crucial battles,' Green Left Weekly, 20 February, www.greenleft.org.au/node/43252.

— (2010) 'Venezuela: Workers' control to solve power problems,' Green Left Weekly, 17 April, www.greenleft.org.au/node/43647.

— (2010) 'Bolivia: When fantasy trumps reality,' Green Left Weekly, 22 May, www.greenleft.org.au/node/44208.

— (2010) 'Bolivia: Social tensions erupt,' Green Left Weekly, 15 August, www.greenleft.org.au/node/45140.

— (2011) 'Fuel backdown shows pressures,' Green Left Weekly, 24 January, www.greenleft.org.au/node/46490.

— (2011) 'Venezuela: Socialist party seeks shake up,' Green Left Weekly, 1 May, www.greenleft.org.au/node/47465.

— (2011) 'Bolivia fights for sovereignty over military,' Green Left Weekly, 7 August, www.greenleft.org.au/node/48426.

— (2011) 'Bolivia: Amazon protest – development before environment,' Green Left Weekly, 8 September, www.greenleft.org.au/node/48774.

— (2011) 'Bolivia: Conflict deepens over disputed highway,' Green Left Weekly, 27 September, www.greenleft.org.au/node/48959.

— (2011) 'Bolivia: Jumble over jungle far from over,' Green Left Weekly, 20 November, www.greenleft.org.au/node/49515.

— (2012) 'Paraguay: US makes gains from coup against Lugo,' Green Left Weekly, 15 July, www.greenleft.org.au/node/51636.

Fuentes, F. and T. Pearson (2008) 'Venezuela: Combating food shortages,' *Green Left Weekly*, 1 February, www.greenleft.org.au/node/38973.

Fundação Perseu Abramo (1981) 'Discurso de Luiz Inácio Lula da Silva na 1ª Convenção Nacional do Partido dos Trabalhadores,' Fundação Perseu Abramo, fpabramo.org.br.

Garcez, B. (2009) 'Zelaya permanecerá em embaixada enquanto for necessário, diz Lula,' BBC Brasil, 25 September, bbc.co.uk/portuguese/noticias/2009/09/090925_lula_honduras_bg_cq.shtml.

García, F. (2003) 'Político, estado y diversidad cultural: a proposito del Movimiento Indígena Ecuatoriano,' in V. Breton and F. García (eds), *Estado, Etnicidad y Movimientos Sociales en America Latina: Ecuador en Crisis*, Icaria Editorial.

García Linera, Á. (2010) 'Bolivia deja el Estado aparente e impulsa el Estado Socialista,' Arzobispado de La Paz, 22 January, www.arzobispadolapaz.org/noticias/Nacional.

— (2010) 'El socialismo comunitario, una aporte de Bolivia al mundo,' *Revista de Análisis, Reflexiones sobre la Coyuntura*, February.

— (2010) *Las Tensiones Creativas de la Revolución: la quinta fase del Proceso de Cambio*, Vicepresidencia del Estado.

— (2011) *El 'Oenegismo', Enfermedad Infantil del Derechismo (o como la 'reconducción' del Proceso de Cambio es la restauración neoliberal)*, Vicepresidencia del Estado.

— (2011) *Las Empresas del Estado: Patrimonio colectivo del pueblo boliviano*, Vicepresidencia del Estado.

Gentile, C. (2008) 'Analysis: Brazil, Cuba sign oil pact,' UPI, 16 January, upi.com/Business_News/Energy-Resources/2008/01/16/Analysis-Brazil-Cuba-sign-oil-pact/UPI-53491200507730/.

Gerlach, A. (2003) *Indians, Oil and Politics: A Recent History of Ecuador*, Scholarly Resources.

Giordani, J., A. Baptista, E. Eljuri, N. Silva, L. Urdaneta de Ferrán, P. Sainz and J. F. Rivas Alvarado (eds) (2006) *Inclusión Social y Distribución del Ingreso*, BCV.

Golinger, E. (2009) 'Newly declassified documents reveal more than $97 million from USAID to separatist projects in Bolivia,' *Bolivia Rising*, 22 May, boliviarising.blogspot.com.au/2009/05/newly-declassified-documents-reveal.html.

González Plessmann, A. J. (2008) 'La desigualdad en la Revolución Bolivariana. Una década de apuesta por la democratización del poder, la riqueza y la valoración del estatus,' *Revista Venezolana de Economía y Ciencias Sociales*, 14(3): 194–5.

Gorz, A. (1967) *Strategy for Labor*, Beacon Press.

Grandin, G. (2009) 'Why stop at two?', *London Review of Books*, 31(20, 22), October.

— (2010) 'Muscling Latin America,' *The Nation*, 21 January, www.thenation.com/article/muscling-latin-america.

Gudynas, E. (2010) 'The new extractivism of the 21st century: ten urgent theses about extractivism in relation to current South American progressivism,' Americas Program, Center for International Policy (CIP), 21

April, news.infoshop.org/article. php?story=20100421011214362.

— (2010) 'Las nuevas intersecciones entre pobreza y desarrollo: tensiones y contradicciones de la sociedad civil y los gobiernos progresistas,' *Surmania*, 4, September.

Hardt, M. and A. Negri (2005) *The Multitude: War and Democracy in the Age of Empire*, Penguin Books.

Harnecker, M. (2005) *Haciendo camino al andar: experiencias de ocho gobiernos locales de América Latina*, Monte Avila.

— (2010) 'Latin America & twenty-first century socialism: inventing to avoid mistakes,' *Monthly Review*, 62(3), July/August.

— (2012) 'Cinco reflexiones sobre el socialism del siglo XXI,' *Rebelión*, 26 March, www.rebelion.org/docs/147047.pdf.

Harnecker, M. and F. Fuentes (2008) *MAS-IPSP de Bolivia: Instrumento político que surge de los movimientos sociales*, Centro Internacional Miranda.

Harnecker, M. with the collaboration of F. Fuentes (2011) *Ecuador: Una nueva izquierda en busca de la vida en plenitud*, Abya Yala.

Hart-Landsberg, M. (2009) 'Learning from ALBA and the Bank of the South: challenges and possibilities,' *Monthly Review*, 61(4), September.

Harten, S. (2011) *The Rise of Evo Morales and the MAS*, Zed Books.

Harvey, D. (2003) *The New Imperialism*, Oxford University Press.

Hellinger, D. (2012) 'Venezuela: movements for rent?', in G. Prevost, C. Oliva Campos and H. E. Vanden (eds) (2012) *Social Movements and Leftist Governments in Latin America: Confrontation or Co-optation?*, Zed Books.

Hernández E., V. and F. Buendía G. (2011) 'Ecuador: avances y desafíos de Alianza PAÍS,' *Nueva Sociedad*, 234, July/August.

Hernández, J. L. (n.d.) 'Sistematización y análisis de la Misión Zamora,' *INNOVAVEN*, www.innovaven.org/quepasa/agropol1.pdf.

Hernández Navarro, L. (2012) 'El pueblo boliviano vive la mayor revolución social,' *La Jornada*, 7 February, pp. 2–3, translation from johnriddell.wordpress.com/2012/02/19/bolivias-garcia-linera-moving-beyond-capitalism-is-a-universal-task/.

Hidalgo Flor, F. (2011) 'Tierra: soberanía alimentaría y buen vivir,' *La Línea de Fuego*, 14 October, lalineadefuego.info/2011/10/14/tierra-soberania-alimentaria-y-buen-vivir-por-francisco-hidalgo/.

Holloway, J. (2002) *Change the World Without Taking Power: The Meaning of Revolution Today*, Pluto Press.

— (2010) *Crack Capitalism*, Pluto Press.

— (2010) 'How far away is Latin America from Nottingham,' *Upside Down World*, 8 November, upsidedownworld.org/main/international-archives-60/2773-how-far-away-is-latin-america-from-vancouver.

Honorio Martínez, J. (2011) 'La política petrolera del gobierno Chávez o la redefinición del estado ante la globalización neoliberal,' *Historia Actual Online*, 24, Winter.

Hoy (2011) 'ONG: 189 indígenas están acusados de terrorismo y sabotaje,' *Hoy*, 19 July, www.hoy.com.ec/noticias-ecuador/ong-189-indigenas-estan-acusados-de-terrorismo-y-sabotaje-488777.html.

Hunter, W. (2010) *The Transformation of the Workers' Party in Brazil, 1989–2009*, Cambridge University Press.

Hunter, W. and T. J. Power (2007) 'Rewarding Lula: executive power, social policy, and the Brazilian elections of 2006,' *Latin American Politics and Society*, 49(1), Spring.

Hurwitz, Z. (2012) 'Dirty business in Brazil: Rousseff backslides on the environment,' *NACLA Report on the Americas*, 45(1), Spring.

IIRSA (n.d.) 'Institutional,' IIRSA official webpage, iirsa.org//Institucional_ENG. asp?CodIdioma=ENG.

Instituto Científico de Culturas Indígenas (ICCI) (2007) 'Uno es el discurso ... otra la realidad,' *Boletín ICCI-Rimay*, 9(105), December.

— (2008) 'Plurinacionalidad, territorios y democracia: los límites del debate,' *Yachaykuna*, 8, April.

Instituto de Pesquisa Econômica Aplicada (Ipea) (2011) 'Comunicado do Ipea n° 77: Energia e meio ambiente no Brasil. Parte da série Eixos do Desenvolvimento Brasileiro,' 15 February, ipea.gov.br/portal/index.php?option=com_content&view=article&id=7263&Itemid=7.

Instituto Nacional de Estadística y Censos (INEC) (2012) 'Pobreza por ingresos,' www.inec.gob.ec/estadisticas/?option=com_content&view= article&id=65&Itemid =35.

Inter Press Service (n.d.) *2009 Annual Political Report*.

— (n.d.) *Resumen Político Anual 2010, La Cuba Real*.

International Rivers (n.d.) 'IIRSA,' International Rivers, internationalrivers.org/latin-america/iirsa.

Jornal do Comércio (2009) 'Investimento é o maior da história da GM,' *Jornal do Comércio*, 16 July, jcrs.uol.com.br/site/noticia.php?codn=3321.

Jornal dos Trabalhadores Rurais Sem Terra (2011) 'Mais venenos nos alimentos, mais doenças,' *Jornal dos Trabalhadores Rurais Sem Terra*, February/March.

Juliboni, M. (2010) 'As 10 maiores empresas de agronegócio do Brasil,' *Exame.com*, 15 September, memes.com.br/jportal/portal.jsf?post=27820.

Katz, C. (2008) *Las disyuntivas de la izquierda en América Latina*, Ediciones Luxemburg.

Kliass, P. (2011) 'Nossas exportações: opção política ou vocação natural?', *Carta Maior*, 27 January, www.cartamaior.com.br/templates/colunaMostrar.cfm?coluna_id=4941.

— (2011) 'Mais uma vez, os incomensuráveis lucros dos bancos,' *Carta Maior*, 5 February, www.cartamaior.com.br/templates/colunaMostrar.cfm? coluna_id=4974.

— (2011) 'Lula's political economy: crisis and continuity,' *NACLA Report on the Americas*, 44(2), March/April.

Kohl, B. and L. Farthing (2005) *Impasse in Bolivia: Neoliberal Hegemony and Popular Resistance*, Zed Books.

La Botz, D. (2011) 'Strike wave sweeps Brazil: no sector unaffected; a new union movement on the march,' *International Viewpoint*, October, internationalviewpoint.org/spip.php?article2317.

Latin American Weekly Report (2007) 'Correa reigns over institutional chaos,' *Latin American Weekly Report*, WR-07-16, 26 April.

— (2008) 'Correa appears to backtrack on debt,' *Latin American*

Weekly Report, WR-08-47, 27 November.

— (2009) 'Correa attempts to define modern socialism,' *Latin American Weekly Report*, WR-09-02, 15 January.

— (2009) 'Anti-drug accord sealed with US,' *Latin American Weekly Report*, WR-09-37, 17 September.

— (2009) 'Correa's get-tough stance founders on one fatality,' *Latin American Weekly Report*, WR-09-39, 1 October.

Latinobarómetro (n.d.) 'Encuesta Latinobarómetro 1999–2000,' www.latinobarometro.org/latino/LATContenidos.jsp.

Lebowitz, M. (2006) *Build it Now: Socialism for the 21st Century*, Monthly Review Press.

— (2010) *The Socialist Alternative: Real Human Development*, Monthly Review Press.

Leindecker, S. and M. Fox (2011) 'After Lula: the Brazilian Workers' Party in transition,' *NACLA Report on the Americas*, 44(2), March/April.

Lema, G. (2011) *La Bolivia que se va, la Bolivia que viene: entrevista a líderes políticos nacionales*, Los Tiempos.

Ley de Consejos Comunales (n.d.) infocentro.gob.ve/archivos/locc.pdf.

López Maya, M. (2000) *Protesta y cultura en Venezuela: los marcos de acción colectiva en 1999*, CLACSO.

Löwy, M. (n.d.) 'O que é o Eco-socialismo?', combate. info/index2.php?option=com_content&do_pdf=1&id=94.

Lula da Silva, L. I. (2010) 'Brazilian President Lula: BRIC countries must forge a transparent system of global governance,' *Christian Science Monitor*, 16 April, csmonitor.com/Commentary/Global-Viewpoint/2010/0416/Brazilian-President-Lula-BRIC-countries-must-forge-a-transparent-system-of-global-governance.

Machado M., J. E. (2009) 'Participación social y consejos comunales en Venezuela,' *Revista Venezolano de Economía y Ciencias Sociales*, 15(1), January–April.

Mancebo, J. P. (2008) 'Una historia económica de Venezuela: balance de realizaciones y desafíos,' in *I Encontro de Historiadores 200 Anos de Independência: Olhar o Futuro numa Perspectiva Sul-Americana*, Fundação Alexandre de Gusmão.

Margolis, M. (2011) 'Dilma thumps for women,' *Daily Beast*, 21 September, thedailybeast.com/articles/2011/09/21/dilma-rousseff-s-u-n-address-championing-women-s-rights.html.

Márquez, H. (2005) 'Venezuela declares itself illiteracy-free,' Inter Press Service, 28 October, www.ipsnews.net/africa/interna.asp?idnews=30823.

Mejía, P. (2012) 'Entrevista a Gonzalo Gomez, co-fundador de Aporrea: "Un general golpista venezolano involucrado en un atentado con explosivos contra la embajada de España en Caracas,"' *Kaos en la Red*, 9 January, kaosenlared.net/america-latina/item/3298-un-general-golpista-venezolano-involucrado-en-un-atentado-con-explosivos-contra-la-embajada-de-espa%C3%B1a-en-caracas/3298-un-general-golpista-venezolano-involucrado-en-un-atentado-con-explosivos-contra-la-embaja-da-de-espa%C3%B1a-en-caracas.html.

MercoPress (2008) 'Lula da Silva praises strength and speed of regional integration,' *Merco-*

Press, 18 July, en.mercopress. com/2008/07/18/lula-da-silva-praises-strength-and-speed-of-regional-integration.

— (2009) 'Last US forces abandon Manta military base in Ecuador,' *MercoPress*, 19 September, en.mercopress.com/2009/09/19/last-us-forces-abandon-manta-military-base-in-ecuador.

— (2010) 'New Brazilian government ratifies Lula da Silva's regional foreign policy,' *MercoPress*, 30 November, en.mercopress. com/2010/11/30/new-brazilian-government-ratifies-lula-da-silva-s-regional-foreign-policy.

— (2011) 'Almost 40 million Brazilians climbed to middle class in the last eight years,' *MercoPress*, 28 June, en.mercopress.com/2011/06/28/almost-40-million-brazilians-climbed-to-middle-class-in-the-last-eight-years.

— (2011) 'Mercosur "structural convergence fund" has distributed 1.1bn USD in 37 projects,' *MercoPress*, 29 June, en.mercopress.com/ 2011/06/29/mercosur-structural-convergence-fund-has-distributed-1.1bn-usd-in-37-projects.

Miller Lana, S. and A. Downie (2010) 'In Brazil Hu Jintao aims for bigger piece of Latin American trade,' *Christian Science Monitor*, 15 April, www.csmonitor.com/Business/2010/0415/In-Brazil-Hu-Jintao-aims-for-bigger-piece-of-Latin-America-trade.

MINCI (2007) *Misiones Bolivarianas*, MINCI.

Ministerio de Economía y Finanzas Públicas (2011) 'Introducción,' *Economía Plural*, Publicación mensual, Year 1, no. 1, September.

Ministério do Desenvolvimento Agrário (2011), 'Portal do Agron-egócio', portaldoagronegocio. com.br/conteudo.php?id=51229.

Ministério do Desenvolvimento, Indústria e Comércio Exterior (n.d.) 'Álcool combustível,' mdic. gov.br/sitio/interna/interna.php? area=2&menu=999.

Ministry of External Relations (2006) 'Africa–South America summit takes place this week in Nigeria,' Press release, Embassy of Brazil in London website, 27 November, brazil.org.uk/press/pressreleases_files/20061127.html.

Molinski, D. (2010) 'Chávez nationalizes auto lubricants company,' *Wall Street Journal*, 11 October, online.wsj.com/article/SB1000142 4052748703385045755448640891 03340.html.

Mommer, B. (2003) 'Petróleo subversivo,' in L. E. Lander (ed.), *Poder y Petróleo en Venezuela*, Publicaciones PDVSA.

Montecino, J. A. (2011) *Decreasing Inequality under Latin America's 'Social Democratic' and 'Populist' Governments: Is the Difference Real?*, Center for Economic and Policy Research.

Moore, J. (2009) 'Swinging from the right: Correa and social movements in Ecuador,' *Upside Down World*, 13 May, upsidedownworld. org/main/ecuador-archives-49/1856-swinging-from-the-right-correa-and-social-movements-in-ecuador-.

Morales, E. (2006) *La revolución democrática y cultural: Diez discursos de Evo Morales*, Editorial Malatesta.

MST (2009) 'Nossos objetivos,' MST, 7 July, mst.org.br/node/7703.

Muller Rojas, A. (2007) 'Adhocracia vs. burocracia,' *Aporrea*, 29 December, www.aporrea.org/ideologia/a48176.html.

Neri, M. (ed.) (2011) 'Os emergentes dos emergentes: reflexões globais e ações locais para a nova classe média brasileira,' Fundación Getulio Vargas, July, cps.fgv.br/pt-br/brics.

New York Times (1992) 'Ecuador set to leave OPEC,' *New York Times*, 18 September, www.nytimes.com/1992/09/18/business/ecuador-set-to-leave-opec.html.

Newsweek (2008) 'Cutting things down to size,' *Newsweek*, 14 November, thedailybeast.com/newsweek/2008/11/14/cutting-things-down-to-size.html.

— (2009) 'Brazil's Lula befriends Iran's Ahmadinejad,' *Newsweek* blog, 12 October, newsweek.com/blogs/wealth-of-nations/2009/10/12/brazil-s-lula-befriends-iran-s-ahmadinejad.html.

Nixon, R. (1971) 'Toasts of the President and President Medici of Brazil,' *American President Project*, transcript, 7 December, presidency.ucsb.edu/ws/index.php?pid=3247#axzz1R6EC1AqK.

O Globo (2010) 'Gasto de Lula com cargos de confiaça cresceu 119%,' *O Globo* (Rio de Janeiro), 22 February, www.pbagora.com.br/conteudo.php?id=20100222150839.

Olivares Alonso, E. (2012) 'La revolución en Bolivia, a caballo de las contradicciones, dice García Linera,' *La Jornada*, 8 February, www.jornada.unam.mx/2012/02/08/politica/o2on1pol.

Ondetti, G. (2008) *Land, Protest, and Politics: The Landless Movement and the Struggle for Agrarian Reform in Brazil*, Pennsylvania State University Press.

Osava, M. (2009) 'World Social Forum: presidents for feminist socialism', Inter Press Service, 30 January, www.globalissues.org/news/2009/01/30/483.

Parker, D. (2008) 'Chávez y la búsqueda de una seguridad y soberanía alimentarías,' *Revista Venezolana de Economía y Ciencias Sociales*, 14(3), September–December.

Pearce, A. J. (ed.) (2010) *Evo Morales and the Movimiento al Socialismo in Bolivia: The First Term in Context, 2006–2010*, Institute for the Study of the Americas.

Petras, J. and H. Veltmeyer (2003) *The New Development Politics: The Age of Empire Building and New Social Movements*, Ashgate Publishing.

Piñeiro Harnecker, C. (2005) 'The new cooperative movement in Venezuela's Bolivarian process,' *MRZine*, 12 May, mrzine.monthlyreview.org/2005/harneckero 51205.html.

— (2008) 'Principales desafíos de las cooperativas en Venezuela,' *Capaya: Revista Venezolana de Economía Social*, 8(15), January–June.

— (2011) 'Empresas no estatales en la economía cubana: ¿construyendo el socialismo?', *Temas*, 67, July–September.

Ponce, J. and A. Acosta (2010) 'La pobreza en la "revolución ciudadana" o ¿pobreza de revolución?', *Ecuador Debate*, 81, December.

Porkworld (2011) 'Exportações do agronegócio ultrapassam US$ 80 bilhões,' *Porkworld*, 12 May, porkworld.com.br/noticias/post/exportacoes-do-agronegocio-ultrapassam-us-80-bilhoes.

Portal ALBA-TCP (2009) '¿Que es el ALBA-TCP?', *Portal ALBA-TCP*, 3 December, www.alianzabolivariana.org/modules.php?name=Content&pa=showpage&pid=2080.

Prevost, G., C. Oliva Campos and H. E. Vanden (eds) (2012) *Social Movements and Leftist Governments in Latin America: Confrontation or Co-optation?*, Zed Books.

PSOL (2011) 'First National Meeting of PSOL Ecosocialists approves Curitiba Charter,' *International Viewpoint*, April, internationalviewpoint.org/spip.php?article2119.

PT (1979) 'Carta de Principios do PT,' 1 May, pt.org.br/arquivos/cartadeprincipios.pdf.

— (1980) 'Manifesto de Fundação,' 10 February, pt.org.br/arquivos/manifesto.pdf.

Reardon, J. (2010) 'Chavez supporters march in Caracas for "radicalization" of the revolution and against "imperialism and bureaucratism,"' *Venezuela Analysis*, 29 November, venezuelanalysis.com/news/5820.

Redacción Bolpress (2011) 'Sudamérica siglo XXI: trascender UNASUR y crear un "Estado región,"' *Bolpress*, 27 May, www.bolpress.com/art.php?Cod=2011052702.

Regalado, R. (2007) *Latin America at the Crossroads: Domination, crisis, popular movements and political alternatives*, Ocean Press.

Rénique, G. (2009) 'Law of the jungle in Peru: Indigenous Amazonian uprising against neoliberalism,' *Socialism and Democracy*, 23(3), November.

República del Ecuador (2008) Constitución de 2008, pdba.georgetown.edu/Constitutions/Ecuador/ecuador08.html.

Reuters (2009) 'VCP e Aracruz formam maior empresa do mundo em cellulose,' Reuters, 1 September, economia.terra.com.br/noticias/noticia.aspx?idNoticia=200909011405_RTR_1251813914nN01483779&idtel=.

— (2009) 'At U.N., Brazil's Lula demands Zelaya reinstatement,' Reuters, 23 September, reuters.com/article/2009/09/23/us-honduras-un-chavez-sb-idUSTRE58M2YW20090923.

— (2010) 'U.S. and Brazil sign defense pact, no decision on jets,' Reuters, 14 April, menwithfoilhats.com/2010/04/u-s-and-brazil-sign-defense-pact-no-decision-on-jets/.

— (2011) 'Factbox: Venezuela's state takeovers under Chavez,' Reuters, 26 April, www.reuters.com/article/2011/04/26/us-venezuela-nationalizations-idUSTRE73P7N620110426.

Ricupero, R. (1995) *Visões do Brasil: Ensaios sobre a história e a inserção internacional do Brasil*, Record.

Riddell, J. (n.d.) 'Progress in Bolivia: a reply to Jeff Webber,' *Socialist Project*, www.socialistproject.ca/bullet/499.php.

Rivera, S. (2003) *Oprimidos pero no vencidos: Luchas del campesinado aymara y qhechwa de Bolivia, 1900–1980*, Yachaywasi.

Rivera Castiñera, B., L. Currais Nunes and P. Rungo (2009) 'Impacto de los programas de transferencia condicionada de renta sobre el estado de salud: el programa Bolsa Família de Brasil,' *Revista Española de Salud Pública*, 83(1): 87.

Robb, P. (2004) *A Death in Brazil: A Book of Omissions*, Henry Holt & Co.

Robertson, E. (2012) 'Revolutionary democracy in the economy? Venezuela's worker control movement and the Plan Socialist

Guayana,' *Venezuela Analysis*, 3 August, venezuelanalysis.com/analysis/7151.

Robinson, D. M. (2006) 'Economic roots of Bolivia's social revolution,' *WikiLeaks*, 17 May, wikileaks.vicepresidencia.gob.bo/ECONOMIC-ROOTS-OF-BOLIVIA-S-SOCIAL.

Robinson, W. I. (2008) *Latin America and Global Capitalism, A Critical Globalization Perspective*, Johns Hopkins University Press.

Rojas Calizaya, J. C. (n.d.) 'Tierra, propiedad y poder,' constituyentesoberana.org/3/docsanal/122011/201211_1.pdf.

Rosset, P., R. Patel and M. Courville, with a Foreword by C. D. Deere (2006) *Promised Land, Competing Visions of Agrarian Reform*, Food First Books.

Rothkopf, D. (2009) 'The world's best foreign minister,' *Foreign Policy*, 7 October, rothkopf.foreignpolicy. com/posts/2009/10/07/the_world_s_best_foreign_ minister.

Ryan, R. (2010) 'John Holloway, crack capitalism and Latin America,' *Upside Down World*, 8 November, upsidedownworld.org/main/mexico-archives-79/2772-john-holloway-crack-capitalism-and-latin-america.

Saavedra, L. Á. (2007) '"We've balanced out the power,"' *Latinamerica Press*, 39(19), 17 October.

— (2008) 'The good with the bad,' *Latinamerica Press*, 40(1), 23 January.

Sader, E. (2011) *The New Mole: Paths of the Latin American Left*, Verso.

— (2011) 'Cuervos y buitres,' 4 November, lalineadefuego. info/2011/11/04/cuervos-y-buitres-por-emir-sader/.

Sader, E. and K. Silverstein (1991) *Without Fear of Being Happy: Lula, the Workers' Party and Brazil*, Verso.

Sahmkow, R. (2010) 'El peso del Estado se hace cada vez mayor en la economía venezolana,' Agence France-Presse, 15 March, economia.noticias24.com/noticia/18349/el-peso-del-estado-se-hace-cada-vez-mayor-en-la-economia-venezolana/.

Saniele, B. (2011) 'Agronegócio pode chegar a 25% do PIB em 2011, diz ministério,' *Terra*, 6 October, alfonsin.com.br/agronegcio-pode-chegar-a-25-do-pib-em-2011-diz-ministrio/.

Schneider, B. R. (2009) 'Big business in Brazil,' in L. Brainard and L. Martinez-Diaz (eds), *Brazil as an Economic Superpower?: Understanding Brazil's Changing Role in the Global Economy*, Brookings Institution.

Secretaria de Formação Politica do Diretório Nacional do PT (2009) *Caderno de Formação, Modulo 1, Conhecer o que foi feito para elhor prosseguir*, Fundação Perseu Abramo.

Silva Querales, N. (2006) 'Organizaciones y redes sociales en las políticas de inclusión social,' in J. Giordani, A. Baptista, E. Eljuri, N. Silva, L. Urdaneta de Ferrán, P. Sainz and J. F. Rivas Alvarado (eds) (2006) *Inclusión Social y Distribución del Ingreso*, BCV.

Sivak, M. (2010) 'The Bolivianisation of Washington–La Paz relations: Evo Morales' foreign policy agenda in historical context,' in A. J. Pearce (ed.), *Evo Morales and the Movimiento al Socialismo in Bolivia: The First Term in Context, 2006–2010*, Institute for the Studies of the Americas.

Sojo, C. A. (2005) 'Venezuela's Chávez closes World Social Forum with call to transcend capitalism,' *Venezuela Analysis*, 31 January, venezuelanalysis.com/print/907.

Soto, S. (2011) 'Encuentro nacional por el control obrero,' Plan Guayana website, 22 May, www.planguayana.com/pgs_documentos/encuentro_nacional_co.htm.

Spoor, M. (2002) 'Policy regimes and performance of the agricultural sector in Latin America and the Caribbean during the last three decades,' *Journal of Agrarian Change*, 2(3), July.

Stefanoni, P. (2010) '¿Pueblo enfermo o raza de bronce? Etnicidad e imaginación nacional en Bolivia (1900–2010),' in M. Svampa, P. Stefanoni and B. Fornillo, *Debatir Bolivia: Perspectivas de un proyecto de descolonialización*, Taurus.

Stefanoni, P. and H. do Alto (2007) *Evo Morales, de la coca al palacio: una oportunidad para la izquierda indígena*, Imprenta Cervantes.

Stewart, P. and R. Colitt (2010) 'Brazil to sign defense cooperation accord,' Reuters, 7 April, reuters.com/article/2010/04/07/brazil-usa-military-idUSN0714692520100407.

Svampa, M., P. Stefanoni and B. Fornillo (2010) *Debatir Bolivia: Perspectivas de un proyecto de descolonialización*, Taurus.

Telesur (2012) 'Tras nacionalización de hidrocarburos Bolivia incremento en mas de un 300% su recaudación,' Hidrocarburos Bolivia.com, 22 January, www.hidrocarburos bolivia.com/bolivia-mainmenu-117/gobierno-relacionamiento-mainmenu-121/49164-tras-nacional izacion-de-hidrocarburos-bolivia-incremento-en-mas-de-un-300-su-recaudacion.html.

Terra Brasil, 'Bolivia rompe contrato con a brasileña Queiroz Galvao "por incumplimiento,"' 14 September 2007, terranoticias.terra.es/articulo/html/av21848931.htm.

Tockman, J. (2007) 'Chávez, Morales seek transformation of MERCO-SUR trade bloc,' *Venezuela Analysis*, 22 January, venezuelanalysis.com/analysis/2187.

US State Department (2011) 'Background note: Venezuela,' 8 February, state.gov/r/pa/ei/bgn/35766.htm.

USDA Foreign Agricultural Service (2010) 'Brazil,' webpage, updated 22 November, fas.usda.gov/country/Brazil/Brazil.asp.

Valdez Mingramm, R., K.-L. Wang, A. Jiménez and J. J. Reyes (2010) 'China–Latin America commodity trade and investment,' *SinoLatin Capital*, November, www.sinolatincapital.com.

Vásquez, W. (2012) 'Un tercio de la subvención se desvió al contrabando,' *La Razón*, 12 January, www.la-razon.com/nacional/tercio-subvencion-desvio-contrabando_0_1539446142.html.

Venezuelanalysis.com (2011) 'Venezuelan workers march again to demand socialism at the workplace,' *Venezuela Analysis*, 31 March, venezuelanalysis.com/news/6106.

Vera Arrata, A. (2005) *Política*, Editorial El Conejo.

Vonk Netherlands and Hands off Venezuela (2010) 'Venezuela and the Netherlands,' *Hands Off Venezuela*, 13 January, www.handsoffvenezuela.org/venezuela_and_netherlands.htm.

VTV (2011) 'Pdte. Chávez convoca a organizaciones sociales a conformar Gran Polo Patriótico,' Venezolana de Televisión, 6 October, www.vtv.gov.ve/index.

php/nacionales/68813-pdte-chavez-convoca-a-organizaciones-sociales-a-la-conformacion-del-gran-polo-patriotico-.

Walder, P. (2011) 'Álvaro García Linera, Vicepresidente de Bolivia: "El movimiento social empuja el cambio político,"' *Punto Final*, 14 October, www.puntofinal.cl/744/movimiento_social.php.

Warnick, R. (2010) 'The Gini index,' *OneUtah*, 13 September, oneutah.org/2010/09/13/the-gini-index/.

Weisbrot, M. and R. Ray (2010) *Update on the Venezuelan Economy*, Center for Economic and Policy Research.

Weisbrot, M. and D. Rosnick (2003) *Another Lost Decade? Latin America's Growth Failure Continues into the 21st Century*, Center for Economic and Policy Research.

Weisbrot, M., R. Ray and L. Sandoval (2009) *The Chávez Administration at 10 Years: The Economy and Social Indicators*, Center for Economic and Policy Research.

Welch, C. (2011) 'Lula and the meaning of agrarian reform,' *NACLA Report on the Americas*, 44(2), March/April.

Wilpert, G. (2007) *Changing Venezuela by Taking Power: The History and Policies of the Chavez Government*, Verso.

World Bank (n.d.) 'Lifting families out of poverty in Brazil – Bolsa Familia program,' go.worldbank.org/QCZI04L470.

— (n.d.) 'Conditional cash transfers,' go.worldbank.org/BWUC1CMXM0.

World Development Indicators (2011) 'Gross domestic product 2009,' Database, World Bank, 14 April, siteresources.worldbank.org/DATASTATISTICS/Resources/GDP.pdf.

Wright, A. (2003) *To Inherit the Earth: The Landless Movement and the Struggle for a New Brazil*, Food First Books.

Zamora, J. (2011) 'China's trade with Latin America raises eyebrows,' Agence France-Presse, 4 September, www.hurriyet dailynews.com/default.aspx?pageid=438&n=china8217s-trade-with-latin-america-raises-eyebrows-2011-09-04.

Zepada, J. (n.d.) 'Entrevista al presidente de Ecuador, Rafael Correa,' Radio Netherlands Wereldomroep, sites.rnw.nl/documento/Entrevista%20al%20presidente%20de%20Ecuador.pdf.

Zibechi, R. (2009) 'Ecuador: The logic of development clashes with movements,' *IRC Americas Program*, 17 March, americas.irc-online.org/am/5965.

— (2010) *Dispersing Power: Social Movements as Anti-State Forces*, AK Press.

— (2011) 'Ecuador: A new model of domination', Latin America Bureau, trans. Alex Cachinero-Gorman, 5 August.

— (2012) 'Will Latin America become the new Middle East?', *La Jornada*, trans. and published through *Upside Down World/ALC*, 10 May, alcnoticias.net/interior.php?codigo=21891&format=columna&lang=688.

Zorrilla, C. (2011) 'Large-scale mining to test rights of nature in Ecuador,' *Upside Down World*, 1 July, upsidedownworld.org/main/ecuador-archives-49/3105-large-scale-mining-to-test-rights-of-nature-in-ecuador.

Index

11 September 2001 attacks, 2

Abrahams, Harlan, with Arturo Lopez-Levy, *Raúl Castro*, 150
Acacho, Pepe, 111
Acosta, Alberto, 108–9
adhocracy, 60
Afghanistan, US invasion of, 56
Africa–South America Summit, 123
agrarian reform: in Bolivia, 85; in Brazil, 131; in Cuba, 147
agribusiness sector: in Argentina, 41; in Brazil, 129–31, 137
agriculture, 18, 50, 63, 85–6, 103; in Brazil, 130; in Cuba, 145, 146–7
Agroisleña company, nationalization of, 68
Ahmadinejad, Mahmoud, 35, 126, 138
Alencar, José, 127
Alianza Bolivariana de los Pueblos de Nuestra América (ALBA), 3, 56, 28–9, 47, 56, 88, 106, 156; Council of Social Movements, 57; Cuba's partnership with, 149; Ecuador summit meeting, 111
Alianza País (AP), 101
Allende, Salvador, 6, 40
Alonso, Aurelio, 145, 151
Amaral, João, 132
Amazon: building of dams in, 135; deforestation of, 131
Amnesty International, 24
Amorim, Celso, 122, 139
Andrés Pérez, Carlos, 18
'Another World is Possible', 31
anti-communism, 118
anti-imperialism, in Ecuador, 105–6
Arce Catacora, Luis Alberto, 80, 82–3
Argentina, 2, 13, 17, 18, 23, 36, 41, 50
Argirakis Jordan, Helen, 95

Arkonada, Katu, 7
Assange, Julian, granted asylum by Ecuador, 106
authoritarianism, in Latin America, 154
Aznar, José María, 58

Bachelet, Michelle, 31
Baduel, Raúl, 66
Báez, René, 112
Banco Bicentenario, 69
Banco de Venezuela, 69
Banco Nacional de Desenvolvimento Econômico e Social (BNDES), 137
Bancosur, 30, 57, 124, 139
Bechtel Corporation, 22
biofuels, 136
Boeing company, 125
boliburguesía, 71
Bolívar, Simón, 4, 30
bolivarianismo, 4, 53
Bolivia, 4, 5, 17, 22, 31–2, 36, 43, 45, 46, 153, 155, 156; communitarian socialism in, 79–96; Constituent Assembly, 87; geopolitical turbulence in, 1; highway link with Brazil, 124; oil exports of, 41; renegotiation of oil contracts, 41
Bolivian Workers Central (COB), 81, 93
Bolsa Familia programme (Brazil), 127–8
bourgeoisie, new, 146
Braskem company, 137
Brazil, 9, 18, 22–3, 25, 36, 43, 46, 115–40; bilateral agreement with USA, 125; Brazil–EU summit, 135; commodity exports from, 156; domestic policy of, 126–7; economic growth of, 129;

financing of highways, 94; foreign policy of, 121–6, 139; Forest Code, 131; Gini coefficient of, 129; oil exports of, 41; relations with Cuba, 149; trade policy of, 136–8; trade with Africa, 123

BRIC countries, 35, 122, 123–4

Bunge company, 130

bureaucracy, 69–73

Bush, George W., 3, 28, 33, 56, 125, 126

CADAFE company, 62, 72

Caldera, Rafael, 17

Camdessus, Michael, 102

Campos, Anderson, 134

capital controls, 14

Caracazo riot, 18, 50, 52

Cardoso, Fernando Henrique, 17, 121, 126

Cargill company, 130

Carmona, Pedro, 54

Castañeda, Jorge, *Utopia Unarmed*, 6

Castro, Fidel, 56, 124, 143, 150

Castro, Raúl, 143–4, 150

Causa R party (Venezuela), 21

Center for Economic and Policy Research (CEPR), 102

Central Intelligence Agency (CIA) (USA), 118

Centro de Estudios Estratégicos de la Defensa (CEED), 88

Chacon, Arne, 71

Chamorro, Violeta, 6

Chávez, Hugo, 2, 9, 13, 22, 28, 31, 32, 35, 39, 45, 49–76 *passim*, 101, 112, 116, 124, 126, 154; diagnosed with cancer, 76; elected president, 52, 149

Chávez, José López, 9

chavismo, 52–4, 67, 74, 75

Chiapas (Mexico), 20

Chile, 23–4, 46; free trade agreement with China, 34; socialism in, 5–6; student rebellion in, 9, 13; US intervention in, 150

China, 145–6; economic involvement in Latin America, 3, 34; relations with Brazil, 125; relations with Venezuela, 57

Cholango, Humberto, 109

Chomsky, Noam, *Hegemony or Survival*, 57

circulos bolivarianos (Venezuela), 53

class struggle, 24, 75

climate change, 88

Clinton, Bill, 56

Clinton, Hillary, 32, 124, 125

coca, decriminalization of, 89

cocaleros (Bolivia), 79

Cochabamba (Bolivia): Declaration of, 89; 'Water War', 22

cogestión, 59, 62

Collor de Mello, Fernando, 120

Colombia, 34, 105, 124; incursion into Ecuador, 31

communal councils (Venezuela), 72–3

Communist Party of Brazil, 119

Communist Party of China, 146

Communist Party of Cuba, 143, 145, 150

communitarianism, 80, 83, 155

Comunidad Andina (CAN), 3, 29

Comunidad de Estados Latinoamericanos y Caribeños (CELAC), 8, 27, 106, 124

Concertación (Chile), 150

conditional cash transfers (CCT), 128

conditionality of loans, 15

Confederación de Nacionalidades Indígenas del Ecuador (CONAIE), 19, 111, 157

Confederación de Pueblos Indígenas de Bolivia (CIDOB), 93

Confederación de Trabajadores de Venezuela (CTV), 53

consulta (Cuba), 144

cooperatives, 84; in Cuba, 148–9; in Venezuela, 61–2

Coordinadora Nacional por el Cambio (CONALCAM) (Bolivia), 87

Corporación Venezolana de Guayana (CVG), 72

Correa, Rafael, 2, 13, 27, 31, 39, 99–113, 153, 154, 156–7; taken hostage, 99

corruption, 64; in Brazil, 139; in Cuba, 144; in Venezuela, 69–73, 75
da Costa e Silva, Artur, 117, 118
Council on Foreign Relations, 28
crime rates, in Venezuela, 73
Cuba, 5, 6, 49, 88, 106, 115, 117, 118, 124, 157; 21st-century socialism in, 143–51; blockade of, 8, 116, 125, 149; economic restructuring in, 47; expelled from OAS, 32; geopolitical turbulence in, 1; medical personnel for Venezuela, 28–9, 60; relations with Venezuela, 56; socialism in, 8
Cuba–Venezuela Agreement (2000), 56
Cuban Communist Party, 8
cut flower industry, 110

dams: building of, in Brazil, 135; Guri dam (Venezuela), 68
Dangl, Benjamin, 43
Dávalos, Pablo, 108
debt, 15; cancellation of, 31; illegitimacy of, 104; of Brazil, 126, 139
democracy, 2, 4, 49, 124, 154; democratization of, 128; forms of, 7; in the workplace, 50; of social movements, 132; participatory, 100
Diaz Vázquez, Julio, 143
Dirceu, José, 121
disappearances, 117
dollar, status of, 3, 14, 29, 104
drought, 68
Drug Enforcement Agency (DEA) (USA), 88
drugs trade, 27

eco-socialism, 133
economic crisis, 2, 18
Ecuador, 4, 5, 19–20, 31, 36, 43, 45, 46, 155, 156; *buen vivir* socialism in, 99–113; constitution of, 101, 107; oil exports of, 41
Ecuarunari organization (Ecuador), 109

education, 104; in Cuba, 148
Ejército Zapatista de Liberación Nacional (EZLN), 20
El Alto (Bolivia), protests in, 13, 46
El Salvador, military in, 1
Empresa de Apoyo a la Producción de Alimentos (EMAPA) (Bolivia), 85
empresas grannacionales, 29
environmental issues, 100, 103, 109
Escobar, Arturo, 153–4
ethanol, production of, 125, 136
European Union (EU), 30
exchange rates, 14–15
export economies, 103
extractive sector, 103; in Ecuador, 106–12 *see also* neo-extractivism

Fedecámaras (Venezuela), 53–4
Federación Indígena y Campesina de Imbabura (FICI), 111
Fernandez, Percy, 90–1
Fernández Barrueco, Ricardo, 71
Fernández de Kirchner, Cristina, 27, 41
Fertinitro company, nationalization of, 68
Fibria company, 135
Fifth International, proposal for, 57
Flor, Francisco Hidalgo, 155–6
Fome Zero programme (Brazil), 127
food sovereignty, 155
Forero, Juan, 154
Fraser, Douglas, 1
Free Trade Area of the Americas (FTAA), 3, 28; rejection of, 88
Frente Nacional Campesino Ezequiel Zamora (FNCEZ), 74
Fuerzas Armadas Revolucionarias de Colombia (FARC), 31, 105
Fujimoro, Alberto, 17

G20 group, 123; creation of, 136
Gaddafi, Muammar, 138
Galeano, Eduardo, *Open Veins of Latin America*, 57
García, Alan, 109–10
García, Marco Aurélio, 122, 138

García Linera, Álvaro, 39, 41–2, 80, 83, 88, 94–5, 155, 157
gas sector, in Bolivia, 84–5
General Agreement on Tariffs and Trade (GATT), 16
Giordani, Jorge, 71
globalization, 13–25
Gold Reserve, Brisas project, 69
Goldberg, Philip, 91
Gomez, Gonzalo, 76
Gorbachev, Mikhail, 146
Gorz, André, 36
Goulart, João, 117
Gramsci, Antonio, 65
Gran Polo Patriótico (GPP) (Venezuela), 75
Grogg, Patricia, 144
Guatemal, Marco, 111
Guatemala, military in, 1
Gudynas, Eduardo, 40–1, 42

Haiti: Brazilian troops in, 122; earthquake in, 34; geopolitical turbulence in, 1
Hanauer, Ana, 132
Hardt, Michael, 24–5
Harnecker, Camila Piñeiro, 61–2, 148
Harnecker, Marta, 46
Harvey, David, 14
healthcare: in Cuba, 148; in Ecuador, 104; in Venezuela, 60
hegemony: construction of, 7; crisis of, 158; definition of, 33
Holloway, John, *Change the World without Taking Power*, 42
Honduras, 32; coup in, 9, 105–6, 154; military in, 1
Huanuni mine (Bolivia), nationalization of, 84
hydroelectricity, in Brazil, 135

import substitution industrialization, 14, 40, 118
indigenous people, 18–20, 79, 156–7; affected by dam building, 135; movements of, 21, 43, 83, 87, 88–9, 92, 95, 96, 109, 110, 111 (rise of, in Bolivia, 88–9)

indignados, 2
Industrias Venoco, nationalization of, 69
inflation, 14
informal sector of employment, 51, 81
Initiative for the Integration of the Regional Infrastructure of South America (IIRSA), 137
Instrumento Político por la Soberania de los Pueblos (IPSP), 79
International Monetary Fund (IMF), 15–16, 126, 139; stops loans to Bolivia, 87
internationalism, 122–3
Internet, use of, 20
Iran, 122; relations with Brazil, 124; relations with Venezuela, 57
Isaías group, 104
Ishpingo Tiputini Tambococha oilfield (Ecuador), 111

Jobim, Nelson, 122, 124, 125; resignation of, 139
Johl, Benjamin, with Linda Farthing, *Impasse in Bolivia*, 80
judicial reform, 100

Katz, Claudio, 46
Kirchner, Nestor, 28
Kliass, Paulo, 129
Kovel, Joel, 133

Lacteos Los Andes company, 68
land: distribution of, in Cuba, 147; occupation of, 68, 120, 134; ownership of, 156
land reform, 59, 61
latifundios, 61, 66; occupations of, 134
Latin American Spring, 153–8
Lebowitz, Michael, 5
Ledezma, Antonio, 67
left, radical, in government, 43–5
liberal paradigm, 155
literacy, in Venezuela, 60
Lobo Sosa, Porfirio, 9, 32, 105
López Obrador, Andrés Manuel, 25

Lówy, Michael, 133
Lugo, Fernando, 2, 9, 31, 39, 112

Macas, Luis, 19–20
Mahuad, Jamil, 105
Manifiesto Colectivo (Bolivia), 93
Marcos, Subcomandante, 20
Mariátegui, José Carlos, 100
Mariel port (Cuba), development of, 149–50
market, function of, 145
Marx, Karl, 83
media luna governorships (Bolivia), 90–1
Meirelles, Henrique, 126
Mendes, Chico, 133
Mendonça, Duda, 121
Menem, Carlos, 23
mensalão, 127
Mercado Común del Sur (MERCOSUR), 3, 29, 35, 116, 124, 138, 139; Structural Convergence Fund, 136
Mercal company, 71
Merida Initiative, 34
Merkel, Angela, 111
Mesa, Carlos, 22
Mesa de Unidad Democrática (MUD) (Venezuela), 73, 74
Mexico, 18
military: dismantling of, 86; reclaiming control of, 52–6
military dictatorships, 117, 118
mining sector, 103, 110; in Bolivia, 80; in Ecuador, 106–8
Misión Barrio Adentro (Venezuela), 60
Misión Vuelvan Caras (Venezuela), 61, 62
Misión Zamora (Venezuela), 61
misiones sociales (Venezuela), 59, 64, 74
Mitrione, Dan, 118
Moral y Luces program (Venezuela), 67
Morales, Evo, 2, 3, 13, 22, 31, 27, 31, 32, 39, 82–4, 89, 91, 96, 112, 124, 154; election of, 79, re-election of, 92

Movimento dos Trabalhadores Rurais Sem Terra (MST) (Brazil), 9, 13, 22–3, 25, 117, 131, 132–4, 156; birth of, 119–21
Movimiento al Socialismo (MAS) (Bolivia), 22, 79, 90, 92, 93, 94, 96
Movimiento Bolivariano Revolucionario (MBR), 52
Movimiento V República (MVR) (Venezuela), 67
Mujica, José, 112
multitude, concept of, 24–5

nation-state autonomy, 33–5
National Endowment for Democracy (NED), 9, 150
National Liberation Alliance (Brazil), 117
nationalization, 6, 65, 101, 104; in Bolivia, 81, 82–6; in Venezuela, 68–9; of the state, 86
Negri, Antonio, 24–5
neo-extractivism, 39–47, 135–6
neoliberalism, 6, 13–25, 136; dismantling of, 153; failure of, 17; resistance to, 82
Netherlands, 58
Neves, Tancredo, 23, 120
New Continentalism, 30
Nicaragua, 46, 115; role of US in, 150
Nixon, Richard, 117
North American Free Trade Agreement (NAFTA), 20, 35
Nova, Armando, 147

Obama, Barack, 8, 32, 34, 57, 125, 138, 149
Occupy Wall Street movement, 2
oil, dependency on, 59
oil sector, 35, 41, 104, 107, 124; in Amazon, 108; in Bolivia, 84; in Venezuela, 45, 50–1, 52–6
oil wealth, redistribution of, 59
Oliveira, José Batista de, 134
Organization of American States (OAS), 9, 27, 31, 32, 106; readmission of Honduras, 105
Organization of the Petroleum

Exporting Countries (OPEC), 56; Ecuador membership of, 107

Ortega, Daniel, 6, 112, 150

Pachamama, 88, 95, 155

Pacto de Unidad (PU) (Bolivia), 87

Palestinians, self-determination of, 138–9

Palocci, Antonio, 126; resignation of, 139

Paraguay, 29, 136, 137; coup in, 9, 154

participation, popular, 60, 128; in Cuba, 144

participatory budgeting (PB), 115, 120–1

Partido Comunista de Venezuela (PCV), 66

Partido da Social Democracia Brasileira (PSDB), 121

Partido do Movimento Democrático Brasileiro (PMDB), 121

Partido Liberal (Brazil), 127

Partido Socialismo e Liberdade (PSOL) (Brazil), 127, 133

Partido Socialista Unido de Venezuela (PSUV), 66–7, 71, 73, 75

partidocracia (Ecuador), 102

Pastoral Land Commission (CPT) (Brazil), 120

Patria Para Todos (PPT) (Venezuela), 66

Patriota, Antônio, 123, 138

pesticides, Brazil's consumption of, 136, 137

Petróleos de Venezuela SA (PDVSA), 45, 51, 53, 54, 59, 62, 107; lockout at, 55

Petras, James, 21, 22

petro populism, in Venezuela, 107

Petrobras company, 135, 137

Petrocaribe company, 29, 57

Petroecuador company, 107

Piñera, Sebastián, 27

'pink tide', 2, 13, 27–36, 40–1, 58

Pinochet, Augusto, 6, 15, 24

piqueteros (Argentina), 13, 23, 50

Plan Colombia, 34

Plan Guayana Socialista (Venezuela), 70–1

plural economy, model of, 82

PODEMOS party (Venezuela), 66

popular justice, 87

popular power, in Venezuela, 69–73

Popular Revolutionary Vanguard (Brazil), 117

Popular Unity government (Chile), 40

Porto Alegre (Brazil), 120–1, 127, 128

Posokoni tin mine (Bolivia), 84

poverty, reduction of, 58–62, 86, 102; in Brazil, 127–8

Preto, Ribeirâo, 126

primary commodities, export of, 41–2, 109

privatization, 16–17, 23, 51, 81, 100, 110, 136; of water, 79, 110

protest movements, 13, 18, 19, 51, 79, 81, 93, 111

public ownership of means of production, 40

puntofijismo, 53

Ramos, Ivonne, 108

Rangel Gómez, Francisco, 71–2

RCTV channel, 65–6

redistribution of wealth, 64

Regalado, Roberto, 45

renewable energy, 135–6

revolution: 'five motors of', 65, 67; in Latin America, 46

Ricupero, Ruben, 118

roads, building of, 124; resistance to, 93–4

Robinson, William, 15, 33

Rothkopf, David, 122

Rousseff, Dilma, 116, 117–18, 121, 124, 130, 135, 138–40

Rua, Fernando de la, 23

Russia, relations with Venezuela, 57

Saab Scania company, strike in, 119

Sader, Emir, *The New Mole*, 6–7, 9, 113, 115, 157–8

Salinas, Carlos, 20

Sánchez de Lozáda, Gonzalo, 22, 88, 90

Sandinista National Liberation Front (FSLN) (Nicaragua), 6
Santa Cruz (Bolivia), separatist movement in, 90
Santi, Marlon, 111
Santillana, Alejandra, 7
Santos, Juan Manuel, 105
Santos, Marina dos, 131
Sanz, Rodolfo, 72
Sarney, José, 23, 120
School of the Americas, 88, 106
self-employment, 144; in Cuba, 148–9
Serrano, Fernando Garcia, 21
Shifter, Michael, 112–13
SIDOR company, nationalization of, 69, 70
Silva, Luiz Inácio 'Lula' da, 2, 23, 28, 31, 32, 35, 112, 115–40; election of, 116, 149
Silva, Marina, 131
Silverstein, Ken, 115
social movements, 10, 43, 45, 57, 103, 110, 112; challenge of, 18–25; in Brazil, 132–4 (decline of, 134); rise of, 13–25
socialism, 9, 133, 157; 21st-century, 4, 27, 39–47, 100, 122, 139, 153, 154 (in Cuba, 143–51; in Venezuela, 49–76); buen vivir, in Ecuador, 99–113, 153, 155; communitarian, in Bolivia, 79–96; definition of, 4–5, 7; 'elementary triangle' of, 49, 65; in Cuba, 5; relation to democracy, 115; renewal of, 1, 13; shift from, 127; socialismo o muerte, 146 see also eco-socialism
Socialist Popular Action (Brazil), 127
solidarity, basis of trade, 28
Soros, George, 126
Sousa Santos, Boaventura de, 100
south–south relations, 121–6
state: as pivot of the economy, 83; conundrum of, 42–3; decolonization of, 87; refounding of, 86–7; role of, 7
state capitalism, 49
state-owned enterprises, 85
Stédile, João Pedro, 131

Stefanoni, Pablo, 92
strikes, in Brazil, 119
structural adjustment programs (SAP), 16, 17–18
subsidies, removal of, 81
sucre currency, 29, 57
sugar, imported by Cuba, 146–7
sumak kawsay, 109, 111
Summit of the Americas, 8, 106, 116
swarm intelligence, 25

Tagaeri people, 111
Taromenane people, 111
Telesur TV channel, 29, 57
Tenesaca, Delfín, 111
Territorio Indígena y Parque Nacional Isiboro Sécure (TIPNIS) (Bolivia), 93, 156
tertiary sector, 63
torture, 117
trade unions, 40, 80, 95, 119, 147; restrictions on, 121
transnational corporations, 16, 33, 35, 51, 84–5
Tratados de Comercio del Pueblo (TCP) (Bolivia), 88
Trigo, Luis, 91
Tupi oilfield (Brazil), 135
Turkey, Brazilian relations with, 124

Unidades de Batalla Electoral (UBE) (Venezuela), 55
Unión de Naciones Suramericanas (UNASUR), 3, 29–30, 31, 88, 106, 124; Declaration of La Moneda, 31–2; emergency summit, 91; South American Defense Council (SADC), 124, 139
Unión Nacional de Trabajadores (UNETE) (Venezuela), 55, 62, 66, 74
Union of Soviet Socialist Rpublics (USSR), 40, 47, 49, 75, 118, 119; lessons of, 146
United Nations (UN): Brazil's reforming push within, 123; conference on climate change, 89
UN Security Council, 138

UN Single Convention on Narcotic Drugs, 89
United States of America, 8, 75; GDP growth in, 14; hegemony of, 28, 32 (challenge to, 1, 10, 27–36, 56–8, 88–9, 116, 123, 140); imperial overstretch of, 33; invasion of Iraq, 33; military bases of, 58, 105; military budget of, 31; military presence in Latin America, 9, 34, 86; relations with Brazil, 118, 122, 125, 138; role in Latin America, 58, 65, 86, 90, 95, 150
Uribe, Álvaro, 105
Uruguay, 36, 46, 136
US Agency for International Development (USAID), 9, 65, 90, 95
US–Central American Free Trade Agreement (CAFTA), 35

Valdes Paz, Juan, 151
Vale company, 135, 136
Vanguarda Armada Revolucionária Palmares (VAP-Palmares), 117
Veltmeyer, Henry, 21, 22
Venezuela, 4, 5, 21–2, 28–9, 36, 46, 88, 105, 107, 122, 124, 128, 155; 21st-century socialism in, 49–76; coup in, 2; geopolitical turbulence in, 1; 'new productive model', 59; oil exports of, 41; oil sector in, 45, 50–1, 52–6
Vietnam, 145
Vietnam War, 14
Villegas, Carlos, 87

Vinto tin smelter (Bolivia), nationalization of, 84
Votorantim Celulose e Papel company, 135

war on drugs, 89, 105
Washington Consensus, 15, 102
Wikileaks, 106; US embassy cables published by, 80
Wisum, Bosco, 111
women, in judiciary, 87
workers' control, 62, 70
Workers' Party (Brazil) (PT), 23, 25, 57, 115–17, 139; birth of, 119–21
working-class organization, fragmentation of, 40
World Bank, 15, 87, 128
World Economic Forum, 30
World People's Summit on Climate Change, 89
World Social Forum (WSF), 30–1, 39, 49, 57, 112, 127
World Trade Organization (WTO), 16; Battle of Seattle, 2

Yacimentos Petrolíferos Fiscales Bolivianos (YPFB), 81, 84
Yasuni National Park (Ecuador), oil exploration in, 109, 111
yuan, status of, 3

Zapatista movement, 2, 7, 24, 25, 155, 158
Zelaya, Manuel, 9, 32, 105, 116, 125
Zibechi, Raúl, 46, 136
Zorrilla, Carlos, 108

About Zed Books

Zed Books is a critical and dynamic publisher, committed to increasing awareness of important international issues and to promoting diversity, alternative voices and progressive social change. We publish on politics, development, gender, the environment and economics for a global audience of students, academics, activists and general readers. Run as a co-operative, Zed Books aims to operate in an ethical and environmentally sustainable way.

Find out more at:

www.zedbooks.co.uk

For up-to-date news, articles, reviews and events information visit:

http://zed-books.blogspot.com

To subscribe to the monthly Zed Books e-newsletter, send an email headed 'subscribe' to:

marketing@zedbooks.net

We can also be found on **Facebook**, **ZNet**, **Twitter** and **Library Thing**.